W9-AUV-585

79827

Latin American
Economic Integration
and U.S. Policy

Latin American Economic Integration and U.S. Policy

JOSEPH GRUNWALD

MIGUEL S. WIONCZEK

MARTIN CARNOY

THE BROOKINGS INSTITUTION

Washington, D.C.

THE BROOKINGS INSTITUTION is an independent organization devoted to nonpartisan research, education, and publication in economics, government, foreign policy, and the social sciences generally. Its principal purposes are to aid in the development of sound public policies and to promote public understanding of issues of national importance.

The Institution was founded on December 8, 1927, to merge the activities of the Institute for Government Research, founded in 1916, the Institute of Economics, founded in 1922, and the Robert Brookings Graduate School of Economics and Government, founded in 1924.

The general administration of the Institution is the responsibility of a Board of Trustees charged with maintaining the independence of the staff and fostering the most favorable conditions for creative research and education. The immediate direction of the policies, program, and staff of the Institution is vested in the President, assisted by an advisory committee of the officers and staff.

In publishing a study, the Institution presents it as a competent treatment of a subject worthy of public consideration. The interpretations and conclusions in such publications are those of the author or authors and do not necessarily reflect the views of the other staff members, officers, or trustees of the Brookings Institution.

Foreword

THOUGH for many years the United States has exercised an important influence on the economic development of Latin American countries, the economic progress of those countries has been and remains largely in their own hands. To accelerate development, they have made serious efforts to achieve some form of regional economic integration—a difficult and thus far elusive goal. Though progress has been slow, Latin America's economic prospects nevertheless appear to the authors of this book to be closely linked to success of the movement toward a regional common market. The authors believe that the United States, though it cannot intervene in this process, can use its economic policies to facilitate Latin American efforts.

This study originated in 1966 as a policy paper on the issues to be debated at the 1967 meeting of Western Hemisphere heads of state at Punta del Este, Uruguay. The scope of research gradually expanded into a broader analysis of past and current U.S. economic policies toward Latin America. Thus the book acquired its present two-part form, the first dealing with the present status of the Latin American integration movement and the second with a discussion of the prospects for U.S. policy toward integration.

Joseph Grunwald, director of the study, is a senior fellow at the Brookings Institution and a lecturer at the School of Advanced International Studies of the Johns Hopkins University. He coordinates a program of joint studies on Latin American economic development conducted by a group of Latin American research institutes known as ECIEL, the acronym for Estudios Conjuntos sobre Integración Económica Latinoamericana. Miguel S. Wionczek, adviser to the Center for Latin American Monetary Studies in Mexico and to the Andean Integration Agreement, was a research fellow at Harvard University when this study was begun. Martin Carnoy, a former Brookings research associate, now teaches at Stanford University. Mr. Grunwald and Mr. Carnoy are co-authors (with Donald W. Baerresen) of another Brookings book, *Latin American Trade Patterns* (1965), and Mr. Carnoy has prepared an ECIEL study, *Industrialization in a Latin American Common Market*, published by Brookings in 1971.

The research for this book was carried out in the Brookings Foreign Policy Studies program, which is directed by Henry Owen. The criticisms and suggestions of Mr. Owen and of his Brookings colleagues Robert E. Asher, Edward R. Fried, Peter T. Knight, and John N. Plank (now at the University of Connecticut) were especially helpful to the authors. Valuable comments were also made by Harvey S. Perloff, Dean of the School of Architecture and Urban Planning at the University of California at Los Angeles, and Walter S. Salant of Brookings; they, together with Luis Escobar of the International Bank for Reconstruction and Development and Isaiah Frank of the School of Advanced International Studies of the Johns Hopkins University, were members of a reading committee.

The following persons also read and commented on the manuscript at various stages: José Cárdenas, Inter-American Development Bank; Ernst Haas, University of California at Berkeley; H. Field Haviland, Jr., Fletcher School of Law and Diplomacy, who was Director of Foreign Policy Studies at Brookings when the project was begun; John R. Karlik, Joint Economic Committee, U.S. Congress; Abraham Lowenthal, the Ford Foundation; Richard D. Mallon, Harvard University; Philip Musgrove, Brookings; David Pollock, United Nations Economic Commission for Latin America; Joseph Silberstein, U.S. Department of State; and Ben Stephansky, the Upjohn Institute. The authors are grateful to all of them and to the Ford Foundation, whose grant helped to support the study.

Joy Dunkerley assisted in the preparation of statistical materials and in preliminary editing. Catita Edward and Rosa Cook provided secretarial assistance; Evelyn P. Fisher checked the accuracy of data and sources; Alice M. Carroll edited the manuscript; and Joan C. Culver prepared the index.

The authors' views are of course their own and should not be attributed to the trustees, officers, or other staff members of the Ford Foundation or the Brookings Institution.

KERMIT GORDON
President

September 1971
Washington, D.C.

Contents

Appendix Tables

PART ONE

The Integration Movement

CHAPTER ONE

The Current Setting

LATIN AMERICAN ECONOMIES, although far from stagnating, did not grow fast enough during the 1960s to alleviate the area's grave economic and social problems. Severe underemployment and unemployment, exacerbated by a rapid population increase, may turn into an unsustainable burden unless the region's economic development can be significantly accelerated. But the promise of the first years of the last decade—the Alliance for Progress, and U.S. aid—has withered. The movement toward economic integration has lost its early, slight strength. Neomercantilist tendencies have emerged in developed countries to bolster traditional restraints against exports, actual and potential, from low-income countries.

The United States and Latin American Economic Development

The forces for change released in the aftermath of the Second World War profoundly affected the poverty-ridden two-thirds of the world's population. As regional isolation ended, awareness of the vast gaps in income levels between the rich and the poor countries grew. The United States interest in the economic development of low-income countries in that period gave rise to aid programs, which became an important instrument of U.S. foreign policy. Those efforts declined during the second half of the 1960s, however, as the disappointing short-term results of foreign

3

aid combined with rising domestic concerns to blur the image of world interdependence and raise doubts about the effectiveness of aid as a foreign policy tool.

Shift in U.S. Policy toward Latin America

The emphasis in U.S. policy toward Latin America has shifted since the early 1950s from a preoccupation with military security and the cold war to consideration of economic and social matters. The tenor of the new policy, increasingly stressing developmental concerns, was first expressed through the Act of Bogotá in 1960, then through the Alliance for Progress subscribed to in Punta del Este in 1961, and again in Punta del Este in 1967 when the United States offered support to a Latin American common market. This change in policy emphasis "constitutes a shift from a concentration upon objectives of primary interest to the United States to those of primary concern to Latin America."[1]

The security and welfare of its own people remain, of course, the primary aim of the U.S. government. But governmental actions have at times appeared incompatible with both United States interests and those of Latin America. Supposed threats to U.S. security led to military interventions in Guatemala in 1954, Cuba in 1961, and the Dominican Republic in 1965. Policy makers' judgments in those, as well as other less serious, actions appeared to many observers to be contrary to the long-run interest of the United States. The same was true of such unilateral economic moves as the withholding of aid from Peru during that country's dispute with a U.S. oil company in the early 1960s and the subsequent Hickenlooper amendment to the U.S. foreign assistance and sugar acts, which provides for the cutoff of assistance to any government that expropriates the property of U.S. citizens or corporations without taking appropriate steps toward equitable and speedy compensation. Strictly interpreted, this amendment would trigger major policy action more or less automatically, thus limiting diplomatic flexibility. The amendment was a major device in another confrontation with Peru in 1969 over the expropriation of the International Petroleum Company. In that dispute the administration failed to put the legislation in force because of its anxiety to avoid negative

---

1. John C. Dreier, "New Wine and Old Bottles: The Changing Inter-American System," *International Organization*, Vol. 22 (Spring 1968), p. 490.

repercussions in Peru and indeed all of Latin America. It cannot be assumed, however, that the conflict between developmental objectives and other considerations has been laid to rest.[2]

Latin American reaction to U.S. policies has been ambivalent. While Latin American governments have almost always sought a special relationship with the United States, the dominant economic, political, and military power in the hemisphere since the First World War, they have often shown hostility to the northern giant. Embraces and admiration of the United States and its ideals have alternated, or frequently existed simultaneously, with rejection and antagonism.

Whatever U.S. policy may be, it will always be found suspect by many Latin Americans, for the region is a conglomeration of nations and peoples, of governments representing a fraction of the population and often only tiny but powerful interest groups. While intellectuals are generally alienated from their governments, the great mass of the population has been, at least until recently, politically uninvolved and inert. Even if U.S. policy were oriented solely toward development and social change, there would be opposition by influential sectors favoring the status quo. As a mixture of developmental, military, and other considerations, U.S. policy may run counter to every conceivable prejudice in Latin America; certain segments of the intellectual community, for instance, may consider a laudable development component only a cover for the true motive of the United States— the political and economic domination of the region.

Since the Alliance for Progress came into being in 1961, Latin American response to U.S. policies has been further complicated by a growing desire among the formerly disenfranchised masses for participation in the social and political life of the region and by the rising nationalism that pervades Latin American societies. Latin Americans' desire for national identity and nationalist achievement dominates many of their actions. While not usually a rational force for economic objectives, nationalism can constitute a powerful unifying force for creating economic dynamism and promoting social change.

Like any society, Latin Americans pursue a multitude of social, political, and economic objectives, and they often differ from those of the United

2. The 1969 Rockefeller Report, for example, full of recommendations to foster development, also urged U.S. military assistance for internal security. (U.S. Presidential Mission for the Western Hemisphere, *Quality of Life in the Americas* [1969]; Nelson A. Rockefeller served as chairman.)

States. Economic growth is only one of them. Continuous access to political power, national independence, preservation of the social status quo, and sometimes a more equitable distribution of income and wealth and a broadening of the political base may also be among the objectives of Latin American leaders. Their diverse and not necessarily consistent aims account for their often perplexing behavior, their seemingly irrational economic point of view. Those aims may explain, for example, why scarce resources are diverted to manufacturing when agriculture so clearly needs more attention; why steel plants are being built when the marginal productivity of investment in another sector is obviously higher; why the currency is overvalued in foreign-exchange terms when devaluation could stimulate exports; why the foreign private investor is not welcomed with open arms in the development of petroleum and other natural resources; why bus fares, telephone and electric power rates, and such, are not increased in order to generate investment funds and improve the services of public utilities, and so on.

The popularly exposed causes of Latin American problems—poor leadership, lack of administrative ability, and demagoguery—certainly exist. But the major deterrent to Latin America's rapid economic development lies in the scale of social and political values of its powerholders. Despite the pronouncements of some Latin American policy makers, maximizing the rate of economic growth is *not* at the top of the list of Latin American priorities.

Economic Dependence

During most of their history the countries south of the Rio Grande have depended on outsiders. Foreign trade has been all important, and the natural resources that dominate Latin American exports have been developed and controlled substantially by foreigners.

Strong political ties with other nations have served the need of those outside powers and of local elites to expand economically. Spain and Portugal maintained trade monopolies with their colonies in the Western Hemisphere. The British followed, penetrating the region through treaties of friendship and free trade. Once the Latin American economies had become sufficiently dependent on exports of raw materials and imports of consumer manufactures, the merchant classes whose prosperity was drawn from that trade worked to preserve the conditions that supported international commerce. Since their governments cooperated, Britain seldom needed to intervene on behalf of British economic interests.[3]

Free trade and investment did not require formal conquest, annexation, or colonization. But "it would be hard to imagine a more spectacular example of a policy of commercial hegemony in the interests of high politics, or of the use of informal political supremacy in the interests of commercial enterprise."[4] At the peak of Britain's "informal imperialism" in Latin America at the beginning of this century, Britons owned roughly a quarter of the region's total commercial assets.

The United States gradually replaced Europe as the principal source of foreign capital. It became Latin America's most important trading partner and the most important source of foreign-exchange revenue. Between 1890 and 1930 the free exchange of Latin American primary commodities for U.S. manufactures, the base of U.S. economic power in the region, provided strong incentives for most governments and local political interests in Latin America to cooperate with the United States.[5] After the Second World War the rapidly emerging protectionism and industrialization in Latin American countries encouraged U.S. investors to enter new fields. As manufacturing enterprises started to prosper behind the rising trade barriers, the United States offered substantial financial and technical assistance, further strengthening its ties with the region.

The Bilateral Relationship

The United States has always considered its relationships and responsibilities toward Latin America special. Latin American countries have largely accepted this status, quarreling among themselves for U.S. favors and rarely, until recently, banding together to countervail its power. The inter-American system established by the United States has promoted neither unity nor independence in Latin America. Following the Second

3. The exceptions include British intervention in Argentina in the 1840s to reopen the River Plate, which had been closed during General Rosas's incursions in Paraguay. The British government also intervened to protect British interests in Guatemala and Colombia in the 1870s and in Mexico and Honduras between 1910 and 1914.

4. John Gallagher and Ronald Robinson, "The Imperialism of Free Trade," *Economic History Review*, Second Series, Vol. 6 (August 1953), p. 8.

5. Before the 1930s, when the Good Neighbor Policy was ushered in by the renunciation of military coercion, the United States frequently intervened directly in the Caribbean nations on behalf of its citizens' commercial and financial interests. See Bryce Wood, *The Making of the Good Neighbor Policy* (Columbia University Press, 1961), p. 5.

World War the system—then embodied in the newly created Organization of American States (OAS)—served primarily as one of many regional security arrangements responding to the emergence of the Soviet Union as a leading world power.

At that time Latin American governments began to concentrate their energies on obtaining the maximum benefits from their special relationships with the United States, seeking with some success U.S. financial aid, capital investment, and technical assistance. As a consequence, commercial and financial ties within the hemisphere are now bilateral, between the United States and each Latin American nation. Development assistance, including aid from multilateral institutions such as the Inter-American Development Bank (IDB), goes for the most part to individual countries for their national programs, rather than to groups of countries for regional purposes. Neither the individual countries nor the aid-giving institutions have seriously worked to identify and promote regional investment projects.

On the contrary, Latin American representatives at Inter-American meetings have been preoccupied with protecting their countries' sovereignty. Nonintervention from within has become as important to them as nonintervention from outside the hemisphere is to the United States. Though their fear is of the overwhelming presence of their northern neighbor, their persistent reaffirmation of national sovereignty has limited their relations with each other. Moreover, because all members of the inter-American system have been considered juridically equal and "to have an equal interest in the prosecution of all the agreed purposes of the system . . . the formation of blocs or subgroups on the basis of special interests" has been strongly opposed.[6] The enormous difference in economic and political power between the "colossus of the North" and Latin American countries has tended to make a true hemispheric partnership impossible.

The Latin American Integration Movement

By the 1950s, strong political motivations for regional integration had begun to emerge. Very few Latin American leaders were ready to speak openly, but the feelings of many were echoed by Chile's President Eduardo Frei in 1964, when he urged that "the twenty poor and disunited [Latin

6. Dreier, "New Wine and Old Bottles," p. 492.

American] nations [form] a powerful and progressive union which can deal with the United States as an equal."[7] Latin American countries have become aware that they would be more powerful in international councils if they spoke as a region, with one voice, rather than dealing individually with the outside world.

While their collective bargaining power is an important motive for regional union, economic considerations have become the main rationale for regional integration. When it became apparent that industrialization based on import substitution within each nation could neither continue indefinitely nor reduce the region's dependence on the outside world, a number of Latin American countries decided to attempt closer economic cooperation among themselves, independent of their individual relations with the United States and therefore outside the inter-American system.

The first successful steps toward economic integration, at the end of the 1950s, resulted in the formation of the Central American Common Market (CACM) and the Latin American Free Trade Association (LAFTA) in 1960. The movement has progressed furthest in Central America, where five small nations have removed most of the tariff barriers to trade among themselves. LAFTA, which now encompasses Mexico and all of South America except the Guianas, has encountered far greater difficulties. The Andean Group, a subregional arrangement of the five western countries in South America that came into being in 1969, holds greater promise in the short run than does LAFTA as a whole.

An ad hoc group created to work out a Latin American position on the United Nations Conference on Trade and Development (UNCTAD), meeting in Geneva in 1964, has continued to meet to deal with questions of international trade and development. In the spring of 1969 this Special Coordinating Commission for Latin America (CECLA) took upon itself the difficult job of coordinating Latin American attitudes on economic issues vis-à-vis the United States. Their Consensus of Viña del Mar was presented to President Nixon in June 1969 (see Appendix E). Though CECLA's establishment "marks a qualitative change in the traditionally submissive attitude of Latin America towards the United States,"[8] its

7. Quoted in Robert N. Burr, *Our Troubled Hemisphere: Perspectives on United States-Latin American Relations* (Brookings Institution, 1967), p. 87.

8. Claudio Véliz, "Latin America and the Visit of the Governor," "EPICA Reports" (Washington: Ecumenical Program for Inter-American Communication and Action, July 1969; processed), p. 3; translated from *Mensaje* (Santiago, Chile), June 1969.

bargaining power is not likely to be significant until it is backed up by a common market arrangement or permanent regional institutions.

Obstacles to Economic Integration

Successful regional integration requires a partial but significant abdication of national power to multinational authority. The problem is compounded in Latin America—as in other less developed countries—by the past efforts of the various nations to develop their own industrial bases. The successes of the major countries prior to 1960, and the smaller countries' designs to imitate them, are a substantial obstacle that did not confront the builders of a common market in Europe after the Second World War. The differing levels of development and degrees of industrialization, as well as autarkic governmental policies, work against intraregional cooperation. Even more crucial, perhaps, is the reluctance of major interest groups in the larger countries to expose themselves to either the present or the potential industrial competitors that a regional common market would create.

Furthermore, regional integration often appears to be incompatible with national integration. In many countries a large part of the population that lives in rural areas and outside the market economy still must be both economically and socially integrated into the individual nations. Felipe Herrera, former president of the Inter-American Development Bank, believes that "the internal conquest of the vast 'new frontiers' in many areas still outside the mainstreams of the national economies, will be greatly facilitated by infrastructure works designed on a regional scale." He sees integration not as an alternative, "but rather a supplement and a stimulus to the internal reforms that must be made without delay in each country so as to extend the benefits of economic and social development to the great majority of the people."[9] And Raúl Prebisch, formerly executive secretary of the United Nations Economic Commission for Latin America (ECLA), holds that "in order to reach internal [national] integration through the incorporation of the great masses of excess and marginal population into the modern economic life of our countries, it is essential to accelerate the growth rate, and in order to accelerate the growth rate, certain steps toward Latin American integration are unavoidable. Thus

9. "Towards a Latin American Common Market" (lecture delivered at Cornell University, May 20, 1966).

progress toward Latin American integration . . . is an essential condition for the efficient attainment of this process [national integration]."[10]

These and other statesmen believe that by creating a network of transportation and communication and putting idle physical and human resources to work, Latin American regional development programs could contribute to solving pressing social problems, whereas national integration alone might require the destruction of the current structure of society. They argue that insofar as regional integration would lead to a general rationalization of production processes, general modernization, and more rapid economic growth, it would greatly facilitate the profound changes that national integration requires.

Sources of Opposition

While regional economic integration has wide emotional appeal as an independence movement, it by no means has the full support of those groups whose collaboration would be needed to translate ideas into action. The concept of integration as an operational mechanism was elaborated in the late fifties by intellectuals and professional economists—"técnicos" (technocrats), in the Latin American jargon. Although their principal base was ECLA's headquarters in Santiago, Chile, they worked in close cooperation with officials in many Latin American governments. They mustered enough political support to make possible the creation of CACM and LAFTA at the turn of the decade, but they failed to enlist sufficient backing of the public and private sectors in most of Latin America for subsequent cooperation in both trade and nontrade fields. This is understandable in countries in which a multitude of industries—financially, managerially, and technologically weak—have been established only comparatively recently and in which the new industrial class—both domestic and foreign—has been comfortably ensconced behind high trade barriers and has never been tested by competition from outside.

Like the United States and other nations, Latin American countries frequently follow short-run policies that are not necessarily in harmony with the long-term development interests of the region. In the United States, however, the electorate can express themselves through many more

10. Quoted in United Nations, Economic Commission for Latin America, *Notas sobre la economía y el desarrollo de América Latina*, No. 24 (Aug. 16, 1969); authors' translation.

channels than can citizens of many Latin American countries, and U.S. policy makers tend to be responsive to a wider variety of interest groups than do most Latin American power holders.

In Latin America, large sectors of the population have no means of communicating with and influencing the government, and in many countries the governments tend to reflect the views only of powerful special interests, who are generally disinterested in changing the socioeconomic status quo. Latin American power holders have in the last few decades begun to respond to the increasing pressure from below to advance social welfare. The objectives of the masses are articulated by a relatively small group of dissenting intellectuals in the academic community, the professions, and more recently the church. While their access to the councils of government has been increasing, their influence at the policy-making level has most often been effectively blocked by vested interests.

The conflict between the long-term objectives of the técnicos and social innovators and the short-run pressures of political and economic vested interests has frequently produced ambivalent policies, especially in such areas as regional integration. When the technocrats and social reformers were in positions of influence, public support for integration was real. The basic integration mechanisms were created during the late 1950s and early 1960s, when most Latin American nations had democratic regimes. By the end of the 1960s, the situation had been nearly reversed: political power in many republics had fallen once again into the hands of military governments, whose occasional pronouncements in favor of integration represented lip service rather than real support. The resurgence of military regimes is a response to the accumulated social and economic problems that more democratic regimes were unable or unwilling to tackle. Some of the military governments have adopted highly nationalistic, even reformist, programs to mobilize broad political support, pushing economic cooperation with neighbors into the background.

Other forces also work against a regional market. Many Latin American governments are genuinely concerned that their economic and financial relations with the United States and other North Atlantic powers would be adversely affected by a common market arrangement. They have become conditioned to dealing individually with the United States, seeking U.S. assistance for their national growth objectives rather than regionwide development.

Moreover, these countries are exposed to a host of external economic problems, ranging from severe fluctuations in their commodity exports to a steadily growing import bill and increased costs of servicing foreign debt. Some of these problems are of Latin America's own making, others functions of the world economy. These overwhelming day-to-day external difficulties are met by day-to-day improvisations. Elaboration of longer-term economic policies is neglected by governments that prefer continuing national industrialization and traditional bilateral economic relations with the United States and other developed countries to the risk of experimenting with regional economic integration.

The genuine interest of the three largest countries in Latin America is critical to regional integration. To many persons the national markets of Argentina, Brazil, and Mexico appear sufficiently large to support vigorous national industrialization. This is particularly true of Brazil with a population expected to approach 100 million by the end of 1971 and a gross national product of nearly $40 billion. Brazil's manufacturing industries, like other Latin American countries', are oriented toward the domestic market; industrialists view exports primarily as a means of using excess capacity. Economic integration is not rejected but appears valuable mainly as a regional tool for negotiating better export conditions and for bargaining generally with the developed countries.[11]

Argentine industrialists are more conscious of the need for exports, but their effectiveness as a pressure group is limited by their fear of being undercut by "cheap labor" production of other Latin American countries.[12] The ambivalent and hesitant attitude toward regional integration is nourished by the nationalist stance of the country's military regime.

Mexico recognized the potential of Latin American economic cooperation by joining LAFTA as a charter member. Although the country's trade with the region, insignificant in 1960, has multiplied, it is still relatively too small to have fostered a strong constituency for integration.

11. See, for instance, "Brazil and Latin American Integration," *Conjuntura Econômica*, Vol. 16 (August 1969), pp. 35–44. This article in the respected economic journal of the Vargas Foundation, which provides the Brazilian government with economic information, claims that Brazil's foreign economic policy is prointegration and shows how the country would benefit from a Latin American trade association.

12. A recent study indicates that LAFTA concessions have benefited Argentine industrialists by stimulating exports. (David Felix, "Import Substitution and Industrial Exporting: An Analysis of Recent Argentine Experience" [paper presented to the Twenty-first Annual Latin American Conference, University of Florida, Feb. 17–20, 1971].)

While its industrial community is probably more export oriented than that in any other Latin American country, Mexico's main trading objectives in manufacturing are concerned with exports to the industrial countries, principally the United States.

Intellectuals remain Latin America's main constituency for regional integration. Politicians and business leaders in most of the countries are ambivalent, but their commitment to the process of economic integration tends to be firmer and more active in the smaller countries of the region.

Economic Integration and Independence

Events in the European and, to a lesser extent, Central American common markets have recently reinforced the ambivalent attitudes toward integration. Many previous proponents of regional economic cooperation decided that a Latin American common market on the European model might be highly vulnerable to economic penetration by the United States. Experience showed that European integration was paralleled by the rapid expansion of giant U.S. international corporations; it appeared that U.S. subsidiaries had grown faster than European firms.[13] Suddenly some of the técnicos and Latin American intellectuals have had second thoughts about integration, arriving at the same position of doubt as some business groups in the region, though mostly for different reasons.

The question has increasingly been raised in Latin America whether regional integration, born of a search for economic independence, might not lead to an even greater dependence on the United States. The first stage of the economic independence movement, in the forties and fifties, concentrated on strictly national, autarkically oriented industrialization. But it neither brought a sound and lasting acceleration of growth nor reduced economic dependence on the outside world.

There is a growing fear in Latin America that a regional effort now to permit more efficient and advanced development and vigorous industrialization might result in even greater foreign dominance. The new industrialization would be much more complex and sophisticated and would require more external capital and expertise. Thus the vision of a strong

13. Jean-Jacques Servan-Schreiber's *Le Défi Américain* (Paris: Editions Denoël, 1967), which analyzes the role of U.S. enterprise in Europe, allegedly sold more copies in Brazil than in France. Published in the United States as *The American Challenge*, trans. Ronald Steel (Atheneum, 1968).

Latin America made independent and powerful by economic union is disturbed by the nightmare of a "hegemony of U.S. macro-enterprises . . . that could eventually relegate Latin America to the status of a minor appendage of the United States."[14] Foreign economic penetration has been increasingly controlled under recent national policies, but many Latin Americans believe that with the progress of economic integration, national control over foreign enterprise would not be replaced by an adequate regional foreign investment policy. These fears are compounded by the knowledge that the United States has been a champion of freedom for foreign investors.

The shift in U.S. policy in favor of a Latin American common market in the middle of the 1960s nourished the new doubts. U.S. expressions of support culminated in the meeting at Punta del Este, Uruguay, in April 1967, when the heads of the states of the inter-American system subscribed to a program for gradually establishing a common market. Latin Americans, looking at the past relationship of the United States with the region and the U.S. coolness to a Latin American common market before the 1960s, have become suspicious of this sudden interest in their integration movement.

A U.S. Policy for Latin American Integration

The obviously poor prospects for Latin American development along traditional lines and the increasing social and political tensions in the area have caused U.S. attitudes to move from indifference toward positive support for Latin American integration. By the mid-1960s U.S. officials had embraced the idea of a Latin American common market as an important vehicle for accelerating economic growth in the region.

Despite official endorsement of regional economic efforts, no effective change has been made in certain key aspects of U.S. policy. This is due partially to U.S. reluctance to interfere in an area that is held to be an exclusive Latin American concern. But the apparent decline in Latin American enthusiasm to make significant sacrifices in support of common arrangements also encourages U.S. apathy. A decisive move by the United States to subordinate its bilateral relations with individual countries in

14. Marcos Kaplan, "Porqué no funciona la A.L.A.L.C.," *Mundo Nuevo*, No. 29 (Buenos Aires and Paris, November 1968), p. 8; authors' translation.

favor of regionwide integration assistance programs might jeopardize those countries' friendship and create new problems in U.S.–Latin American relations. Such a shift in policy is the more difficult to support because of the uncertain prospects for Latin American economic integration. And there is still a lingering question whether a regional common market is compatible with the free trade policy that the United States has subscribed to since the Great Depression; moreover, there is still doubt whether regional support for Latin American development would be more productive than traditional bilateral aid.

A potential conflict with private economic interests in the United States may also restrain institution of a policy change. Some U.S. investors, like indigenous industrialists in the area, prefer to operate with a minimum of competition behind the protection of high national trade barriers rather than be exposed to the uncertainties of regional free trade. Furthermore, Latin American economic integration poses a threat to the traditional export markets of U.S. firms; in a highly protected area, imports would be replaced; in an efficiently integrated area without high tariff walls, imports might not be replaced but regional exports might become competitive. Protectionist sentiment in the United States and other developed countries has been stirred by Latin American production of goods other than traditional exports at competitive world market prices. Economic integration could further reduce production costs and increase the conflict between U.S. domestic producers' interests and Latin America's development needs.

But the basic reason for U.S. failure to reduce its bilateral ties in favor of regional relations is the lack either of any compelling need to do so or of any significant pressure from Latin American governments to change the bilateral system.

U.S. and Latin American Roles

No evidence is available to justify great concern about threats to U.S. security in Latin America.[15] The first inter-American attempt to emphasize

15. The economic burdens of USSR support of Cuba are very considerable. Substantial evidence indicates that neither the USSR nor Communist China is genuinely interested in revolution in Latin America. (For example, see Herbert S. Dinerstein, "Soviet Policy in Latin America," *American Political Science Review*, Vol. 61 [March 1967], pp. 80–90.) Expanded diplomatic and commercial exchanges between Latin

development instead of conventional political and security considerations was the Alliance for Progress. Yet fear that Castro would export revolutionary governments to all of Latin America, thus threatening U.S. security, was an important motivation for U.S. support of the Alliance. Probably the most important reasons for the Alliance's deterioration were its use by Latin American governments as just another vehicle for getting more external aid in order to avoid undertaking difficult but necessary reforms, and the decrease in the Castro challenge and hence in effective U.S. support after 1963. The shift to concern for economic and social development has more recently resulted in a clash between the U.S. view that more rapid development implies an unreserved welcome for U.S. capital, technology, and managerial know-how and the growing nationalism in Latin American countries and their demands for more control over their economic destiny.

The integration movement is a Latin American solution to its own development problems; it was born as a movement toward greater independence from developed countries, particularly the United States, under the assumption that such independence is compatible with the long-term interest of the region as well as of the United States. The halting progress toward a common market and the concurrent dissipation of the Alliance for Progress have produced a very touchy situation in which Latin Americans feel more dependent on the United States than they actually are.

At the 1967 Punta del Este conference the United States made a formal commitment to cooperate in the integration effort. But the problems of regional integration must be solved by Latin Americans themselves; they will ultimately have to come to grips with the politically complex issues of mutually adjusting their economic policies and of accepting a certain degree of regional policy making. They must create the institutional mechanisms to facilitate the reduction of trade barriers within the region and to insure a reasonably equitable distribution of the benefits from integration.

While all these decisions cannot be dictated by the United States, their feasibility, shape, and timing will depend greatly on U.S. policy toward

---

American republics and the USSR and Eastern European countries cannot qualify as Soviet intervention in Latin America. Furthermore, the rise of military governments in Brazil, Argentina, Peru, and Bolivia in the late sixties was clearly not related to internal or external military danger. These governments often exaggerate the threat of domestic guerrillas in order to disarm domestic opposition to repressive internal policies.

Latin American economic integration and the general state of hemispheric political and economic relations. If accelerated growth through regional integration is to be the objective, the United States will need to modify its existing bilateral relations, especially the form of its financial aid, which work directly and indirectly against the formation of a common market. Latin Americans must, of course, retain responsibility for the region's development. But the United States can play an important role in that process. This study focuses on such a role against the background of Latin American initiatives to promote regional integration.

CHAPTER TWO

The Economic
Rationale

IF THE MODERNIZATION OF Latin American society depends upon economic development and if a key objective of U.S. policy is to foster economic development, it is important to consider whether economic integration would contribute toward that end.[1] Many countries of Latin America demonstrated in the 1960s that they could not sustain alone the rapid growth and high rates of industrialization they had reached during the 1940s and 1950s.

The economic slowdown is often attributed to an overemphasis on development of the industrial sector, aided by high protective tariffs, primarily at the expense of agriculture and mining. Industrialization was able to provide the impetus for growth during the 1940s and 1950s because of particularly favorable conditions for commodity exports, foreign investment, and financial assistance. Growth possibilities now are diminishing

1. In strict technical terms the various degrees of economic integration are the free trade area, in which barriers are eliminated to the movement of goods among members without adoption of a common external tariff; the customs union, a free trade area with a common external tariff; the common market, a customs union with free movement also of labor and capital among members; and the economic union, a common market with harmonization of all major economic policies. The terms common market, customs union, and economic union are used interchangeably in a general sense in this study.

because they depend on industrial production for small home markets, traditional exports, and foreign aid.

It has become clear that a less protective trade policy can help the stagnant Latin American economies develop more rapidly through more efficient resource allocation. But for Latin Americans a fundamentally important aim of industrialization is the political and economic independence provided by self-sufficiency in manufacturing. A development policy for the region, then, must count industrial self-sufficiency as important as an increase in the rate of growth. Economic integration must be aimed not only at leaving the region better off than the autarkic development policies that the individual Latin American republics have followed but also at meeting the political goals of the region.

Industrialization to Replace Imports

Some countries of Latin America began to industrialize during and after the First World War; and in Argentina, Brazil, and Mexico manufacturing was significant even in the nineteenth century. This industry developed within a relatively free market where local products competed on equal terms with imports. Exports of primary products remained the source of growth, however.

The Great Depression ended that era of economic development. The collapse of international commodity and capital markets in the 1930s caused enormous balance-of-payments problems in countries that were accustomed to satisfying most of their consumer wants through imports paid for by the sale abroad of one or two principal commodities and that had been financing a large part of their domestic investments through the sale of bonds in the capital-exporting countries. Adversity induced Latin American republics to limit their imports severely through increased tariffs, exchange restrictions, import quotas, and outright import prohibition. In the larger countries, industries sprang up haphazardly to produce domestic substitutes for imports. High protection fostered the establishment of uneconomical plants, which often worked at a fraction of their capacity and produced a variety of goods. The Second World War, by cutting off traditional sources of supply, further encouraged import substitution.

The smaller countries, on the other hand, whose markets were very limited, had little choice in the matter and could not undertake any significant industrialization. They remained essentially open economies with low trade barriers, and their economic growth continued to reflect the magnitude and fluctuations of their export proceeds. Until the 1960s these economies, including all the Caribbean and Central American states, grew less rapidly than the industrializing countries of Latin America.[2]

The impetus for growth through import substitution in the larger countries slowed down in the early 1960s. By that time most of the consumer goods that had previously been imported were being produced domestically. Industrial growth has since been largely dependent on the slow increase in national markets, and industrial investment has consequently diminished significantly. Because of an upsurge in economic activity at the end of the 1960s in the three largest countries—Argentina, Brazil, and Mexico—the decade's per capita growth rates averaged somewhat higher than those of the 1950s, as Table 1 illustrates.

Import-substituting industrialization is obviously in large part the consequence of serious balance-of-payments difficulties. But it also reflects a long-standing drive of Latin American societies to achieve some degree of independence from the vagaries of international trade and to strengthen their position vis-à-vis the advanced countries of the world. During the past quarter of a century, industrialization in the region has become synonymous with growth and economic independence. This indeed was the concept of industrialization espoused by many leaders in the now developed countries, including the United States, at an earlier time.[3]

Industrialization in the past few decades has brought about fundamental changes in the internal economic structure of Latin American countries. Import replacement has failed, however, to reduce dependence on traditional exports for foreign exchange. Internally, the roles of agriculture and manufacturing have shifted profoundly. Before the Second World War,

2. See United Nations, Economic Commission for Latin America (ECLA), *The Economic Development of Latin America in the Post War Period*, UN-E/CN.12/659/Rev. 1 (1963), Table 6. Small countries generally appear to be at a disadvantage in the international trade of manufactured goods (see Donald B. Keesing, "Population and Industrial Development: Some Evidence from Trade Patterns," *American Economic Review*, Vol. 58 [June 1968], Pt. 1, pp. 454–55; and Bela Balassa, "Country Size and Trade Patterns: Comment," *American Economic Review*, Vol. 59 [March 1969], pp. 201–04).

3. Compare, for instance, Alexander Hamilton's report to the Congress in 1791 on manufactures (Joseph Grunwald, "Some Reflections on Latin American Industrialization Policy," *Journal of Political Economy*, Vol. 78 [July/August 1970], Supplement, pp. 826–56).

Table 1. Population and Gross National Product in Latin American Countries and the United States, End of 1960s

	Population		Gross national product, per capita		
		Average annual growth, 1965-70	*1969 (in 1960 dollars)*	*Average annual growth (percent)*	
Country	*Total, 1970 (millions)*	*(percent)*		*1950-60*	*1960-69*
LAFTA					
Argentina	24.4	1.5	902	1.2	1.9
Bolivia	4.7	2.4	196	−1.6	3.0
Brazil	93.2	2.9	338	2.6	2.6
Chile	9.8	2.3	593	1.2	2.0
Colombia	22.2	3.5	358	1.6	1.5
Ecuador	6.0	3.4	287	2.3	1.1
Mexico	50.7	3.5	649	2.8	3.3
Paraguay	2.4	3.5	268	0.1	1.1
Peru	13.6	3.1	372	2.7	2.1
Uruguay	2.9	1.2	666	0.6	−0.5
Venezuela	10.8	3.4	731	3.6	1.1
Total	240.7				
CACM					
Costa Rica	1.8	3.8	517	3.2	2.9
El Salvador	3.4	3.3	312	1.5	2.3
Guatemala	5.3	2.9	336	0.9	2.2
Honduras	2.6	3.4	231	0.6	1.8
Nicaragua	2.0	3.0	346	2.2	3.2
Total	15.1				
Others					
Cuba	8.3	2.0	n.a.	n.a.	n.a.
Dominican Republic	4.3	3.4	205	2.4	0.1
Haiti	5.2	2.4	88	−0.2	−0.8
Panama	1.4	3.3	651	1.9	4.8
Total					
Latin America[a]	275.0	2.9	479	2.0	2.2
United States	205.0	1.0	3,452	1.4	3.2

Sources: Centro Latinoamericano de Demografia (CELADE), *Boletín Demográfico*, Vol. 4, No. 7 (Santiago, Chile, January 1971), pp. 4–5; United Nations, Economic Commission for Latin America (ECLA), *Economic Survey of Latin America, 1968*, E/CN.12/825/Rev. 1 (1970), Table 7, p. 10; ECLA, "Economic Survey of Latin America, 1969, Part 1: Basic Aspects of Latin American Development Strategy," E/CN.12/AC.62/2/Corr. 1 (April 28, 1970; processed), Table 2, and "Part 2: The Latin American Economy," E/CN.12/AC.62/2/Add.1/(1) (April 21, 1970; processed); ECLA, "Notas sobre la economía y el desarrollo de América Latina," various issues; U.S. Bureau of the Census, *Statistical Abstract of the United States, 1970*, pp. 5, 312; U.S. Department of Commerce, *Survey of Current Business*, Vol. 51 (July 1971), p. 5.

n.a. Not available.

a. In this study Latin America refers to the members of LAFTA and CACM and to the Dominican Republic, Haiti, and Panama, except as otherwise amended (for example, this table includes Cuba).

agriculture contributed about twice as much to the regional gross product as did manufacturing. By the 1950s the contributions were about equal, and in the late 1960s the share of manufacturing was well above that of agriculture (see Table 2). In countries like Argentina, Brazil, Chile, and Uruguay the contribution by the various economic sectors (agriculture, manufacturing, services, and so forth) to gross national product now seems similar to that of some industrial countries in Europe.

Import substitution has not induced any major changes in the size of Latin America's external trade. Contrary to expectations, total import requirements have not decreased significantly as a result of import replacement by domestic production. Haphazard industrialization and the rise of a vast array of assembly industries in smaller countries have in some cases brought an increase in imports. The cost of imported inputs for small-scale, inefficient domestic industries may be greater than the value of their output at world market prices. Overvalued currencies and multiple exchange rates, which most Latin American countries have resorted to during the import substitution phase, have combined with tariffs to make import-competing goods and services more profitable investments than exports, thus constricting the supply of exportable products.

The composition of imports has changed. The percentage of consumer goods has generally declined in favor of a higher proportion of capital and intermediate goods (machinery, equipment, replacement parts, fuels, chemicals, and other materials and supplies). Thus import substitution, which originally was intended to improve the balance of payments, has often aggravated a country's dependence on the external sector. It is easier in a balance-of-payments crisis to compress imports if they consist primarily of final consumer goods, as was the case in the past, than if—as is the case now in many Latin American republics—they are largely vital supplies for industrial plants employing a significant (and articulate) part of the labor force.

National import substitution has not been, and was not intended to be, helpful as a stimulant to exports. Almost by definition, this kind of industrialization is geared to the domestic market and therefore does not help raise export earnings appreciably. About 90 percent of the exports of even the most industrialized countries in the region still consist of primary goods, Latin America's traditional exports. Attempts to expand exports of manufactures and semimanufactures to the rest of the world run into very serious difficulties because of the high cost and low quality of produc-

Table 2. Composition of Gross Domestic Product of Latin American Countries and the United States, 1969

Percent of total

Country	Agriculture	Mining	Manufacturing	Construction	Electricity, gas, water	Transportation, communication	Commerce, finance	Government	Miscellaneous services
LAFTA									
Argentina	15.2	1.7	35.4	4.6	2.2	7.4	19.0	6.1	8.6
Bolivia	23.1	13.9	13.3	8.1	1.2	9.6	9.9	8.0	12.9
Brazil	19.9	0.7	24.4	1.1	2.5	7.6	20.2	7.7	15.9
Chile	10.1	9.7	25.9	4.1	1.5	10.3	17.6	4.7	16.0
Colombia	30.3	3.3	18.4	4.5	1.2	6.8	16.7	6.0[a]	12.9[a]
Ecuador	31.7	2.3	17.0	4.6	1.5	3.6	13.3[a]	7.8[a]	18.4[a]
Mexico	12.8	4.3	22.2	4.9	1.4	3.4	30.3	6.1	14.6
Paraguay	34.2	0.2	19.0	3.1	1.0	5.1	18.3	5.1	14.0
Peru	18.1[b]	7.1	22.0	3.4	1.1	5.4	15.4	8.2	19.3
Uruguay	21.2	c	21.3	3.3	2.0	7.3	21.4	7.9	15.6
Venezuela[a]	6.5	19.3	18.7	6.2	2.1	4.6	15.9	c	26.7
CACM									
Costa Rica	22.4	c	20.5	5.1	c	c	c	c	46.8
El Salvador[a]	26.1	0.2	18.2	3.4	1.9	5.3	24.1	7.9	12.8
Guatemala	27.3	0.1	13.2	1.8	1.2	4.5	33.3	5.3	13.2
Honduras	38.5	2.2	15.6	5.7	0.9	6.6	15.6	2.5	12.4
Nicaragua	27.5	1.4	14.3	3.9	3.1	4.7	20.8	10.3	14.0
Others									
Dominican Republic	24.8	1.6	12.6	5.9	1.6	6.9	18.5[a]	10.2[a]	18.8[a]
Haiti[a]	45.9	3.4[d]	13.7	d	1.1	2.5	10.8	6.1	16.5
Panama	21.8	0.3	16.6	6.1	2.6	6.6	12.9	2.9	30.2
United States	3.2	1.7	27.8	4.7	2.3	6.3	30.2	12.6	11.3

Sources: ECLA, "Economic Survey of Latin America, 1969, Pt. 2: The Latin American Economy," E/CN.12/AC.62/2/Add.1/(I) and (II) (April 21, 1970; processed); U.S. Department of Commerce, *Survey of Current Business*, Vol. 51 (April 1971), p. 17.

a. 1968 data.   b. Includes fisheries.   c. No separate data available.   d. Construction is included in mining.

tion, the restrictive import policies prevailing in the rest of the world, and the market-sharing arrangements followed by many foreign industrial corporations operating in Latin America.

New Strategies

Internally oriented industrialization has ceased to be an avenue to development. Less than fifteen years after he had called for a policy of accelerated national import substitution as an antidote to the declining economic prospects of primary goods suppliers,[4] Raúl Prebisch had concluded, with other Latin American economists, that in several countries the dynamic phase of national import substitution was ending.[5] Policy makers in many Latin American countries have become increasingly aware of the economic cost of autarkic industrialization. Even the largest national market in Latin America is not one-fourth the size of the domestic market of West Germany, or the United Kingdom, or France.[6] Latin American national development policies have led to highly protected, inefficient industrial production on a scale so small that even the most skilled entrepreneurs cannot compete in the world market. Lack of competition in many industries has created national monopolies and oligopolies, which further increase the prices of their products. Prebisch believes that "had it been possible to develop industrial exports, the process of industrialization would have been more economical, for it would have made possible the international division of labour in manufacturing."[7]

Latin American economists agree that the way out of the current economic impasse is through new development strategies oriented toward promoting international trade. A return to an emphasis on exports, however, should not mean concentrating production once more on traditional

4. Raúl Prebisch, "The Economic Development of Latin America and Its Principal Problems" (1950; processed); printed in *Economic Bulletin for Latin America*, Vol. 7 (February 1962), pp. 1–22.

5. *Towards a Dynamic Development Policy for Latin America* (United Nations, 1963).

6. Albert O. Hirschman argues that import-substituting industrialization is not dead but that sociological barriers and bottlenecks that appear in industries producing final goods that need a larger market are holding it back ("The Political Economy of Import-Substituting Industrialization in Latin America," *Quarterly Journal of Economics*, Vol. 82 [February 1968], pp. 1–32).

7. *Towards a Dynamic Development Policy*, pp. 21–22.

commodities for export at the expense of manufactures. Specializing in primary goods production might maximize the region's welfare in the short run, although the poor prospects for expanding such production significantly and the import restrictions, domestic subsidies, and other means of protecting inefficient competition in the advanced industrial countries make even that dubious.[8] Comparative advantages in international trade can be altered by development policies that seek to increase a country's economic welfare over the long run. Not only is the volume of production important to the economy, but the kinds of goods produced. Thus a country or region whose current comparative advantage does not favor industrialization may elect to incur the short-run costs for the long-run advantages of industrialization.

Integration and Industrialization

Latin American industrialization may continue to be inefficient in idealized free-trade terms but may promote a broader sort of social welfare. The region's new development strategy aims at accelerating the industrialization process by orienting it to exports. A general reduction in trade barriers without discrimination against countries outside the region is not, however, one of its primary objectives.

The cost of Latin American manufacturing production is higher than that of industrially advanced countries. There is little possibility that Latin American industries could match the superior technology and overall efficiency of the industries of developed countries in the short run. The foreign manufactures that would pour in after substantial nondiscriminatory tariff reductions could stifle Latin American industrialization, weakening incentives to build up industries even in those sectors in which Latin America could eventually develop a comparative advantage.

The main thrust of a long-run development policy is to enlarge markets for protected Latin American manufactured goods. Heavy and medium industry, with expanded markets, would realize the benefits of economies of large-scale production[9] and resources could be more efficiently allocated

8. See Joseph Grunwald and Philip Musgrove, *Natural Resources in Latin American Development* (Johns Hopkins Press for Resources for the Future, 1970), Pt. 1, Chap. 2, and Pt. 2, the commodity chapters.

9. Unit costs of production decrease because of utilization of idle machinery and equipment or the introduction of new machinery and equipment, mass production tech-

and used. The two main avenues currently considered for increasing exports of manufactured products of the Latin American countries are special treatment in the markets of the developed countries and protected trade in a common market.

Although an increase in the scale of operations of a firm can significantly reduce unit costs of production, the benefits would not be great enough to permit Latin American firms to compete in the markets of the advanced countries. Undertaking new investments in order to expand production for exports to new and untried markets would require a degree of risk-taking and modern entrepreneurship that cannot be expected in less developed countries. The technological gap between Latin America and the industrial countries is vast; nearly all technical innovation in Latin America is imported, usually with some time lag. It would take years for Latin Americans to acquire managerial and labor skills equal to those in the industrialized world and to keep up with technical and scientific progress there; to acquire innovative competence or adapt the knowledge and techniques of developed nations to newly industrialized countries would take both time and a great effort in human resource development.

Moreover, trade restrictions in the economically advanced nations, while on the whole not as great as restrictions in the developing countries, have tended to discriminate against the latter, thus dampening the Latin American businessman's enthusiasm for exporting. The progressive Latin American entrepreneur needs a strong incentive to confront the adverse export conditions and the difficulties of access to developed-country markets. Tariff reductions and other preferences extended by the advanced countries to the manufactures of the developing areas—but not to those of other developed nations—could provide the stimulus by compensating for cost differentials and creating export possibilities to accelerate industrialization in the less developed countries.

Another route to larger markets for Latin American products is through economic integration. While preferences would have to be substantial to induce a Latin American manufacturer to compete in developed nations' markets, reducing trade barriers among Latin American countries would more readily attract efficient Latin American producers. A Latin American customs union, although it would be much smaller than the combined

---

niques, and other technological improvements occasioned by a wider market. Economies of scale tend to be large in heavy industries and mass-production industries.

markets of developed countries, would open up a market many times greater than that of the average individual Latin American republic. Such a regionwide market might appear more durable to the Latin American business community than would markets opened up through special trade preferences in developed countries. The permanence of developed countries' concessions would always be uncertain in view of the recurring pressures of vested interests and frequent balance-of-payments problems. On the other hand, an external tariff around the region, combined with stable markets, would protect regional industry during the "learning period." It would give firms incentives and time to make technological changes, to undertake large new investments and plant expansion in order to benefit from the economies of large-scale production, to improve their use of resources, and to make other cost-cutting efforts that could eventually make their goods competitive with imports from advanced countries. Simultaneously it would give the countries time to improve their educational systems in order to raise the skill levels of their labor force.

Preferential arrangements with developed countries' markets and a regional common market are not mutually exclusive alternatives. They can be mutually reinforcing instruments for Latin American development. Nevertheless, the hope of gaining access to markets of advanced countries through preferences tends to draw attention away from the difficult problems of regional integration.

Latin American economic integration could expand industrialization through regional instead of national import substitution, but Latin American statesmen do not accept this as the ultimate objective of development. Integration is considered "the most important mechanism for stimulating the diversification of exports"[10] and a step in the direction of worldwide free trade: "As a first stage, this competition should be primarily among the Latin American countries themselves. In a second stage these countries should gradually accept competition from outside as their industries become stronger through the operation of the Latin American Common Market. . . . In this way, Latin American countries could participate more and more in a truly world-wide movement of trade liberalization."[11]

An economically integrated Latin America thus could be viewed as a subsystem of the world economy. The purpose of such a subsystem would

10. Carlos Sanz de Santamaría, in *Journal of Commerce*, April 14, 1967.
11. Raúl Prebisch, in *ibid.*

be to change the structure of comparative advantage within which Latin American foreign trade takes place. At present the region finds itself "trapped" by the international division of labor, exporting primary commodities and at best only processed raw materials and light manufactures, and importing the products of technologically more complex industries. Regional integration would permit Latin America to enter some of the dynamic sectors of manufacturing, not as a move toward regional self-sufficiency but toward less unequal partnership in the world trading community. Latin Americans are quite aware that the bulk of international trade takes place among the industrial countries of the world. They want to participate in this interchange with products of growth industries in which they do not now have a comparative advantage.

The Impact on Intra-Latin American Trade

Reduction of tariffs and other restrictions within Latin America cannot, of course, be expected to lead immediately to a large diversion of the region's foreign commerce to intra-area trade. Nations that to a considerable extent still compete in raw material production will have little to trade with one another until their industrialization reaches higher levels. While fuller utilization of present manufacturing capacity might increase trade within the area, the immediate thrust of Latin American integration will be to increase regional investment. Only after new investments have borne fruit can a significant increase in intraregional trade be expected.

Integration is intended primarily to accelerate the region's industrialization, not per se to aid the production and marketing of bananas or solve the coffee surplus problem; it can be expected, however, to have a significant impact on area trade in minerals and other industrial raw materials. In the past only a small part of the region's natural resources has been absorbed by the manufacturing sector of the area. Aside from some intra-Latin American trade in food, only petroleum (mainly Venezuelan) has been traded in substantial amounts within Latin America.[12] By far the major share of raw materials exports still goes to markets outside the region. If economic integration succeeds in accelerating industrialization, Latin American countries could use more and more of the region's natural resources as inputs for their plants. Integration, therefore, can eventually

12. The largest proportion of intra-area trade in food has been accounted for by wheat from Argentina to Brazil and Chile.

increase trade not only in manufactured products but also in primary goods within the area.

The Economic Benefits of Integration

Customs unions traditionally have been held to bring the greatest gains to regions with highly developed trade and economic relations, in which the partner countries' industries are at similar levels of development and well diversified and in which financial intermediaries are well established. Those conditions were present in Europe before economic integration. They were not present in Latin America at the end of the 1960s: differences in income levels were considerable;[13] productive structure varied greatly; and trade within the area was a small fraction of the region's total international trade. If the supposedly proper conditions are mandatory to the success of a customs union, a Latin American common market is unlikely to succeed.

The welfare of an area is expected to increase through economic integration if the member countries shift to less expensive sources of supply. But a high, protective common external tariff for Latin America would divert trade from low-cost suppliers outside the region to high-cost regional suppliers and thus lead to a net welfare loss for the area in the short run.

Integration and Developing Countries

Most developing countries do not fit the assumptions underlying the traditional model for a customs union. Because many of their resources are unemployed or underemployed, diverting trade to higher cost producers within an integrated area might cause a loss that could be more than offset even in the short run by fuller utilization of resources. Latin America would continue under an integration scheme to import from low-cost suppliers outside the area as long as export earnings permitted; but by importing a different mix of goods it could increase efficiency, even with a

13. If the top income countries (Argentina and Venezuela) and the bottom income countries (Haiti, Bolivia, Dominican Republic, and Honduras) are eliminated (see Table 1), relative income differentials in Latin America are not much greater than in Europe, but because they occur at much lower income levels, they create greater difficulties than did differences among European countries.

seemingly unprofitable trade diversion. Several Latin American writers have argued that trade diversion does not necessarily lead to a decrease in welfare. It can be considered "efficient" in developing countries if trade is being diverted from the efficient developed country outside the region to the efficiently developing country within the region.[14] If national import substitution has already diverted a large share of trade to domestic producers, they may be capable of supplying an integrated market at reasonable costs. The amount that can be saved by buying from efficient regional producers instead of producing nationally in a number of countries can be considered trade creation.

Moreover, economies of scale help decrease costs of production, as do such external economies as those gained by locating an industry where it can take advantage of a skilled labor pool, service industries, expert management, and perhaps cheaper raw materials, energy, and other inputs. External economies can also be broadly conceived as accruing to the community, in the upgrading of the labor force and in the modernization brought about by industrialization. Increased market size stimulates investment not only in direct production, but also in transportation, communications, and other infrastructure works.[15] Taking account of these dynamic elements in the traditional theory of customs unions would more accurately depict the benefits of economic integration in less developed areas such as Latin America.

Latin American economies have become so distorted through national import substitution that integration offers an attractive means of rationalizing the industrial structure. Certainly, integration will lead to trade diversion as imports shift away from advanced countries. But increased regional trade will help to reduce costs as industries where economies of scale are important take advantage of enlarged markets. Furthermore, regional import substitution will free foreign exchange for imports of

14. See Ana María Martirena-Mantel, "Integración y desarrollo económico," *El Trimestre Económico*, Vol. 36 (April–June, 1969); and Jorge Sakamoto, "Industrial Development and Integration of Underdeveloped Countries," *Journal of Common Market Studies*, Vol. 7 (June 1969), pp. 283–304.

15. "Infrastructure" generally denotes physical works fundamental to the economic and social development of a region. It encompasses transport facilities (such as roads, ports, railroads, and airports); energy developments (such as hydroelectric works and other facilities for generating and distributing electricity); and social projects (such as schools, hospitals, housing, and recreation facilities). It sometimes applies to institutional and administrative organizations of governments designed to foster development.

capital goods and equipment for investment in the industrialization process.

Economic integration could change Latin America's production advantages in the long run; industrial growth would bring technological advances and new labor skills and contribute to the modernization and diversification of the productive structure. Even if regional costs of production should remain higher than world market prices, Latin American countries would have industrialized at less cost under integration than under national autarkic development schemes.

Research has shown that improvements in the allocation of resources in a customs union are of relatively little benefit to the member countries.[16] But the research is based primarily on the European experience. The disregard for benefits of scale economies is likewise based on conditions in European countries; production levels before economic integration may well have been so high that creation of the European Economic Community did not yield large economies of scale.[17]

The Latin American Case

In a less developed region like Latin America, where the small size of national markets limits production, the possibilities of gains from economies of scale appear to be great. The larger markets created by a customs union should lead to lower manufacturing costs, higher rates of investment, and more efficient allocation of resources in the region. In addition, existing idle industrial capacity could be put to use to increase production. Indications are, therefore, that a Latin American common market would

16. See Harry G. Johnson, *Money, Trade and Economic Growth* (London: Allen & Unwin, 1962), and Harvey Leibenstein, "Allocative Efficiency vs. 'X-Efficiency,'" *American Economic Review*, Vol. 56 (June 1966), pp. 392–415. Tibor Scitovsky suggests that the most important effect of liberalizing trade in Europe is not the welfare gains from increased specialization or economies of scale, but an increased rate of investment that results from the risk-spreading influence of larger markets (*Economic Theory and Western European Integration* [London: Allen & Unwin, 1958]).

17. Edward F. Denison has shown that market growth and associated economies of scale were responsible for a large part of the increase in national growth rates in Europe in the postwar period (*Why Growth Rates Differ: Postwar Experience in Nine Western Countries* [Brookings Institution, 1967], pp. 225–35). Bela Balassa has shown that scale economies through horizontal specialization may bring considerable gains, even in the large European industrial countries (*Trade Liberalization among Industrial Countries: Objectives and Alternatives* [McGraw-Hill, 1967], Chap. 5).

have a direct and important influence in accelerating economic growth in the region.

Tariffs are obviously not the only obstacle to intraregional trade in Latin America. During the 1950s and 1960s approximately 10 percent of Latin America's foreign trade was intraregional, and about 40 percent of that was accounted for by two of the region's most industrialized countries, Argentina and Brazil.[18] Geography has undoubtedly been an important factor in limiting trade within the area. The Andean mountains separate the countries on the Pacific from those on the Atlantic coast. Jungles and deserts interfere with east-west as well as with north-south trade, and large bodies of water, jungles, and mountains isolate Mexico and Central America (and the Caribbean Islands) from South America. Natural barriers have helped steer foreign commerce outside the area. Are these natural barriers between the Latin American countries so prohibitively expensive that intraregional trade would remain uneconomical even after tariffs and other institutional barriers were removed?

Historical and institutional forces have done much more to bias Latin American trade toward outside areas than have geographical barriers. Almost every country's production, transportation, and other trade mechanisms were developed by Europeans and North Americans interested primarily in purchasing Latin American raw materials and agricultural commodities and in turn using Latin America as an outlet for their manufactures. Transportation systems were therefore geared mainly to external trade, connecting ports with the centers of primary goods production and with the capital.

Furthermore, the fear of neighboring countries was so strong that transportation arteries along national borders were purposely neglected. Not only are there few roads crossing from one country to another, but those that do exist are left in disrepair. Transshipment of cargo at frontier points on railroads and highways, still frequently required by national authorities (even when rail gauges do not differ), has imposed a heavy burden on intra-area trade.

Perhaps the most important manmade barriers to intra-Latin American trade have been tariffs and other restrictions imposed to protect national production and foreign-exchange reserves. National tariffs have not only helped to fragment the Latin American market but have also discriminated

18. Donald W. Baerresen, Martin Carnoy, and Joseph Grunwald, *Latin American Trade Patterns* (Brookings Institution, 1965).

against intraregional trade. Latin American countries applied tariffs and other restrictions indiscriminately against goods from all other countries, through most-favored-nation agreements. "Thus, protectionist restrictions that might or might not be justified by the 'infant industry' argument were applied against the infant industries of sister nations in Latin America as well as against the industrially developed nations of Europe and North America. Insofar as this protection was often of very limited effectiveness, it encouraged imports from the latter countries, while handicapping severely the development of adequate markets for Latin American production."[19]

The distortions in the structure of trade that are the result of historical and institutional rather than physical factors are uneconomical. The elimination or substantial reduction of tariffs among the Latin American countries, and retention of existing tariffs to the rest of the world, should provide a strong incentive for the development of commerce within the region. The meagerness of intra-area trade can "be viewed as an indication of the existence of a large pool of untapped trading opportunities which could be developed in the future."[20]

The results of a study of the effects of economic integration on six Latin American industries are striking. Projections of demand and of production and transportation costs for each of the industries at different output levels and locations in the Latin American Free Trade Association (LAFTA) were made for 1975.[21] For most of the products of the six industries the increase in market size from a national to a regional market would bring substantial benefits from economies of scale in a free trade area. Latin America could be competitive with U.S. imports in thirteen of the fourteen products examined and with worldwide imports in twelve. The annual benefits to LAFTA countries of producing the fourteen products at the minimum-cost locations within the region rather than importing them from the United States is estimated to range from $180 million to $230 million, depending on transport costs and rates of exchange. This

19. Robert Triffin, "International Monetary Arrangements, Capital Markets and Economic Integration in Latin America," *Journal of Common Market Studies*, Vol. 4 (October 1965), p. 79.

20. *Ibid.*, p. 78.

21. Martin Carnoy, *Industrialization in a Latin American Common Market*, an ECIEL study (Brookings Institution, 1971). Fourteen products in the following product groups were studied: nitrogenous fertilizers, methanol and formaldehyde, pulp and paper, lathes, tractors, and powdered milk and cheese.

gain equals 10–15 percent of the projected total value of production of the six product groups in 1975. It would also bring an annual gain of 3–4 percent in the region's gross domestic product (GDP). Assuming a 15 percent average rate of return to capital, the 3–4 percent gain is translated into an increase of 0.4–0.6 percentage points in the growth rate of the region.

This means that formation of a customs union would not only allow Latin America to compete with U.S. imports in the production of manufactured goods, but would free almost 4 percent of GDP annually for further investment or consumption.

Economic Efficiency and the Distribution of Benefits

Elimination of trade barriers might result in a polarization of economic development, with the more industrial countries attracting most of the investment and the least developed losing some of their infant industries in regional competition. Economies of scale, transportation costs, and external economies would all work to distribute production in such a way that the optimum results for the region would not necessarily coincide with the optimum results for the individual nations. Thus while the region's prosperity increased, economic growth in the member countries might not be equalized.

Integration would produce benefits as well as costs for each member nation, and the difference between the two determines the net effect of integration on a country's welfare. The benefits arise from the employment of idle resources, increased industrialization, diversification of exports, and other structural changes, some of which fall under the heading of "modernization." The costs represent the higher regional prices paid for products formerly imported from the outside. If the benefits outweigh the costs, there will be a net gain. Smaller and weaker countries would tend to have a smaller net gain—perhaps even a net loss—than the more industrial countries. They might not be able to attract more industry, possibly even less than they would have had they instituted national policies of import substitution; in addition, because they must import a greater share of consumer goods than their more advanced partners, they must bear a higher proportion of the costs of trade diversion.

In weighing long-run gains against short-run benefits it is not possible to translate the elements of a growth policy for a national economy to a regional economy. Some claim that national development may depend upon the "paradoxical but inevitable fact that in order to accelerate the future development of retarded regions the growth of industrially more advanced areas must be encouraged."[22] But even within a single country the radiation and feedback effects between developed and depressed areas are often very slow, as they have been between the north and the south of the United States and of Italy. Certainly they would be even weaker and slower between nations and perhaps overwhelmed by the effects of polarized development, which would tend to widen differences between the less developed and the more advanced countries in Latin America. The realities of regional development have been recognized by the United Nations Conference on Trade and Development (UNCTAD):

> Countries, be they developing or developed, will envisage the establishment of a unified market only if they can expect that the benefits of the integration process will be distributed among them in an equitable manner. . . .
>
> . . . In general, it would appear that the problem of ensuring an equitable distribution of the benefits of integration is more difficult to solve as between developing than as between developed countries. . . .
>
> . . . Ideally, no doubt, the objective would be the narrowing of the gap between the more advanced and the less advanced partner countries. In reality, each country interprets the meaning of equity in the light of its own evaluation of the prospective advantages and disadvantages of a particular scheme. It will not judge an ideal scheme, but appraise chances of arriving at, or the probable results of a specific negotiated compromise. . . .
>
> . . . despite all calculations, public opinion in the partner countries will not judge the benefits of integration by comparing hypothetical rates of growth, nor will it easily trust long-term appraisals. What is more important is that even for the short term there should be tangible evidence of the benefits of integration, particularly for the less advanced country [of an integration group]. . . . At any rate, probably the most important reason for the failure of integration schemes or for the reluctance to enter into them is the insufficient consideration given to this problem of the fair sharing of the ensuing gains.[23]

Political reality demands that member countries of a customs union be assured that all will share in the benefits of economic integration and that none will be disadvantaged. Some economic efficiency will have to be

---

22. L. Lefeber, "Regional Allocation of Resources in India," in P. N. Rosenstein-Rodan (ed.), *Pricing and Fiscal Policies* (M.I.T. Press, 1964), p. 18.

23. United Nations Conference on Trade and Development (UNCTAD), *Trade Expansion and Economic Integration among Developing Countries*, Sales No. 67.II.D.20 (1967), Chap. 4, pp. 20–22.

sacrificed in the process of trading regional growth for a reasonable distribution of income among individual countries. Latin American interest in an equitable distribution of integration benefits is evidenced by the fact that LAFTA provides for special treatment of the least developed countries in the region, offers fewer privileges to the middle level countries, and offers none to the three most industrialized (Argentina, Brazil, and Mexico). The Andean subregional integration agreement makes an even sharper distinction. Such mechanisms as complementarity agreements also provide a safeguard against the benefits from integration accruing to the big countries at the expense of the smaller.

Thus economic efficiency is not the sole objective of Latin American economic integration. Its aim is to achieve the highest output for the region consistent with a "balanced"distribution of economic development among the member countries; this would not necessarily result in maximum regional production.

Investments therefore must be oriented toward achieving a more balanced distribution of integration benefits in the short run than might otherwise occur. While it would be folly to make certain only that each member country share equally in the benefits of a Latin American customs union, it would be nonsensical to expect any country to join if it had only a small chance of participating promptly in the economic growth of the region.

The study of free-trade effects on the six industry groups indicates that at least seven of the ten LAFTA countries studied (Bolivia was excluded) would qualify as the optimum (minimum-cost) location for one or more of the fourteen products.[24] A geographically more diversified distribution of industrial production might not be particularly costly, for several less desirable locations of production for most of the industries would cost the region little more than production at the minimum-cost location. There is thus some leeway for the political orientation of investments—particularly since more than six industries will in reality be involved—that would not do violence to the precepts of economic efficiency.[25]

24. Carnoy, *Industrialization in a Latin American Common Market.*
25. For instance, there are 75 combinations of places where the production of methanol and formaldehyde might be located in the ten countries. At one of these the costs of production and transportation would be a minimum for the region; but at 28 other locations these costs would be less than 10 percent higher than at the optimum location. Most of the remaining alternatives would be grossly inefficient. (*Ibid.,* Chap. 5.)

Summary

A Latin American common market could increase economic growth rates in Latin America and also permit the other goals of Latin American development—industrialization, a more equitable distribution of income among countries, and reduced dependence on the United States and other advanced countries. The characteristics of the common market would not fit the traditional image of economic integration but would accord with the welfare objectives of developing countries. Primarily, integration would be aimed at the acceleration of development through industrialization, carried out by the promotion of investments in export industries. An export-oriented industrialization can help to end the slow growth trend. Regional industrialization could be fostered through "infant industry" protection via a common external tariff against outside competition from the advanced countries. The goal of economic efficiency would therefore be subordinated to the development of an indigenous industrial structure. Within the common market, the principal objective would be a balanced distribution of economic benefits among the partner countries.

Regional integration might not be the ideal way for Latin America to develop economically. But because the gaps in technological knowledge, resources, and entrepreneurial skill are immense, because resources are underutilized and capital and labor have limited mobility, because both advanced and less developed countries restrict the international flow of goods and services, and because industrialization and such noneconomic considerations as national and regional sovereignty are deemed important, economic integration looks like a good alternative to free trade, and regional import substitution appears more efficient than national import substitution.

CHAPTER THREE

Integration Efforts

DESPITE THE TIES THAT would seem to unite Latin American countries—a common colonial heritage, cultural affinities, and two, very similar, dominant languages—early movements toward economic cooperation and political unification ended in failure. The philosophical discourse on Latin American cooperation in the nineteenth and the early twentieth century failed to make a concrete case for regional union. Even Bolívar, who is proclaimed—probably wrongly—the father of Pan Americanism and of the inter-American system, gave no evidence of an integration philosophy in his writings. Bolívar's plans for international cooperation in the Western Hemisphere called for a close relationship among the former Spanish colonies, with Great Britain as their protector against the other European powers and the United States.

The doctrine of Pan Latin Americanism arose in the twentieth century as a defense against the overwhelming political and economic power of the United States. While it was openly directed against the expansionist and interventionist policies of Theodore Roosevelt, it was more than a political protest. The writings of such influential Latin American intellectuals of the early years of the century as José Enrique Rodó of Uruguay, Manuel Ugarte of Argentina, Rubén Darío of Nicaragua, and Francisco García Calderón of Peru abound in exhortations for Latin American economic cooperation. Their purpose was to bring some measure of political and economic independence to a continent hopelessly divided into a score of weak, quasi-independent republics.[1] They sought to build on the common cultural and political traditions of the Spanish empire and the early postindependence period. And they offered examples of other unifications to convince their broad audiences:

Our century tends to synthetical action. As modern nations were formed by overcoming the old feudal anarchy, so metropolis and colonies are uniting in our days to form formidable empires which merely commercial interests could not explain. ... The enormous power of the North American nation is the result of this unity. ... But there are economic ties between the Latin nations, which may assist the preparation of respectable unions. ...

Latin America cannot continue to live divided, while her enemies are building up vast federations and enormous empires. Whether in the name of race or commercial interests, of common utility or true independence, the American democracies must form themselves into three or four powerful States. The Latin New World is alone in resisting the universal impulse toward the establishment ... of increasingly vast and increasingly powerful organisations.[2]

In spite of such exhortations, Latin America continued to live divided. In the years following the Great Depression various attempts were made to form regional trading arrangements, but only bilateral schemes prospered until 1960. Argentina, Brazil, and Chile promoted bilateral trade with other Latin American countries in the forties and the early fifties for political reasons and because their traditional export trade with the industrial countries was disappointing, not because they supported the idea of regional economic cooperation.

The few attempts to expand these bilateral arrangements failed. For example, in early 1941, at the initiative of Argentina, a conference of the River Plate countries was held in Montevideo, with Argentina, Bolivia, Brazil, Paraguay, and Uruguay participating. The conference agreed to establish a customs union that would offer preferential tariff treatment for Bolivia and Paraguay, the lowest income countries of the group. Moreover, arrangements were made to promote river and road traffic, communications, and tourism among the five nations.[3] Because the treaty did not extend to out-

1. The cry against a disunited Latin America reappeared in the forties and the fifties: "An empire was destroyed in the south, while one was built in the United States. A process of integration made the United States; a process of disintegration divided the twenty nations to the south." (Carlos Dávila, *We of the Americas* [Ziff-Davis Publishing Co., 1949], p. 17.)

2. Francisco García Calderón, *Latin America—Its Rise and Progress* (Charles Scribner's Sons, 1913), p. 350.

3. Acta Final de la Conferencia Regional de los Países de la Plata (Montevideo, Feb. 6, 1941).

side countries the trade privileges that were granted within the region, the United Kingdom and the United States expressed opposition. The treaty was never ratified by the signatory nations, not only because of the opposition of the member countries' major trading partners but also because of the other members' fear of Argentine hegemony.

Bilateral trading arrangements continued in Latin America after the war, and some progress was made toward economic integration. For example, Colombia, Ecuador, and Venezuela formed a multinational merchant fleet, Flota Grancolombiana, in 1947. Although Venezuela withdrew in 1953, the joint operation by Colombia and Ecuador has brought benefits to both parties.

When the Central American Common Market (CACM) and the Latin American Free Trade Association (LAFTA) were established in 1960, the world at large was surprised in view of the failure of previous integration efforts. If nothing else, they seemed to indicate a considerable improvement in Latin America's political and psychological climate for cooperation in economic matters. It is difficult to say whether this improvement reflected a better perception of a regional unity of interests or whether it arose from dissatisfaction with traditional economic relations with the outside industrialized world, in view of the post-Korean War dampening of the international commodity markets, which seriously affected Latin America.

The commitment to integration of key groups in Latin American countries later proved weaker than it appeared at first. The military, the most powerful group in many Latin American countries, was never enthusiastic, the business sector at best ambivalent. Intellectuals and bureaucrats, the main support of the integration movement, do not make an effective political constituency.

The Central American Common Market

The first attempts after the Second World War to bring about some degree of economic cooperation among five minuscule Central American republics began in the early 1950s. At that time only Africa seemed to have a lower priority than Latin America among the vital political and economic interests of the United States. It was while the United States was preoccupied with the Korean War, the final years of the Marshall Plan, its involvement in the Middle East, and the peak of the cold war that the idea of Central American economic integration was conceived by a group of Latin

American economists in the United Nations Economic Commission for Latin America (ECLA).

Except for the East African Common Market (whose experiences neither the ECLA experts nor Central Americans were aware of), Central American economic integration was the first contemporary experiment of its kind in the underdeveloped world. Leaving aside economic reasons—the obvious lack of viability of five small economies, each of them having an internal market the size of a medium-sized city's in an industrial country—ECLA could hardly have chosen a less promising field for such an experiment. The Central American republic established when Spanish colonial rule ended in the first quarter of the nineteenth century had disintegrated after fifteen years into five small units ravaged by external invasions, regional wars, and domestic strife. These conditions prevailed for over a century. The report that the U.S. minister to Central America, George M. Williamson, sent to Secretary of State Hamilton Fish in 1874 could have been written after the end of the Second World War: the memory of past bloody struggles made intra-Central American friendship and alliances practically impossible; the extent of local prejudices against neighboring countries was unimaginable; each state considered itself superior to all the others; no identity of interest could be found even among big landowners; the absence of communications prevented cooperation; and one of the countries—Costa Rica—followed a traditional policy of isolationism.[4] Between 1840 and 1930 there were some thirty-five attempts at uniting Central America. All ended in dismal failure.

Central America has been among the poorest areas in Latin America. Just before the formation of the common market, per capita gross national product was about $250—two-thirds of the regional level. The range was from about $180 in Honduras to $350 in Costa Rica. The combined population was about 11 million, and the largest country, Guatemala, had about 3.5 million inhabitants. Close to 70 percent of the economically active population in the area as a whole was in agriculture, living largely outside the market economy.

Preliminary Steps

The Central Americans and ECLA took close to ten years to create the basic preconditions for the economic cooperation scheme embodied in the

---

4. Thomas L. Karnes, *The Failure of Union: Central America, 1824–1960* (University of North Carolina Press, 1961), pp. 181–82.

Managua Treaty of 1960. The preliminary stage consisted of building up local technical elites, politically neutral but convinced of a need for regional economic cooperation. Their education was left to regional institutions created for that purpose and manned in the great majority of cases by Central Americans and "neutral" foreigners, mainly other Latin Americans. Consequently, at no point in the preparatory work for regional cooperation could charges be made that the program was managed, inspired, or abetted from the outside. When in 1959 the United States offered financial support for integration, the ground-work for close regional economic cooperation had already been laid.

This early "Central Americanization" of the regional scheme and the insistence upon its neutrality vis-à-vis the political power groups within the area and the United States paid dividends. By the time of the Managua Treaty the provision for establishing a common market within six years (by mid-1966) seemed reasonable because local technical leaders were available to run it and various regional institutions designed to assist them either were at hand or being planned. Today there is an impressive array of executive and supporting organizations: the Economic Integration Secretariat (SIECA), the Central American Bank for Economic Integration (CABEI), the Monetary Council, the Central American Clearing House, the Regional Industrial Research Institute (ICAITI), and the Central American Public Administration Institute (ICAP), all of them run by Central Americans.

The basic instruments for economic integration were established between 1951, when ECLA and Central American leaders began to negotiate bilateral free trade agreements, and 1961, when SIECA, CABEI, and the Central American Clearing House started operations. The first major step toward integration was the signing of the Multilateral Treaty on Central American Free Trade and Economic Development in Tegucigalpa, Honduras, in 1958. It provided for the expansion of a system of free trade and common external tariffs for a limited list of goods over a period of ten years. It was followed in 1959 by the convention on the equalization of import tariffs vis-à-vis third countries that established the framework for the protection of the regional market through common import duties.

Simultaneously with the 1958 treaty a scheme to develop Central American "integration industries" was adopted in order to promote industrialization in the region. The scheme was designed to insure an equitable distribution of modern, large-scale industrial production among the five member countries. It provided for the licensing by common consent of integration industries in every country. Such industries were given free trade privileges for their products within the region; they were also entitled to import raw materials and intermediate goods duty free for a period of ten years. Tariffs on competing goods produced in the region were to be gradually eliminated over the ten-year period, and tariffs against outside competitors equalized and raised in order to protect the regional market. The scheme provided each member country the opportunity to establish an integration industry within its borders before any other could be assigned a second. Safeguards against the ten-year semimonopoly power of the integration industries included maximum prices the industries could charge for their products and maintenance of quality standards that would be set and controlled by ICAITI. If an industry failed to meet the standards or charged "excessive" prices, its special status could be revoked and competitive imports would be authorized.

Despite such safeguards, the possibility that monopolies would be created evoked strong opposition in the United States to the integration industries scheme.[5] This opposition resulted in the denial not only of U.S. financial assistance but of loans from the Inter-American Development Bank and the World Bank for integration industries in Central America. No integration industries were established until the mid-sixties, when the pronounced U.S. skepticism declined and internal political obstacles were overcome.

The Managua Treaty

The most important step in the formation of the Central American Common Market was the signing of the General Treaty on Central American Integration in Managua at the end of 1960 by Guatemala, El Salvador, Honduras, and Nicaragua, joined later by Costa Rica. It granted free regional trade to Central American products not specifically exempted in the treaty itself. Duties were eliminated on about three-quarters of the items in the tariff schedule as soon as the agreement went into effect and on an addi-

5. An aide-mémoire by the U.S. State Department outlining the United States position on the scheme was presented to the Central American governments in May 1962. See statement of Emilio G. Collado in *Latin American Development and Western Hemisphere Trade*, Hearings before the Subcommittee on Inter-American Economic Relationships of the Joint Economic Committee, 89 Cong. 1 sess. (1965), pp. 33–34; James D. Cochrane, "U.S. Attitudes Toward Central American Economic Integration," and "Central American Economic Integration: The Integrated Industries Scheme," *Inter-American Economic Affairs*, Vol. 18 (Autumn 1964), pp. 73–91, and Vol. 19 (Autumn 1965), pp. 63–74.

tional 20 percent during the following five years. By 1967 there were intra-regional trade restrictions on very few products. Among the exempted products, however, were some of Central America's principal export commodities, such as coffee and cotton.

The Managua Treaty and its corollary legal instruments were based on a recognition of the conditions that would insure cooperation among the five countries. Tangible and substantial economic benefits were offered to every party concerned, and distribution of these benefits among the participating countries was provided for. The participants' individual means of access to external assistance were not disturbed, and considerable additional external aid was made available that probably would not have been forthcoming without the common market. The integration commitments did not present any threat to the existing structure of economic investment or political power within the area.

Aware of political realities and the significance attached by developing countries to industrialization, the builders of Central American integration acted at an early stage through the integration industries scheme to assure relatively equal participation in the benefits of industrialization. The Central American Economic Integration Bank (CABEI), which was created to provide financing for infrastructure projects and productive activities of regional interest, followed the principle of "equitable economic development," so that the gains from regional integration would not accrue only to the richer member countries.

CACM Achievements

Central American economic cooperation increased the value of intra-regional trade almost eightfold between 1960 and 1968. The exports of member countries to their CACM partners increased from 4 percent of their foreign trade in 1956 and 7 percent in 1960 to 25 percent in 1968, thus belying the claim of skeptics that countries producing mainly bananas and coffee have nothing to trade among themselves (see Table 3). The composition of trade changed markedly. Industrial exports rose more than eightfold, so that in 1968 about three-fourths of intraregional trade was composed of manufactures and semimanufactures. Practically all intra-regional transactions were carried out in domestic currencies through settlements in the Central American Clearing House. Despite currency restrictions, which some member countries were forced to introduce for a

Table 3. Intraregional Exports within Latin America, 1950–68

Year	Intra-Latin American exports		Intra-LAFTA exports		Intra-CACM exports	
	Total (millions of dollars)	As percent of total Latin American exports	Total (millions of dollars)	As percent of total LAFTA exports[a]	Total (millions of dollars)	As percent of total CACM exports
1950	517	8	426	8	8	3
1952	616	9	515	9	10	3
1954	703	9	631	10	14	3
1956	653	8	566	8	16	4
1959	718	9	540	8	28	6
1960	689	8	570	8	31	7
1961	580	7	498	7	35	8
1962	694	8	550	7	39	8
1963	741	8	579	7	69	12
1964	958	10	754	8	105	16
1965	1,082	10	834	9	133	17
1966	1,171	11	867	9	172	20
1967	1,162	11	835	9	205	24
1968	1,367	10	993	10	245	25

Sources: For years through 1956, United Nations, International Bank for Reconstruction and Development (IBRD), International Monetary Fund (IMF), *Direction of International Trade*, various issues; for years after 1956, IMF and IBRD, *Direction of Trade: A Supplement to International Financial Statistics*, various issues; and Latin American Free Trade Association (LAFTA), *Newsletter*, various issues.
a. Because Venezuela accounts for about 30 percent of total Latin American exports, any change in its exports is important. Excluding Venezuela, intra-LAFTA exports as a percentage of LAFTA exports to the world would have been 8 percent in 1963; 10 percent in 1964, 1965, 1966, and 1967; and 12 percent in 1968.

limited time, the Central American payments arrangements greatly facilitated the flow of regional trade.

By 1968 CABEI had approved loans totaling about $120 million—about half to the private sector primarily for industrial projects and the other half to the public sector for investment mainly in transportation, communications, and power. Loans were distributed fairly evenly among the five countries, the largest proportion (26 percent) going to Nicaragua, the smallest (15 percent) to Costa Rica, which is roughly the inverse of the distribution of per capita income: Nicaragua with about a 10 percent larger population has a national income only three-quarters that of Costa Rica. CABEI also distributed loans from the Central American Integration Fund whose purpose is almost exclusively to finance regional infrastructure projects. The fund is supported by contributions from the U.S. government, the Inter-American Development Bank, and the Central American states. Nontrade programs and institutions supporting the common market also helped considerably to improve the region's physical infrastructure and the use of human resources.

In the late 1960s the approximately 97 percent of Central American tariff items that were traded freely represented about 80 percent of the value of intra-area commerce. Efforts were being made to remove such important exceptions as coffee, wheat, and sugar. But international commodity arrangements complicate the task; for example, free trade in coffee might upset the quota system of the International Coffee Agreement. Petroleum products constitute the most important single category of goods that have not been traded freely.

Uniform external tariffs had by mid-1966 been set on more than 80 percent of the items imported from countries outside the region. The levels of tariffs to the outside world were increased under integration in the following fashion:[6]

Commodity group	Average national tariff before integration	Common external tariff after integration
Consumer goods	64	82
Raw materials and intermediate goods	30	34
Building materials	26	32
Capital goods	12	13

Central American economic integration has strongly attracted foreign investment. The inflow of foreign capital more than tripled between 1960 and 1968, the annual rate jumping from $20 million to over $60 million. By 1968 the book value of U.S. investment alone amounted to nearly $0.5 billion.

Partly as a result of trade liberalization within the framework of the Central American Common Market and the concurrent increase in the levels of investment in the area, economic development of the region has accelerated. The average yearly growth rate of the gross regional product rose from 4.4 percent during the five years preceding 1960 to 7 percent between 1962 and 1965. At least 1 percentage point of the 7 percent growth rate has been at-

6. United Nations, Economic Commission for Latin America (ECLA), "General Situation and Future Outlook of the Central American Integration Programme," E/CN.12/CCE/265 (Feb. 20, 1963; processed), p. 19. The effective rate of protection (see p. 146, below) for the region as a whole has been estimated to have increased by about 40 percent (Roger D. Hansen, *Central America: Regional Integration and Economic Development* [Washington: National Planning Association, 1967], p. 51).

tributed to the expansionary effect of the common market; about 4 percentage points were due to minimum "normal" growth, and 2 percent to the increase in export earnings.[7]

Both internal and external conditions were favorable to the first stage of Central American integration. Levels of industrialization were low and did not differ greatly among member countries. Practically all the countries had a great deal of unused or easy-to-mobilize productive capacity. Between 1960 and 1968 Central America's outside trade grew faster than Latin America's because the region was able to rapidly mobilize the resources available from the export-oriented plantation agriculture that flourished in a semifeudal land tenure system not seriously challenged by the poor rural masses. The region's balance-of-payments position was comfortable enough to permit minimal concern about intraregional trade imbalances.

The integration process has only slightly affected the social structure and the structure of production of Central America. Progress in industrialization—a major goal of integration—seems to have been limited to the increased use of capacity in existing manufacturing enterprises and the appearance of some assembly industries, which put pressure on the area's import bill. More complex, new industries have not yet appeared. Agriculture still accounted for almost one-third of gross domestic product and employed over one-half of the region's labor force in 1968.

A tragic setback for the integration movement was the outbreak of open hostilities in July 1969 between the neighboring states of El Salvador and Honduras. Although the fighting was quickly brought under control, the conflict—based on traditional antagonism and caused indirectly by the migration of people from crowded El Salvador to low-population-density Honduras—has seriously damaged the rapid progress of Central American integration.[8] It is too early to assess the extent of the setback; intra-area trade declined only slightly from 1968 to 1969, and the slowdown after the short-lived war had been reversed in 1970. At the end of 1970, one and a half years after the war, however, trade between El Salvador and Honduras was still interrupted, and trade between El Salvador, Nicaragua, and Costa

---

7. Donald H. McClellan, "The Common Market's Contribution to Central American Economic Growth: A First Approximation," in Ronald Hilton (ed.), *The Movement Toward Latin American Unity* (Praeger, 1969), pp. 508–36.

8. Honduras withdrew from the common market in December 1970. It is as yet uncertain whether this is a definite break or a transitory tactical maneuver; in July 1971 Honduras signed bilateral trade treaties with all CACM members except El Salvador.

Rica had to be rerouted because of Honduras' refusal to let Salvadorian goods pass through its territory in transit to other members of CACM.

Even more worrisome, negotiations begun in late 1969 about a new modus operandi for the ailing Central American Common Market had made no headway by the fall of 1970, leading to the resignation of the common market's able secretary general, Carlos Manuel Castillo of Costa Rica. The fruitless negotiations dealt with issues that had complicated CACM life since its successful first stage ended in the mid-sixties: the "unequal" participation of the least developed countries, Honduras and Nicaragua, in regional industrial and agricultural activities; the stagnation of regional industrial policy; the high level of protection against the rest of the world; the absence of coordination in the agricultural sectors; and, finally, the lack of rules of origin for intra-Central American trade. Agreeing that the problem of unequal participation in the benefits of regional integration was the main obstacle to the revival of CACM, the majority of member countries showed willingness to establish within CABEI a special fund for financing industrial and agricultural expansion that would give priority to Honduras and Nicaragua. But El Salvador refused to adhere to that fund, nullifying any other progress toward a new modus operandi for the CACM.

It is obvious that the Central American experiment is facing a new and extremely difficult stage, confirming the lesson of Western Europe. Broad economic cooperation among sovereign or even quasi-sovereign states, whether developed or underdeveloped, does not develop automatically, and any program for cooperation in the long run faces serious problems of political as well as economic readjustments among the participants. Assuming that the Central American customs union does eventually provide for the free movement of both goods and people, the subsequent goals of integration, including a unified fiscal and monetary policy, cannot be met so easily. These goals involve a gradual renunciation on the part of the member countries of freedom of action in fields that are universally considered the legitimate domain of a sovereign state. But even supposing that mutually acceptable solutions can be found on economic policies, in order to forge ahead the Central American Common Market will have to tackle difficult sociopolitical issues dealing with the distribution of income and the role of foreign investment. These issues were left in abeyance during the first years after the Managua Treaty, when neutrality of the integration process vis-à-vis external and internal interest groups was considered of paramount importance.

The Latin American Free Trade Association

The Montevideo Treaty, which brought the Latin American Free Trade Association (LAFTA) into existence in mid-1961, was originally signed by seven Latin American countries in early 1960, by Colombia and Ecuador shortly afterwards, and most recently by Venezuela and Bolivia. Now LAFTA covers all of South America (with the exception of the Guianas) and Mexico.

The treaty established a rather complicated trade-negotiation system aimed at the gradual elimination within twelve years—or by mid-1973—of customs duties and any other restrictions on substantially all reciprocal trade. To achieve a free trade zone by the end of the period, each party to the treaty was committed to grant annually to all others reductions in duties and charges equivalent to 8 percent of the weighted average applicable to countries outside the agreement. Every three years these concessions, open in the meantime to withdrawal through renegotiation, were to be consolidated into a common schedule of products on which all customs duties and other charges on intrazonal trade would be eliminated before mid-1973. This common schedule was to constitute 25 percent of the aggregate value of trade among the member countries by mid-1964, 50 percent by mid-1967, 75 percent by mid-1970, and "substantially all of such trade" at the end of the period.

An impressive number of escape clauses was applicable to trade in agricultural products and in cases of intrazonal trade disequilibria and seriously unfavorable overall balance-of-payments situations. The treaty offered special provisions for the less developed countries within the region: nonreciprocal trade concessions, special nondiscriminatory measures aimed at protection of their industries, and collective arrangements for financial and technical assistance.

Commitments outside of trade liberalization were put in extremely vague language. They envisaged the reconciliation of overall import and export policies vis-à-vis the rest of the world and the coordination of the treatment of capital and services coming from outside the area. They also pledged "progressively closer coordination of the corresponding industrialization policies" through agreements "among representatives of the economic sectors concerned" and the negotiation of nondiscriminatory complementarity agreements to insure an equitable division of labor within LAFTA.[9]

9. Implementation of the treaty was assigned originally to the Conference of Con-

During the first eight years of LAFTA, a maze of about 11,000 concessions on individual trade items was negotiated in successive annual meetings of the Conference of Contracting Parties.[10] Partly as a result of these concessions and partly because the emergence of LAFTA led to the discovery of many trade opportunities (regardless of the height of tariffs), trade among LAFTA members increased from about $500 million in 1961 to about $1 billion in 1968. This represents a doubling in intra-LAFTA trade against an increase of only 40 percent in the value of the members' total exports for the same period.

Even though LAFTA did not inject any dynamism into Latin America's economic development, it did succeed in raising regional interchange during a particularly difficult period. The intraregional share of total trade rose from 7 percent in 1961 to 10 percent in 1968 (see Table 3). The LAFTA performance is much less impressive, though, when compared with the mid-1950s when the intraregional share was almost the same as at the end of the 1960s. While LAFTA has not met the expectations of its promoters or the broader needs of the Latin American economies, it cannot be considered a failure as a trade liberalization mechanism.

During its first eight years, LAFTA encountered several major difficulties. The Montevideo Treaty began the long process of reconciling the political and economic differences among a group of countries that had followed very different economic paths. The large and middle-sized republics had followed an autarkic industrialization policy and depended on the developed outside world. The Montevideo Treaty tried to accommodate simultaneously the southernmost countries, where the bulk of intraregional

---

tracting Parties, the Permanent Executive Committee, and a Secretariat. In 1966 a Council of LAFTA Foreign Ministers was established as the supreme organ of the Conference of Contracting Parties. In effect, each LAFTA member has a veto power on all major substantive issues.

10. About half of the concessions are accounted for by Argentina, Brazil, and Ecuador, which had granted concessions on about 1,700 items each by the end of 1967. Chile and Mexico accounted for about 10 percent each; Colombia, Paraguay, and Uruguay, about 7 percent each; Peru and Venezuela, about 4 percent each; and Bolivia, 2 percent. As of Jan. 1, 1968, a total of 10,382 concessions had been granted within LAFTA. (Asociación Latino-Americana de Libre Comercio [ALALC], *Sintesis Mensual*, Vol. 4, No. 41 [November 1968], Table 4.) Over half of the concessions are on manufactured goods, almost one-third on semimanufactures, and the rest on primary products. Because of highly overvalued foreign exchange rates, nontariff trade restrictions, and difficulties in the financing of regional commercial transactions, Latin American exporters made use of only about one-third of all LAFTA concessions from 1962 through 1965.

trade has been concentrated for about a century, and the rest of the continent (excluding Central America, whose involvement in Latin American economic relations has been almost nil). It was a compromise between ECLA "globalists" and those who held national political and economic power, between technical experts and vested interests. It had to offer a formula acceptable to the three leading industrial countries as well as to the others with their varying degrees of bargaining power. Finally, it had to consider the interests and attitudes of international organizations and of industrial powers outside the region.

Not only were the commitments of member countries relatively weak, but during the first stage of LAFTA the attitudes of the outside world toward this experiment were—contrary to those in the formative period of CACM and the European Economic Community—confusing and contradictory. No coordinated steps were taken to help Latin America alleviate the cumulative effects of the economic difficulties it had suffered during the fifties. From 1960 on, the attitude of the high-income countries toward the rest of the world changed only marginally: at best, they saw more clearly the inadequacies in the way the international economy worked and the need for social change.

The unequal development levels of LAFTA countries proved to be an important stumbling block to rapid integration progress. The informal division of members into three classes, which emerged rapidly in the course of LAFTA meetings, was formally confirmed by resolutions of the Conference of the Contracting Parties. Argentina, Brazil, and Mexico, as the most industrialized and economically advanced members, make up the first group. Bolivia, Ecuador, and Paraguay are known as the "countries of lesser relative development," a euphemism for their extreme state of underdevelopment. The remaining countries, Chile, Colombia, Peru, Uruguay, and Venezuela, fall into a middle group of "countries with insufficient domestic markets."[11] At the beginning of the negotiation process the least developed states claimed and received preferential treatment, consisting mainly of unilateral trade concessions on the part of the rest of the group and of the acceptance by LAFTA of their highly protective policies on behalf of a few local industrial activities. The trade preferences have not resulted, however, in a significant reduction of Ecuador, Bolivia, and Paraguay's trade deficit

11. Because of serious economic problems, Uruguay was temporarily transferred to the least developed class in August 1967. However, the country's per capita income is still considerably above the Latin American average.

with the zone, nor have the middle countries that later asked for special treatment been able to improve their trade positions within the area. Although the Montevideo Treaty provided for nontrade measures of assistance from the more developed to the less developed members, a program of technical and financial aid that was subsequently elaborated has not yet been put into effect. The economically advanced countries are unwilling or do not consider themselves sufficiently developed to transfer real resources to their poorer neighbors or to support their requests for assistance from the international aid-giving organizations.

Cooperation also has been minimal in the area of regional industrialization. Two schools of thought on the problem developed. One emphasized a rapid dismantling of regional trade barriers, a thorough revision of tariff policies vis-à-vis the rest of the world, and elimination of the overvaluation of currencies. The other advocated development of a regional industrialization program by gradually including different industrial sectors and offering a broad scheme of incentives and disincentives to entice private financial resources, both domestic and extraregional, and foreign technology into key industrial activities.

As a result of the nationalist outlook of Latin American governments and the pressures from domestic and foreign interests, little progress has been made on industrial specialization, whether in private or state-controlled activities. The absence of effective regional agreements in many heavy industries—especially steel, petroleum, and chemicals—in which the state has a strong hand indicates that their programming continues to follow exclusively national lines.

In the area of private industry, sixteen complementarity agreements had been signed and ratified by the end of 1970, many of them on the initiative of foreign enterprises operating in various countries at the same time.[12] These agreements provide for eliminating customs duties and other restrictions on both final products and components and necessary raw materials, permitting better horizontal and vertical integration of productive units. The agreements benefit a small number of foreign-owned corporations; their contribution to the expansion of intrazonal trade and the growth of the involved industries has so far been negligible. The value of trade in goods covered by complementarity agreements did not exceed $4 million in 1967, about 0.5 percent of the intraregional trade in that year.

12. Seven of these were signed in 1970, the only apparent achievement of LAFTA during that year.

After more than a decade of technical studies and meetings, monetary and financial cooperation is still at a rudimentary level. A complicated agreement, signed in the fall of 1965, provides an elementary system for the settlement of net balances arising from regional trade transactions, and an arrangement entered into in October 1969 establishes the beginnings of a regional balance-of-payments assistance fund.[13] The agreements provide for periodic meetings of LAFTA central bankers to study the working of this new mechanism. The present arrangements are still too weak and complicated to contribute significantly to the expansion of trade.

Even less progress would have been made toward integration had it not been for the Inter-American Development Bank, which tried to become the bank of Latin American integration. Although it has continued to support autarkically oriented national projects, it has begun to extend loans for regional infrastructure projects, particularly in border areas, and to promote intraregional exports and finance preinvestment studies. The bank has also established a research and training Institute for Latin American Integration (INTAL) in Buenos Aires.

New Initiatives

The lack of progress in the free trade zone has led to new initiatives aimed at the complete overhaul of LAFTA. In 1965, upon the invitation of Chile's President Eduardo Frei, four eminent Latin Americans—Raúl Prebisch, then secretary-general of UNCTAD and formerly executive secretary of ECLA; Felipe Herrera, president of the Inter-American Development Bank; José Antonio Mayobre, executive secretary of ECLA; and Carlos Sanz de Santamaría, chairman of the Inter-American Committee on the Alliance for Progress (CIAP)—submitted to all the Latin American heads of state a broad program for accelerating the economic integration process.[14]

Their report recommended establishment of a regional common market by 1975. All participating countries would be committed within the preparatory ten-year period to annual across-the-board tariff cuts on intrazonal trade. In addition, maximum duty levels would be defined at each stage of trade liberalization, quantitative and other nontariff restrictions on intraregional trade would be gradually eliminated, and a common external tariff

13. See pp. 103–04.
14. "Document: Proposals for the Creation of the Latin American Common Market," *Journal of Common Market Studies*, Vol. 5 (September 1966), pp. 83–110.

would be set up. Emphasis was to be given to integration agreements for such key industries as steel, petrochemicals, motor vehicles, ships, and heavy industrial equipment, where benefits from large-scale production are great and improvements in operational efficiency are of paramount importance for progress in industrialization. The report also contained recommendations regarding the institutional machinery for administering a Latin Americanwide common market.

The first conference of LAFTA foreign ministers, held in November 1965, considered the report of the four "wise men." While the conference did not adopt any of its major proposals, various decisions were taken to further its aims and purposes. The resolutions were not followed up, however, so little progress was made toward revising the LAFTA structure. Another LAFTA conference at the end of 1966 also failed to resolve any major issues.

Thus when the presidents of Latin America and the United States met at Punta del Este in April 1967, it was recognized that bold new efforts were needed if a common market was to become a reality. While the summit conference could not have been expected to eliminate the obstacles to effective integration, the program of action that the presidents signed (see Appendix D) might have, if seriously implemented, enabled the Latin American countries to accelerate the integration process.

The Treaty of Montevideo had envisaged completion of a free trade zone by 1973. In view of the slow progress in LAFTA's first eight years, a target date of 1985 for a common market was agreed on at the summit meeting. Yet the Council of Ministers meeting in Asunción, Paraguay, a few months later failed to reach agreement on several key resolutions, including the rescheduling of the reductions of still existing tariffs, the reduction of such nontariff barriers as quotas, the preferential treatment of the least developed countries within LAFTA, and the establishment of a common external tariff on goods originating outside the LAFTA zone. Their only major achievement was approval of the formation of subregional groupings—in particular the Andean Group—with the proviso that other LAFTA members could join them without hindrance.

By the end of 1968, LAFTA's most serious failure was the inability of its members to agree on the second common schedule of tariff concessions, which was to have eliminated all customs duties on 50 percent of their intra-area trade before 1973. The first list, covering 25 percent of intra-area trade, had been agreed on according to schedule in 1964. The second was to have emerged in 1967. An acceptable number of tariff concessions (subject to escape clauses) was agreed on in 1968 (about 600 concessions), but the second common schedule, which would be irrevocable, was still pending at the end of 1969 when the LAFTA Council meeting in Caracas agreed to a slowing down of the implementation of the Montevideo Treaty. The establishment of a free trade zone was delayed from 1973 to 1980, the annual rate of tariff reduction was lowered from 8 to 2.9 percent, and the further expansion of common lists of tariff concessions was postponed to 1974 when a full review of integration progress is to take place.

New Regional Groupings

Other integration arrangements have emerged either as subregional groupings within LAFTA or outside to fill a geographic gap. The Andean Group falls within the former, the Caribbean Free Trade Association (CARIFTA) within the latter class.

The Andean Group

Motivated partly by political considerations (the desire to offset the power of Argentina, Brazil, and Mexico) and partly by the slow progress of LAFTA, the presidents of Colombia, Venezuela, and Chile and the personal representatives of the presidents of Peru and Ecuador met in Bogotá in August 1966 and signed a declaration with the objective of promoting closer economic cooperation among their countries. Bolivia joined the group in 1967. The action program of the Bogotá Declaration called for establishment within the framework of the Montevideo Treaty of a subregional common market known as the Andean Group. It envisaged the coordination of commercial, industrial, and financial policies, as well as technical cooperation, among the participants. A Mixed Commission representing the member countries was established to recommend specific integration measures, draft necessary legal documents, and periodically review achievements.

One of the commission's first accomplishments was an agreement establishing the Andean Development Corporation to function as a subregional development bank. Its authorized capital stock of $100 million includes $25 million to be contributed by the member countries over a five-year period, the larger members (Chile, Colombia, Peru, and Venezuela) providing $5.5

million each and the smaller (Bolivia and Ecuador) $1.5 million each. Apparently similar in purpose to CABEI, the Andean Development Corporation's guiding principle is to distribute investment among the partners of the group in such a way as to favor the less developed members. If the corporation succeeds in raising additional funds in the industrial countries and from international financial organizations, it may become an important vehicle for eliminating regional frictions that arise from the extreme underdevelopment of some Latin American republics.

The Mixed Commission also agreed, in July 1968, to integrate the petrochemical industry within the Andean Group, which accounts for about 80 percent of the petroleum output of all of Latin America. The agreement, patterned on the LAFTA complementarity arrangements, provides for specialization, by country or industrial concern, in the production of some twenty products. It goes beyond the LAFTA provisions by committing the participants to abstain from any production outside of their designated fields. In this way it resembles the Central American integration industries scheme, about which the United States had strong misgivings. The distribution of petrochemical plants is to be negotiated before the end of 1971. It is estimated that trade in petrochemical products within the Andean Group could reach $60 million in five years and provide substantial foreign-exchange savings.

Other fields in which cooperation among the Andean countries was envisaged encompass not only other complementarity agreements for key industries, including food processing, but also a payments union, elimination of double taxation, harmonization of economic policies, and technical cooperation, including the setting up of a subregional research and postgraduate training institute.

The Andean Subregional Integration Agreement (Acuerdo de Integración Subregional Andina) creating the common market was finally signed by Bolivia, Colombia, Chile, Ecuador, and Peru in May 1969, nearly three years after the declaration that initiated the movement. At the last moment the Venezuelan government decided not to sign, principally because of Colombia and Chile's insistence that most products be included in the trade liberalization program. The Venezuelan government, pressured by domestic and foreign industrial interest groups, wanted to protect its recently established industries through a lengthy list of exceptions; it also objected to the speed with which the trade liberalization program and the common external tariff were to be implemented. Venezuela is, nevertheless, a member of the Andean Development Corporation and the door has been left open for it to join the common market.[15]

The Andean treaty provides for the automatic and irrevocable reduction of tariff and nontariff barriers to intra-Andean trade, aiming at free intra-regional trade by the end of 1980. Products included in the LAFTA common list were completely freed 180 days after the agreement went into effect, and goods not produced in any of the Andean countries were, with some exceptions, freed by the end of February of 1971. Schedules for reducing trade barriers on products included in the Andean industrial development programs are to be specified in the industrial agreements. Duties on other goods produced in the region, apart from those on special lists of exceptions, will be reduced by 10 percent annually, starting at the end of 1971; all exceptions are to be eliminated by the end of 1985.

A common external tariff is to be established gradually. Beginning with a minimum external tariff to go into effect at the end of 1975, external duties of the partner countries are to be automatically equalized over a five-year period, with a common tariff anticipated by the end of 1980.

The treaty provides for establishment of sectoral industrial development programs. Not only are new industries to be assured regional markets, but the financing and location of new plants within the area is to be included in the planning. These provisions and the projected establishment of multinational enterprises with regional capital for the installation of new industries and the expansion of existing industries would in effect replace LAFTA-type industrial complementarity arrangements.

The treaty further calls for harmonization of economic policies and coordination of development plans, including in particular a common regime for the treatment of foreign capital and technology. Programs designed to accelerate agricultural development are included. And Bolivia and Ecuador are given special treatment as less developed nations within the Andean region.[16]

15. Some Latin American intellectuals argue that the Andean Group is better off without Venezuela because that country is too closely tied to the United States (Claudio Véliz, "Latin America and the Visit of the Governor," in "EPICA Reports" [Washington: Ecumenical Program for Inter-American Communication and Action, July 1969; processed], p. 3, translated from *Mensaje*, June 1969).

16. "Acuerdo de Integración Subregional," in *El Proceso de Convergencia de la ALALC y el MCCA*, CEP-Repartido 1154 (Montevideo: June 10, 1969), and "Informe Mensual de la Integración Latinoamericana," *Comercio Exterior* (Mexico), June 1969, pp. 410–13.

The Andean common market, formally approved by LAFTA as compatible with the Montevideo Treaty, started operating on January 1, 1971. The common policy on foreign investment and technology transfer that went into effect bars foreign investment in banking, domestic trade, and most other service activities and provides that within fifteen years (twenty years for less-developed Bolivia and Ecuador) all foreign-owned enterprises will be transformed into joint ventures with majority domestic control.[17]

The Andean experiment, despite Venezuela's refusal to join in the agreement, probably has a greater chance of success in the near future than does LAFTA. If Venezuela is included, the group accounts for about one-fourth of Latin America's gross national product, population, and area; successful economic integration of the region could provide the stimulus for effective integration of LAFTA and, indeed, of Latin America as a whole (see Table 4).

Table 4. Area, Population, and Gross National Product of Latin American Regional Groups, 1968

Group	*Area (millions of square kilometers)*	*Population (millions)*	*Gross national product*	
			Total (billions of dollars)	*Per capita (dollars)*
LAFTA	19.3	226.7	95.3	421
Andean Group, including Venezuela	5.4	62.2	26.7	429
CACM	0.4	14.0	4.5	322
Latin America	19.9	250.8	102.2	407
CARIFTA[a]				
Including Jamaica and Trinidad and Tobago	0.2	4.4	2.2	510
Excluding Jamaica and Trinidad and Tobago	0.2[b]	1.5	0.5	326

Sources: *Oxford Economic Atlas of the World*, 3rd ed. (Oxford University Press, 1965); International Bank for Reconstruction and Development, *World Bank Atlas: Population, Per Capita Product and Growth Rates* (IBRD, 1970).

a. CARIFTA is not included in the computations for Latin America as a whole in this study.

b. Guyana's territory alone amounts to 215,000 square kilometers; Jamaica and Trinidad and Tobago have less than 17,000 square kilometers; the remaining islands combined are less than 4,150 square kilometers.

17. "Tercer Período de Sesiones Extraordinarias de la Comisión, 14–31 de diciembre de 1970" (Lima, Peru, 1970; processed); "Andean Common Market Investment Rules," *Peruvian Times*, Jan. 8, 1971, pp. 3–5. See discussion on pp. 116–17 below.

River Plate Basin

The old idea for subregional development, the development of the River Plate basin, evolved into a formal arrangement signed in Brasilia in April 1969. The agreement among Argentina, Brazil, Paraguay, Uruguay, and Bolivia, which limits the field of action primarily to infrastructure works, should stimulate the development of electric power, the fishing industry, road and rail communications, and navigation on the Paraná, Paraguay, and Uruguay rivers. It also provides for "regional complementarity by means of the promotion and establishment of industries which are of interest for the River Basin development," and for "cooperation in matters of education, health and disease control."[18] Formation of a common market group between these five countries is unlikely in the near future, however.

The Caribbean Free Trade Area

The most recent integration movement in the hemisphere, the Caribbean Free Trade Area (CARIFTA), is a very loose association of the former and present British Commonwealth countries and territories of the Caribbean, launched for the purpose of increasing trade and bringing about closer economic cooperation.[19] The arrangement originated in late 1965, when Antigua, Barbados, and the then British Guyana signed an agreement to create a free trade zone for selected product groups. In October 1967 a conference of heads of governments of the Commonwealth Caribbean countries, held in Barbados, proposed a wider free trade area based upon the original CARIFTA agreement with suitable modifications. In February 1968 a meeting of ministers of trade of the countries of the former British West Indies was held in Georgetown, Guyana, to consider a new draft treaty. The participants—Guyana, Barbados, Trinidad and Tobago, and all smaller Caribbean islands—accepted a treaty that calls for the liberalization of a considerable part of intraregional trade by the end of 1980 through the gradual elimination of tariffs on different groups of products contained in separate products lists. The more developed CARIFTA countries—

18. *Comercio Exterior*, June 1969, p. 413; authors' translation.
19. The CARIFTA members are Jamaica, Trinidad and Tobago, Guyana, Barbados, Antigua, Montserrat, Saint Kitts-Nevis-Anguilla, Dominica, Saint Vincent, Saint Lucia, and Granada. (Entry of the Dominican Republic has been explored.) Per capita income varies from about $900 in Trinidad and Tobago to less than $200 in Saint Vincent.

Trinidad and Tobago, Barbados, Guyana, and Jamaica—will remove duties on imports of these products from other members by 1975.

In October 1969 a Caribbean Development Bank, to promote the development of the region, was established with an initial equity capital of $50 million, of which $20 million would be contributed by Canada and the United Kingdom.[20] Those countries have made available a $20 million fund—in addition to the $50 million in the bank's ordinary capital resources—for long-term low-interest loans with extended grace periods.

Trinidad and Tobago reportedly increased its CARIFTA trade by 41 percent in 1969 compared with 1968, and Jamaica doubled its exports to the region.[21]

CARIFTA is at the margin of the movements toward common markets in the hemisphere. Because of its small size and weakness, it is not likely to stimulate the progress of Latin American integration.

Conclusion

Of the two major Latin American integration schemes established in 1960, the Central American Common Market has been by far the more successful, despite the difficulties that resulted in the withdrawal of Honduras from the group. LAFTA, after early success, progressively deteriorated and by the beginning of the 1970s was merely languishing. The road to a Latin American common market may well lead through such subregional arrangements as the Andean Group whose size and homogeneity make their integration easier than that of the highly diverse LAFTA membership.

20. In addition to the CARIFTA group, bank members include British Honduras and the Bahamas.
21. Alliance for Progress, "Weekly Newsletter," Vol. 8 (Feb. 2, 1970).

PART TWO

U.S. Policy toward Integration

CHAPTER FOUR

The Historical Setting

FROM THE END OF THE LAST CENTURY, when the idea of Latin American economic cooperation emerged, to about 1960, when the idea began to be implemented, U.S. economic policy toward Latin America underwent remarkably few changes. The United States viewed Latin American countries as export economies dedicated to the sale of their natural resources overseas. The economic interest of the United States lay principally in promoting private investment and enterprise and serving the business interests of its citizens in the area. Even the great alterations in the economic environment and in Latin America's development needs during the 1930s did not change this posture. The United States continued to see the Latin American republics as simple agrarian countries and producers of raw materials for export even while Latin America turned toward industrialization.

Politically the United States has been guided by a sense of special responsibility toward Latin America. As the senior member of the inter-American system the United States has established a rule of dealing separately with each republic in pursuit of its interests. This bilateralism did not disappear even during periods of close hemispheric cooperation such as the First World War, the Good Neighbor era, and the early years of the Alliance for Progress. Cooperation among Latin American countries could never prosper within the bilateral framework.

Economic integration for Latin America is a move toward both economic and political viability that demands the region's increasing independence from the United States and the rest of the world. Because this objective goes against the traditions of U.S. policy in the Western Hemisphere—although not necessarily against the long-term interests of the United States —the United States has been reluctant to accept the integration movement and its probable consequences.

Early U.S. attitudes toward Latin American economic cooperation were reflected in the government's recommendation at the end of the last century of a hemispheric customs union embracing both Latin America and the United States. Rising protectionism in the United States resulted in the quick abandonment of this idea for bilateral trade agreements between the United States and individual Latin American nations. In the 1930s the United States turned from a protectionist to a relatively free trade position. It continued to deal with Latin American countries bilaterally, strengthening these relations in the name of hemispheric security. Only in the late 1950s did the United States begin to accept Latin American integration efforts, as long as they conformed with the rules set for regional trade groupings by the General Agreement on Tariffs and Trade (GATT), which appeared to be concerned primarily with developed countries.

In the first four years of the Alliance for Progress (1961–65) U.S. thinking began to shift from the idea of hemispheric free trade and pure bilateralism to a concept of economic integration as a means of developing Latin America. Under the Alliance for Progress, U.S. assistance was made available to the Central American Common Market (CACM). But U.S. policy makers viewed economic cooperation among the larger economies of the region as a Latin American affair and avoided any direct relationship with the Latin American Free Trade Association (LAFTA) lest it be regarded as interventionism. Since 1966 a Latin Americanwide common market has had the formal support of the United States.

Yet inconsistencies from the past dominate current U.S. attitudes. While the United States supports an accelerated move toward a common market, it is deeply committed to, and conditioned by, its bilateral trade relations and aid programs in Latin America. Since the Korean War, aid has been the front-line instrument of U.S. policy in the region. It has been concerned with the progress of individual Latin American countries rather than of the region as a whole. Both U.S. aid practices and other policies must change if Latin American integration is to become a serious objective of U.S. policy.

The whole relationship between Latin American countries and the United States that has grown up over the last century must be modified.

The Idea of a Hemispheric Customs Union

The original advocate of an inter-American system based on a hemispheric customs union was James G. Blaine, U.S. secretary of state under Presidents Garfield and Harrison. A leading spokesman for expansionism at the turn of the century, Blaine was deeply concerned with eliminating the last vestiges of European political and economic influence in Latin America and expanding U.S. foreign trade.[1] As chairman of the First International Conference of American States, held in Washington in the winter of 1889–90, he sought to cultivate "such friendly, commercial relations with all American countries as would lead to a large increase in the export trade of the United States, by supplying fabrics in which we are abundantly able to compete with the manufacturing nations of Europe."[2] Five of the eight points on the conference's agenda dealt specifically with hemispheric economic integration: formation of an American customs union; setting up of regular communications between American ports; promotion of a Pan American railway; establishment of a uniform system of customs regulations, weights and measures, and laws to protect copyrights and trademarks; and institution of a common silver coin.

Contrary to Secretary Blaine's expectations, the conference failed completely on the central issue of a continental customs union. Not only was it adamantly opposed by Argentina, which considered the proposal inimical to its close economic relations with Europe, but the scheme lacked appeal for other Latin American countries.[3] Another cause of failure was the grow-

1. Julius W. Pratt, *Expansionists of 1898—The Acquisition of Hawaii and the Spanish Islands* (Johns Hopkins Press, 1936), pp. 22–27.

2. Quoted by Joseph B. Lockey, "James Gillespie Blaine," in Samuel F. Bemis (ed.), *The American Secretaries of State and Their Diplomacy, 1776–1925* (Alfred Knopf, 1927–29), Vol. 7, p. 275.

3. Some Latin American misgivings were expressed many decades later by a leading Mexican diplomat: "Since the first Pan American conference . . . the United States has proposed—and Latin America rejected—the creation of a customs union embracing the entire hemisphere, which would have ruined any future possibility of industrialization in Latin America and would have condemned it to the never-ending extraction of raw materials for industry in the United States." (Jorge Castañeda, *Mexico and the United Nations* [Manhattan Publishing Co., 1958], p. 170.)

ing protectionist sentiment in the U.S. Congress, shortly translated into the McKinley Tariff Act of 1890. The new chapter in U.S. trade policy was to last until 1934. The new tariff bill did include reciprocity provisions, inserted at the last moment under pressure from the Department of State, to provide the United States with bargaining power in trade negotiations with Latin American producers of raw materials. Congressional action made it clear, however, that Blaine's desire to protect U.S. industries against European competition was of more interest to the legislators than his idea of a Pan American customs union.

As a result, the hemispheric free trade scheme was not presented at the Second International Conference of American States, held in Mexico City in 1901–02. In fact, the Mexico City conference, coming in the aftermath of the Spanish-American War and shortly before Theodore Roosevelt's enunciation in 1904 of the Corollary to the Monroe Doctrine, did not address itself to major economic problems. It recommended the development of continental transport links, the simplification of customs and harbor regulations, and the establishment of a Pan American bank. It also called for an international customs congress to facilitate continental trade. Its results, however, were insignificant.

During the ensuing period of bilateral relations the United States used various political, economic, and—in the Caribbean—military means in dealing with individual Latin American countries to foster U.S. interests. None of the numerous inter-American political and technical conferences of that era dealt with, or signified a need for, any kind of hemispheric or regional economic cooperation.

Free Trade and Hemispheric Security

The return of the United States to more liberal trade policies under U.S. Secretary of State Cordell Hull did not significantly modify its bilateral economic relations with Latin America. The reciprocal trade agreements act of 1934, like Secretary Blaine's 1890 call for a hemispheric customs union, sought the rapid expansion of U.S. exports through bilateral and multilateral tariff reductions. Secretary Hull's thesis was that the radical decline in world trade during the Great Depression was due in large part to the protectionist policies of the United States and other leading industrial powers over a period of forty years, from the McKinley Act of 1890 to the Smoot-

Hawley Act of 1930. The increased scope of the proposals from Blaine's hemispheric to Hull's worldwide free trade was a natural expression of the change in the U.S. role from dynamic but still weak newcomer to leading participant in international commerce.

The relative position of Latin America in world commerce changed very little between 1890 and 1934. Furthermore, Latin American governments continued to be highly dependent on tariffs for revenue. Thus, when Cordell Hull proposed a tariff-cutting program for increasing inter-American trade at the Seventh International Conference of American States at Montevideo in December 1933, Latin American countries would not accept that as a remedy for the stagnation of intra-American trade and the backwardness of their economies. Even then the southern republics were interested more in financial assistance for trade and development than in reciprocal tariff cuts to aid in their economic growth. On Latin America initiative, the Montevideo conference considered a proposal to establish an inter-American bank, but no action was taken. The concept of equality among nations, which underlay the Hull free trade proposals, was openly challenged by some of the less equal partners in the inter-American system.

During the period between the First and Second World Wars Latin America did not seriously try to develop regional economic cooperation. In the Great Depression, most, if not all, of the republics followed the line of least resistance and defended the "chauvinistic autonomy of small countries."[4]

The late thirties and early forties efforts to promote customs unions in South America were considered inconsistent with Secretary Hull's most-favored-nation principle that extended tariff reductions granted to "favored" nations to all others. Thus, the Conference of the Commissions of Inter-American Development, held in New York in 1944, recommended that customs unions in the Western Hemisphere meet the following conditions: (a) duties and other trade restrictions among the countries forming the union should be eliminated either immediately or within a reasonable predetermined period; (b) if two or more American governments proposed to establish a customs union, they should communicate its terms to the non-participating countries and open participation to them; (c) tariff rates against nonparticipating nations on individual commodities should not on the whole be increased as a result of the establishment of the union; and

4. The phrase is from Francisco García Calderón, *Latin America—Its Rise and Progress* (Charles Scribner's Sons, 1913), p. 349.

(d) the customs union should not stand in the way of a more comprehensive international program designed to eliminate or reduce barriers to world trade.[5]

An inter-American economic conference that was to meet in Washington in mid-1945 was postponed for nine years. In the meantime, the United Nations Economic Commission for Latin America (ECLA) was formed in 1948 and started to work on various aspects of Latin American economic policy. When the long-awaited Inter-American Conference of Ministers of Finance or Economy was finally convened at Rio de Janeiro in November 1954, ECLA submitted a report on practical measures for Latin American development, including development financing and the problems of international trade. The report, after noting that "the tariff concessions granted by the United States since the policy of reciprocity began, have not had outstanding effects upon over-all exports of [Latin American] primary products," strongly recommended liberalization of trade among Latin American countries, together with a regional industrialization policy.[6]

The United States also submitted a report outlining its position on Latin American development problems.[7] It argued that economic union among countries having little trade with one another would probably result in a net diversion of trade from low-cost imported goods to high-cost regionally produced goods. It emphasized the need for expansion of multilateral inter-American trade, improvement of the investment climate for the flow of private capital, and promotion of tourism and industrial fairs. But on economic union it stated:

Latin America faces some of the same problems which led to the European Payments Union, the Schuman Plan, and other "integrating" devices in Europe, and in the long run, maximum, most efficient and durable economic development will surely involve greater integration of the national economies into which Latin America is now divided. However, we do not believe these devices in their present form can be applied to Latin America because they were designed to meet the special requirements of European economies which for many years have been closely integrated.[8]

5. Julian G. Zier, "First Conference of the Commissions of Inter-American Development," *Bulletin of the Pan American Union*, Vol. 78 (July 1944), pp. 382–85.

6. United Nations, Economic Commission for Latin America (ECLA), *International Co-operation in a Latin American Development Policy*, E/CN.12/359 (1954), p. 70.

7. *An Economic Program for the Americas*, Report of the International Development Advisory Board (September 1954).

8. *Ibid.*, p. 16.

The Rio de Janeiro conference ended without U.S.-Latin American trade policy deviating from the most-favored-nation principle introduced twenty years earlier. The United States stuck to its belief that a customs union was not advisable or feasible in the case of Latin America in the mid-1950s.

New Attitudes toward Latin America

At the end of the decade the attitude of the United States toward intra-Latin American trade began to change. The United States participated in a resolution of the Economic Conference of the Organization of American States (OAS) held in Buenos Aires in the late summer of 1957 that declared "the advisability of establishing gradually and progressively, in multilateral and competitive form, a Latin American regional market."[9] A year later the official communiqué of the informal meeting of American foreign ministers contained a slightly longer paragraph related to the call by Juscelino Kubitschek, then president of Brazil, for closer regional economic cooperation:

It would be well for the governments directly concerned and the international organizations directly interested, chiefly the Organization of American States, the Economic Commission for Latin America, and the Organization of Central American States, to expedite their studies and concrete measures directed toward the establishment of regional markets in Central and South America.[10]

Yet economic integration was still far down on the U.S. list of priorities for Latin American development, and the United States clearly was not ready to support it actively. Although the United States showed signs of shifting its policy, it was still hesitant to move significantly away from the concept of freer world trade on the most-favored-nation principle.

The Act of Bogotá, subscribed to by OAS members in September 1960—six months after the establishment of LAFTA and two years after the signature of the first Central American integration treaty—did not mention the two regional cooperation schemes. Its chapter on "Multilateral Cooperation for Social and Economic Progress" dealt exclusively with

9. Organization of American States, "Economic Conference of the Organization of American States, Buenos Aires, Argentina, August 15–September 4, 1957, Final Act," OAS Conferences and Organizations Series, No. 58 (OAS, 1957; processed), p. 66.

10. OAS, " 'Operation Pan America' and the Work of the Committee of 21," OEA/Ser.X/3.1.1 (Aug. 15, 1960; processed), p. 15.

administrative and procedural measures for improving the functioning of the Inter-American Economic and Social Council (IA-ECOSOC). In the debates preceding adoption of the final text, various small countries proposed that priority in the disbursement of new financial resources offered by the United States go to the least developed countries and to projects for regional economic integration. Neither the more developed Latin American republics nor the United States supported the idea, and the resolution that was adopted recommended only that credit institutions take into account "the needs of groups of countries that are in the process of relating and/or integrating their economies."[11]

The slowness of change in U.S. policy toward Latin American economic integration at the turn of the decade was due not only to a reluctance to deviate from the principles of free trade but also to the "foot dragging" of the larger countries in the region. The traditional policy of political and economic bilateralism was strengthened by the cold war, which "furthered not hemispheric solidarity, but the concept of reciprocity: economic assistance for Latin America as a reward for supporting United States policies to meet the threat from international communism."[12]

The coolness of the United States toward ECLA helped to limit U.S. interest in Latin American economic integration, as did the apprehension that expansion of intraregional trade might be detrimental to U.S. exporters. The small concern for Latin America's economic integration among U.S. economists and political scientists at that time did not help to dispel the fear.[13]

Nevertheless, the United States did evolve a position on Latin American economic integration at the time the Montevideo Treaty establishing LAFTA was signed: it might favor a regional common market that met standards similar to those it had agreed to for European integration. Its representatives on the committee on President Kubitschek's Operation Pan America indicated the standards for a Latin American common market:

11. OAS, "Final Report of the Secretary General of the Organization of American States on the Third Meeting of the Special Committee to Study the Formulation of New Measures for Economic Cooperation," OAS/Ser.G/IV, C-i-487, Rev. 2 (Nov. 26, 1960; processed), p. 15.

12. Gordon Connell-Smith, *The Inter-American System* (Oxford University Press, 1966), p. 148.

13. Raymond F. Mikesell appears to be the only scholar in the United States who wrote on Latin American economic integration problems before mid-1960, when the Council on Foreign Relations set up a study group to analyze the Montevideo Treaty.

trade restrictions against third countries should not be higher after the formation of a common market than before; virtually all barriers to intraregional trade should be eliminated for all products within a reasonable period of time, and labor and capital should also be free to move in response to economic forces; any cooperative arrangement should be reconciled with the principles of GATT; no monopoly privileges should be given to particular industries, and no agreements should be made to restrain competition; no restrictions should be placed on private foreign investment; any regional arrangement should provide for the financing of trade with convertible currencies; and bilateral payments agreements and restrictive regional payments regimes should not discriminate against nonmembers.

These standards, however relevant to relations among economically advanced countries, made no concessions to Latin American conditions. The National Planning Association noted in 1960 that "the intensity of their [Latin Americans'] desire for development, diversification, and higher standards of living, in the face of changing market conditions abroad and instability in their terms of trade, has created issues involving fundamental principles of trade and finance which do not have the same historical significance and the same practical implications for underdeveloped countries that they have for industrialized countries."[14] The same study, however, resurrected Secretary Blaine's 1889 proposal for a hemispheric common market: "The nations of the Western Hemisphere may find themselves becoming more and more dependent on one another as sources of supply and as markets," and, therefore, "acceptance of the goal of increasing Western Hemisphere integration by the United States, Canada, and the Latin American States would do much to increase hemisphere morale and to improve hemisphere relations in the short term as well as to foster progress toward the long-range objective."[15] The gross inconsistency of such thinking with Latin American industrialization objectives was pointed out by Lincoln Gordon: A Western Hemisphere common market or free trade area "is neither desirable nor feasible. It would cut across the developmental aspirations of the industrializing nations of Latin America, nations whose governments differ in many economic policies but agree on the importance of pro-

14. Statement by the National Planning Association in *United States-Latin American Relations*, Compilation of Studies Prepared under the Direction of the Subcommittee on American Republic Affairs of the Senate Committee on Foreign Relations, 87 Cong. 1 sess. (1960), p. 525.
15. *Ibid.*, p. 430.

tecting their infant industries from being throttled at birth by massive American competition. The very proposal would raise charges of a new form of economic imperialism from the 'Yankee colossus of the north'."[16]

Felipe Herrera was equally unsympathetic to a hemispheric common market: "Obviously, such an approach underestimates the vast differences in political power and in economic, financial, industrial and technological capacity between the United States and the Latin American republics. A common market for them all does not seem feasible and, on the contrary, might indeed be counterproductive for Latin America, at this stage of its development."[17]

Events in Cuba as well as signs of increasing anti-American feeling in other parts of Latin America prompted the United States to start reappraising its postwar policies toward the region. One of the earliest unequivocal and visionary proponents of Latin American economic integration was Senator Mike Mansfield, who wrote early in 1960, shortly before the signing of the Montevideo Treaty:

> To date the Administration has taken the view that a common market in this hemisphere is a Latin American affair. While the idea has not been discouraged, little has been done to encourage it. . . . The present concern of Latin America with the common market concept affords the U.S. one more opportunity to end the downward spiral in inter-American relations. What is needed is a policy initiative which is at once dynamic, understanding and creative. Unless we act promptly in displaying that initiative we shall leave the impression, as we have done so often in the last few years, that we are little concerned with Latin America's interests unless we are prodded and shocked. Should that impression once again take hold in connection with the [Latin] American common market concept, any subsequent positive action on our part will be stripped of much of its value.[18]

Gradually it was recognized that the aspiration of Latin America and other underdeveloped regions for regional economic integration was not an irrational reaction designed to harm the United States and the world economy, but was based on economic development objectives.

> [All of the underdeveloped nations] are rightly preoccupied with economic development as one of their major objectives. All want to diversify their economies, to improve agricultural productivity, and to industrialize. . . . It can be

16. Lincoln Gordon, "Economic Regionalism Reconsidered," *World Politics*, Vol. 13 (January 1961), p. 253.

17. "Towards a Latin American Common Market" (lecture delivered at Cornell University, May 20, 1966), p. 6.

18. "Common Market for Latin America," *New Leader*, Jan. 25, 1960, p. 9.

predicted with some assurance that most or all of these countries will seek to promote industrialization through protection of domestic industry from foreign competition. . . .

In these circumstances, the realistic question is whether such protection will be based on the very small markets of the individual sovereign units, leading inevitably to inefficient small-scale production and the frustration of many developmental opportunities, or whether it will be on a regional basis with some promise of adequate market size and investment scale, and even some hope for competitive pressures within the regional areas. These are the most pressing reasons for fostering deliberately a form of "developmental regionalism."[19]

Forward-looking sectors of the U.S. business community began to come out in favor of regional integration. The Committee for Economic Development, an organization supported by businessmen, stated as early as the spring of 1961:

The United States should encourage the movements toward economic integration in Latin America. . . . Many of the Latin American countries do not subscribe to the General Agreement on Tariffs and Trade and we should not expect their regional arrangements to conform to the provisions of the GATT governing free trade areas and customs unions.[20]

At the August 1961 Punta del Este conference that launched the Alliance for Progress, the new approach in U.S. policy was still pushed into the background. An expert group preparing for the meeting had concluded that regional economic integration should be considered a dynamic factor in the economic development of the region. Among their recommendations were proposals to step up trade liberalization within Latin America, to reconcile national development plans and investment programs with regional integration efforts, and to have international aid-giving agencies give special attention to the investment needs of regional economic cooperation. However, the draft agreement to establish the Alliance for Progress, formulated by the U.S. government and distributed among OAS members in the middle of July 1961, made no reference whatsoever to regional economic integration.

Nevertheless, in his major address at the Punta del Este conference, Secretary of the Treasury Douglas Dillon made it clear that the United States was not opposed to regional integration. The U.S. delegation agreed to the inclusion in the final text of the Punta del Este Charter of a paragraph com-

19. Gordon, "Economic Regionalism Reconsidered," p. 247.
20. Committee for Economic Development, *Cooperation for Progress in Latin America* (New York: CED, 1961), p. 35.

mitting the signatories "to accelerate the integration of Latin America so as to stimulate the economic and social development of the Continent. This process has already begun through the General Treaty of Economic Integration of Central America and, in other countries, through the Latin American Free Trade Association."[21] The same section of the charter urged the establishment of ties between LAFTA and the Central American Common Market and recommended that special attention be given to applying external resources to investment in multinational projects that would help strengthen the integration process; that part of these resources be channeled through financial institutions devoted to integration; that negotiations be undertaken with the International Monetary Fund and other aid sources to persuade them to supply the means needed to solve transitory balance-of-payments problems that might arise in countries belonging to economic-integration systems; and that steps be taken to coordinate transport and communications facilities that would accelerate the integration process.

Despite its acceptance of these principles in 1961, the United States did not discernibly raise the priority given to integration. No resources were earmarked in support of integration. As an assistant secretary of state for inter-American affairs later wrote, Latin American integration "has only in recent years won the wholehearted endorsement of the United States. Six years ago [1961], the Charter of Punta del Este, although it included a chapter on Latin American integration, did not even venture to use the words 'Latin American Common Market'."[22]

The LAFTA countries, beset by balance-of-payments and other short-term difficulties, as well as economic and political pressures from business groups inside and outside the region, likewise failed to pursue with any vigor the integration program they had instituted with the Montevideo Treaty. No powerful groups in Latin America were pushing for it or willing to make sacrifices to achieve it. But U.S. policy was also a factor; for lack of positive U.S. action, Latin American governments were not encouraged to drive more rapidly toward intra-LAFTA cooperation. At least some of the governments thought that promoting integration would harm their bilateral relations with the United States.

21. OAS, *Alliance for Progress: Official Documents Emanating from the Special Meeting of the Inter-American Economic and Social Council at the Ministerial Level Held in Punta del Este, Uruguay, from August 5 to 17, 1961*, OEA/Ser.H/XII.1.Rev. 2 (English) (OAS, 1967), p. 4.

22. Lincoln Gordon, "Punta del Este Revisited," *Foreign Affairs*, Vol. 45 (July 1967), p. 626.

On the other hand, the United States gave active support to the Central American Common Market. Over one-quarter of U.S. aid to that region consisted of financial assistance for the common market, helping to overcome the obstacles to Central American integration. But U.S. help for LAFTA was almost nonexistent during its formative years.

Latin American Integration as Part of U.S. Policy

The United States began to reexamine its policies toward regional economic integration schemes in the developing countries in preparation for the first United Nations Conference on Trade and Development (UNCTAD), which met at Geneva in the spring of 1964. While its position on the great majority of issues raised by the developing countries was negative,[23] the United States supported four of the fifteen UNCTAD General Principles, one of them declaring that regional trade groupings should not harm outsiders, and another encouraging integration. The latter, Principle Ten, states: "Regional economic groupings, integration or other forms of economic co-operation should be promoted among developing countries as a means of expanding their intra-regional and extra-regional trade and encouraging their economic growth and their industrial and agricultural diversification, with due regard to the special features of development of the various countries concerned, as well as their economic and social systems."[24]

Developments within the Western Hemisphere forced the reevaluation of U.S. attitudes toward Latin American integration efforts. Four years after the Alliance for Progress had been launched no acceleration of the region's economic growth could be detected, and the program was obviously languishing. While the Alliance had been very popular during the Kennedy era, Congress was showing signs of rebellion against foreign aid programs whose lack of conspicuous success seemed not to justify their costs. The Alliance for Progress in particular was in need of some new dynamism. Chile's President Eduardo Frei, in his impatience with economic stagnation, had sponsored the experts' study that the Latin American heads of state received early in 1965.

Thus, by the spring of 1965, a new U.S. policy was mandatory, and the

23. Harry G. Johnson, *Economic Policies Toward Less Developed Countries* (Brookings Institution, 1967), App. B.
24. United Nations, *Proceedings of the United Nations Conference on Trade and Development*, Vol. I: *Final Act and Report*, E/CONF. 46/141 (1964), pp. 18–22.

search for it led to regional economic integration. Vice President Hubert H. Humphrey in an address to the Protocolary Session of the Council of the Organization of American States on April 14, 1965, welcomed integration efforts:

We support effective economic integration because it is essential to economic and political development under the Alliance for Progress. We support it because the modern Latin America which can emerge from effective economic integration will be a more effective partner in all the great common world tasks which confront those who share the common values of Western civilization. We support it because, as our post-war experience demonstrated, our most fruitful and mutually advantageous trade and financial relations are with industrialized and diversified areas of the world. Finally, we support it because economic integration is a fundamental part of the Alliance for Progress, the Alliance program to which we committed ourselves at Punta del Este.[25]

But the subsequent U.S. military action during the Dominican crisis made the United States appear more committed than ever to a policy of unilateral action; the evident need for a new U.S. policy made support of Latin American economic integration even more attractive. Integration was approved by Latin America's intellectual leaders as a symbol of a healthy multilateral approach. Support for integration might be favorably viewed in the U.S. Congress as a demonstration of the administration's interest in establishing a strong link between self-help efforts of the aid-receiving countries and the distribution of aid funds. The U.S. business community meantime had begun to take an interest in a Latin American common market. Experience with the European and the minuscule Central American common markets showed that integration could bring benefits to U.S. as well as regional business groups. A number of large U.S. companies with branches in several Latin American countries had discovered that LAFTA might afford them the opportunity to enlarge operations and reduce costs.[26]

The United States now had a wealth of reasons to implement the changes in policy toward Latin American integration that had been gestating for a decade. Consequently, President Johnson, in commemorating the fourth Alliance anniversary, declared that "we must try to draw the economies of Latin America much closer together. The experience of Central America re-

25. "Acta de la Sesion Protocolar Celebrada el 14 de Abril de 1965," OEA/Ser. G/II, C-a 567 (Protocolar) (April 14, 1965; processed), p. 13.

26. See Business International Corp., *LAFTA, Key to Latin America's 200 Million Consumers* (New York: Business International Corp., 1966).

affirms that of Europe. Widened markets—the breakdown of tariff barriers—leads to increased trade and leads to more efficient production and to greater prosperity."[27] He recommended that a continental fertilizer community be established and offered a financial contribution for a new fund for preparing multinational projects.

In November at the Second Special Inter-American Conference, held in Rio de Janeiro, Secretary of State Dean Rusk assured his colleagues that, although it was up to Latin Americans themselves to decide the future of the regional integration program, they could expect some U.S. aid for its acceleration. The United States, he added, was not afraid of Latin American union and would like to have close and friendly relations with a common market. Rusk's statement passed practically unnoticed in the region, mainly because the meeting, held in the wake of the Dominican crisis, was concerned primarily with the structure of the inter-American system, including a highly controversial U.S. proposal to organize a "permanent peace force" under the OAS.

The United States continued to pursue its Latin American relations primarily on a country-to-country basis, and the Alliance for Progress came under increasing criticism from Latin Americans interested in regional integration. The executive secretary of LAFTA said in the spring of 1966 that "on balance Latin American integration—the most important basic reform and the most important of internal efforts undertaken by Latin America as a whole—is being made more difficult by the Alliance (bilateral) practices than helped by some financial contributions directed mainly to Central America."[28]

By the time the United States recognized Latin American economic integration as being in its long-run interest in the Western Hemisphere, developments within Latin America, and especially within LAFTA, made dialogue on the subject very difficult. The great expectations of 1960 for drawing the national economies of LAFTA members closer together through trade liberalization were far from being realized. Five years later, despite substantial growth of intra-LAFTA trade, the member countries were seriously at odds over the distribution of benefits from economic

27. *Public Papers of the Presidents of the United States: Lyndon B. Johnson, 1965*, Bk. 2, p. 887.
28. Romulo Almeida, speech delivered before the fourth meeting of the Inter-American Economic and Social Council; reproduced in *Comercio Exterior* (Mexico), May 1966, p. 309.

integration. Continuing bilateral trade and aid and lackluster national economic performance severely curtailed the effectiveness of groups pressing in each republic for regional economic cooperation. Not only was the trade liberalization program deadlocked, but little progress was achieved in cooperation on nontrade matters, which might have made trade liberalization easier and more rapidly implemented.

In the meantime highly nationalistic military groups had taken over power in several republics, including Argentina and Brazil, and the drive toward integration was being progressively paralyzed. When the United States finally decided to give firm support to Latin American regional cooperation, conditions within the region itself were much less propitious than they had been since the beginning of the integration effort.

The Summit and After

In mid-1966 Argentina's President Arturo Illia, searching for a way to strengthen his domestic position (he was soon deposed by the military), suggested a hemispheric summit conference. The resurgence of military governments and the waning fear of Castro had crippled the Alliance for Progress, leaving the Johnson administration without much of a Latin American policy; President Johnson seized Illia's suggestion as a manifestation of Latin American interest and as a way of stimulating the growing congressional interest in Latin American integration (motivated partly by the hope that it would cut U.S. aid needs).

The search for an attractive agenda for a summit conference eventually led to regional economic integration as an important item if not the central theme.[29] It was the major subject of President Johnson's fifth anniversary observation of the Alliance for Progress in August 1966, when he offered "to work in close cooperation toward an integrated Latin America."[30] But again, as in the Rio de Janeiro conference of 1965, the United States wanted

29. According to one observer, President Johnson wanted "to provide the kind of political allure for his Latin American program that President Kennedy had been able to evoke when he proposed the Alliance for Progress" (Richard Eder, "United States Seeks Ideas with Allure for Latin Presidents' Parley," *New York Times*, June 27, 1966, p. 13). Also, the President's special assistant for national security, Walt Rostow, persuaded him that Latin American integration made sense.

30. *Public Papers of the Presidents of the United States: Lyndon B. Johnson, 1966*, Bk. 2, p. 826.

to include in the agenda political proposals, such as the creation of an inter-American peace force. This was a clearly disruptive issue because, while it had the support of Argentina, Brazil, and Bolivia—countries ruled by the military—most republics wanted to concentrate on economic matters only.

In order to make a meeting feasible, the United States abandoned the peace force idea, and a consensus on drafting a purely economic agenda was finally reached. Preparations for the presidents' meeting took several months. The United States wanted to give consideration primarily to economic integration through automatic reductions of trade restrictions and to Latin American development through foreign private investment.[31] Latin Americans wanted to emphasize U.S. international trade policies affecting Latin American exports. The United States was not prepared to discuss trade issues but wanted to come to the summit meeting with a concrete offer of financial aid for integration. The U.S. Congress, however, did not endorse President Johnson's request early in 1967 for a $1.5 billion five-year aid commitment for Latin America that would have included $180 million annually for education and increased food production, $150 million (distributed over a three-year period) for the Fund for Special Operations of the Inter-American Development Bank, as well as a contribution of about $100 million per year for an adjustment fund to help overcome balance-of-payments problems and industrial and labor force dislocations that might arise from the regional integration process.

The summit conference resulted in a Declaration of the Presidents of America signed by the United States and all but one of the Latin American countries.[32] The essential part of the declaration was an Action Program that dealt with regional integration, multinational infrastructure projects, international trade matters, agriculture, and education.[33] The Action Program looked toward the establishment of a Latin Americanwide common market. However, it did not contain any provisions for automatic tariff reductions or a date for negotiation and signature of the common market treaty. It stated only that in order to implement the decision "to accelerate the process of converting LAFTA into a common market ... starting in

31. U.S. State Department, "Annotated Agenda for the Inter-American Meeting of Presidents" ([1967]; processed).

32. Ecuador's refusal to sign, intended as a show of strength by its president to counter his weak internal position, came as a surprise both to Latin Americans and to the United States.

33. The chapters of the Action Program dealing with integration are reproduced in Appendix D.

1970, and to be completed in a period of not more than fifteen years, LAFTA will put into effect a system of programmed elimination of duties and all other nontariff restrictions."

The fear in Latin America of domination by external private investors was reflected by the fact that a special section of the original U.S. draft agenda dealing with foreign investment was dropped. Instead, two brief references to external private capital were inserted in Chapter 1: "Foreign private enterprise will be able to fill an important function in assuring achievement of the objectives of integration within the pertinent policies of each of the countries of Latin America." In addition the presidents agreed "to mobilize public and private resources within and without the hemisphere to encourage industrial development as part of the integration process and of national development plans."

For Latin America, perhaps the most important part of the summit document dealt with measures regarding international trade. Latin Americans were apprehensive about the great gap in the region's trade balance with the developed countries. A regional common market might "help to correct this trade gap by facilitating industrialization and import substitution efforts on a much wider basis than is possible at present. But it could assist in bridging only part of the 'trade gap'."[34]

It was recognized that implementation of the Punta del Este Action Program would take time. Yet by 1971 few steps had been taken to follow up the measures contained in the program. No politically powerful business groups had emerged in Latin America to press their governments to implement the Punta del Este exhortations; Latin Americans were not prepared to make a bold move toward a common market without any insurance against real or imagined risks. The United States, because of the Vietnam war and the Congress's attitude toward foreign aid, was in no position to make substantial and definite commitments in support of Latin American integration.

The absence of tangible progress within Latin America and the lack of financial commitments from Washington have hardened the skeptics' view of the 1967 conference as just another hemispheric meeting devoid of any serious substance. Further delay in implementing the Action Program could seriously damage the economic development of Latin America as well as hemispheric political and economic relations.

34. Raúl Prebisch, "Joint Action Held Imperative," *Journal of Commerce*, April 14, 1967.

CHAPTER FIVE

Foreign Aid

THE SHORTAGE OF ENTHUSIASM among Latin Americans for the summit meeting in April 1967 reflected not only the coolness of some new leaders to the idea of a common market but their realistic view of the possible magnitude of U.S. financial commitments. Latin Americans were unwilling to forgo bilateral assistance, whose familiar rules and limits they understood, for the unknown effects of integration.

U.S. policy makers seem to have recognized the need to change the structure of relations if a common market is to receive effective support, but decades of commitment to bilateral diplomatic contacts are difficult to overcome. During the preparations for the Punta del Este meeting, the dilemma of change became very real. The United States sought to avoid infringing the autonomy of Latin American policy makers and simultaneously to protect U.S. investors and traders. Shortly before the meeting Secretary of State Rusk recognized the common market as a Latin American undertaking. He warned, however, that:

the United States will only support a common market that is commercially outward looking and receptive to foreign investment on reasonable terms. Furthermore, the United States will have opportunities to make known its views in various inter-American meetings between now and the establishment of an integration adjustment fund. Moreover, the common market's policies will be reviewed as an important part of the negotiations incident to any United States contribution to such a fund.[1]

1. Dean Rusk, in *Latin American Summit Conference*, Hearings before the Senate Committee on Foreign Relations, 90 Cong. 1 sess. (1967), p. 28.

Table 5. Latin American Aid Authorized by the United States and International Institutions, 1961–68[a]

Millions of dollars

Source of aid	1961	1962	1963	1964	1965	1966	1967	1968	Total
United States	605	827	770	1,262	751	906	1,052	942	7,114
Agency for International Development	372	441	508	817	479	619	464	404	4,103
Export-Import Bank	139	184	86	239	161	151	470	428	1,859
Public Law 480[b]	94	202	175	205	111	137	117	110	1,152
International Bank for Reconstruction and Development	276	349	307	135	384	342	166	578	2,539
Inter-American Development Bank[c]	290	330	261	301	372	396	493	427	2,870
Total	1,172	1,506	1,338	1,698	1,507	1,644	1,711	1,947	12,524

Source: Organization of American States (OAS), *External Financing for Latin American Development* (Johns Hopkins Press, 1971), p. 2. Figures are rounded and may not add to totals.

a. Credits and donations; does not include compensatory finance operations.
b. Agricultural Trade Development and Assistance Act of 1954; reenacted with amendments by the Food for Peace Act of 1966
c. Includes Fund for Special Operations, authorized in 1961 to finance commercially risky projects.

The direct integration assistance of $100 million per year proposed by the United States at Punta del Este was only about one-ninth of the current bilateral aid. While bilateral foreign aid in its traditional form offers no encouragement for a customs union, few governments would volunteer to sacrifice the support for their countries' national development to the integration cause. Perhaps the only significant action the United States can take to further Latin American economic integration is a shift in its support to multinational rather than national projects.

Current Financial Aid

Since the Korean War, U.S. policy toward Latin America has been expressed chiefly through foreign aid. While that assistance constitutes only a small percentage of total investment in Latin America, many countries have become increasingly dependent on it for solving balance-of-payments and other problems.

The total gross U.S. aid authorized for Latin America during the period 1961–68 (see Table 5) was just over $7 billion, averaging close to $900 million annually. Approximately one-third was given in the form of grants, and almost all of the remaining two-thirds through Export-Import Bank loans, project and program loans of the Agency for International Development (AID), and other credits, most of them tied to buying U.S. goods.

The two largest multilateral sources of financial aid to Latin America— the International Bank for Reconstruction and Development (IBRD or World Bank) and the Inter-American Development Bank (IDB)[2]—during the eight years authorized $5.4 billion in aid to the area. Of the $12.5 billion in credits and donations authorized to Latin America over this period, more than 70 percent represents assistance from the United States government, including U.S. funds channeled through the IDB. Total disbursements by these donors (see Table 6) lagged well behind authorizations, and the flow of assistance net of amortization and interest payments was only half as great as the disbursements.

2. The United States holds 32 percent of the subscribed shares of the World Bank. It holds 43 percent of the shares of the IDB, which was created in 1959 to promote the development, individually and collectively, of its members (nineteen Latin American countries and the United States). The IDB figures include lending from the Social Progress Trust Fund, a soft-loan fund established in June 1961 to finance commercially risky projects.

**Table 6. Latin American Aid Disbursed by the United States
and International Institutions, 1961–68**

Millions of dollars

Source of aid	Total disbursed	Amortiza- tion of loans	Interest on loans	Net flow^
Inter-American Development Bank	1,331	168	154	1,009
Agency for International Development	3,097	96	131	2,870
Export-Import Bank[b]	2,285	1,889	717	−321
International Bank for Recon- struction and Development	1,562	492	490[c]	580
International Development Association	98	...	2	95
Total	8,372	2,645	1,494	4,233

Source: OAS, *External Financing for Latin American Development*, p. 19. Figures are rounded and may not add to totals.
a. First column minus the second and third columns.
b. Includes compensatory finance, such as the refinancing of loans.
c. Estimated.

U.S. aid is highly concentrated in a few countries, roughly in accordance with their share in Latin America's population (see Table 7): Brazil, Chile, and Mexico received half of total U.S. government assistance in the period 1961–67; these countries together with Colombia, Argentina, and Venezuela accounted for 76 percent of the total. Since 1960, per capita authorizations for U.S. aid to Latin America have been high relative to other areas, but as a percentage of the gross domestic product, Latin American aid is relatively small. Total economic assistance to the region was 17 percent of U.S. economic aid to all foreign countries during 1961–65, and only 11 percent when military assistance is included.[3]

The Transfer of Real Resources

Because of domestic balance-of-payments difficulties, the President and Congress of the United States have instructed the Agency for International Development to require recipient countries to use assistance credits to buy goods in the United States. The U.S. policy of tying aid, introduced

3. The region received about 7 percent of total U.S. foreign aid between July 1, 1945, and Dec. 31, 1967, and 9 percent if military assistance is excluded. (U.S. Department of Commerce, Office of Business Economics, *Foreign Grants and Credits, Calendar Years 1965–67.*)

in the 1950s, was progressively tightened until 1969, when President Nixon eased the requirement. According to AID data, well over 90 percent of U.S. aid dollars were spent in the United States in 1968, 1969, and 1970.

Most donor nations—even those with no balance-of-payments problems—have used aid-tying as an instrument for expanding their export trade. This policy tends to reduce the real value of a fixed amount of aid because project costs are usually greater than they would be in free com-

Table 7. Development Loans for Latin American Countries Authorized by the United States, 1961–67

Country	Total loans (millions of dollars)	As percent of regional total	Average annual authorization per capita (dollars)
LAFTA			
Argentina	750	9	5
Bolivia	201	2	9
Brazil	1,786	21	3
Chile	1,210	14	20
Colombia	944	11	8
Ecuador	175	2	5
Mexico	1,168	14	4
Paraguay	101	1	7
Peru	440	5	6
Uruguay	106	1	6
Venezuela	590	7	10
CACM			
Costa Rica	129	2	13
El Salvador	97	1	5
Guatemala	90	1	3
Honduras	107	1	7
Nicaragua	114	1	10
Others			
Dominican Republic	186	2	8
Haiti	11	a	b
Panama	126	2	15
Trinidad and Tobago	61	1	9
Total	8,393c	100	

Source: OAS, *External Financing for Latin American Development*, p. 14.
a. Less than 0.5 percent.
b. Less than $1.
c. Excluding regional credits and P.L. 480 funds.

petition; purchases for a specific project must come from the donor country, even if sources elsewhere are cheaper.[4]

Aid-tying is so costly that "untying" aid to Latin America might increase the region's resources substantially. If the cost to Latin American countries of buying U.S. goods and transporting them in U.S. ships is, on an average, 20 percent greater than the cost elsewhere (see Table 8 for examples), the total saving to Latin America could be in excess of $100 million a year. Untying aid is of greater benefit to the borrower than increasing aid because there are no additional amortization and interest payments.

On the other hand, the U.S. Congress can more readily legislate tied than untied assistance for developing countries, given the balance-of-payments difficulties in the United States. Thus, although aid-tying may reduce the effective resource transfer and limit efficient intraregional trade, its net effect may be to make more resources available than otherwise. Such political considerations must be balanced against the negative psychological impact in the countries receiving tied aid. Whether the added assistance that tied aid might make available would or would not outweigh the loss of effective aid caused by tying, it is clear that tied aid lowers the value of a given amount of assistance in terms of goods and services.

In his first major speech on U.S.–Latin American relations in late 1969, President Nixon announced some revisions in U.S. policy. The major thrust of his speech was a less dominating U.S. posture in Latin America and a desire to leave major decisions on Latin America's future in Latin American hands. Among President Nixon's decisions was to drop the "additionality" principle, a particularly onerous feature of aid-tying aimed

---

4. The Organization of American States (OAS) estimates the cost of tying adds from about 12.5 to 25 percent to the cost of goods, not including the requirement that 50 percent of U.S. shipments be carried in U.S. bottoms (OAS, "Project Loan Tying," CIES/1382 [June 1969], Tables 1 and 2, pp. 3 and 7). A study of twenty development projects in Pakistan indicates that their weighted average price was about 50 percent higher from the tied source than on the international bids (cited in Harry G. Johnson, *Economic Policies Toward Less Developed Countries* [Brookings Institution, 1967], p. 83). Bhagwati estimates that the average direct costs of aid-tying account for at least 20 percent of the value of tied aid, and that inclusion of indirect costs (monopoly pricing, and so forth) would increase this proportion considerably; "in specific cases, price differentials amounting to 100 percent or more are not uncommon" (Jagdish N. Bhagwati, "The Tying of Aid," UNCTAD/TD/7/Supp. 4 [Nov. 1, 1967], p. 3). He also shows that "the balance of payments gain for the donor country corresponds to only about one-third of the value of the tied aid."

Table 8. Costs of Aid-Tying in Selected U.S. Loans to Latin American Countries

Lending agency and goods purchased	Cost of goods (thousands of dollars)		Cost of tying	
	Tied source	Cheapest source	In thousands of dollars	As percent of total cost
Export-Import Bank (equipment for electric power stations)	1,524	1,056	468	30.7
[Agency not indicated] (cement pipe)	461	294	167	36.2
IDB-Social Progress Trust Fund (passenger elevators)	245	138	106	43.5
AID (cement)	291	162[a]	130	44.5
IDB-Social Progress Trust Fund (miscellaneous building materials)	16	12	4	25.6
IDB-Social Progress Trust Fund (cast iron pipe)	1,291	1,169	122	9.5
AID (miscellaneous equipment for electrification project)	216	191	24	11.3
Total	4,044	3,022	1,022	25.3

Source: OAS, IA-ECOSOC, "Project Loan Tying," OEA/SER.H/X 14, CIES/1382, Add. 2 (June 1969; processed), pp. 3 and 7. Figures are rounded and may not add to totals.
a. A Latin American country was the lowest bidder.

at preventing substitution of AID exports for imports that would have otherwise been made.[5] He also indicated that the concept of tied aid would eventually be widened to include all members of the Organization of American States (OAS) so that Latin American countries could compete in the bidding to supply goods for U.S.-financed projects in Latin America.

Only a part of the flow of resources from governmental and international agencies can be considered pure "aid." The aid component of a loan, for instance, consists primarily of the savings in interest charges, terms, and repayment schedules over commercial loans. The OAS Secretariat estimated that real aid to Latin America amounted to about 47 percent of all official loans and grants from the United States and international

5. While additionality was an open device for promoting U.S. exports that could not compete well in world markets, it did not significantly benefit the U.S. economy but did hurt Latin American countries (see William S. Gaud, administrator of AID, in *A Review of Balance of Payments Policies*, Hearing before the Subcommittee on International Exchange and Payments of the Joint Economic Committee, 91 Cong. 1 sess. [1969], pp. 85–97).

agencies to the region during 1961–67, and 38 percent if only loans are taken into consideration.[6]

If amortization and interest payments—which constitute a significant burden on the Latin American economy—are deducted from the total loan disbursements by the United States and international agencies, just over half remains as net flows to Latin America (see Table 6). According to data of the UN Economic Commission for Latin America, the foreign net contribution in the 1960s was negative, if private capital movements are included, resulting in a net outflow from Latin America of $0.5 billion in 1967 (see Table 9). Amortization and interest payments and repatriated profits on direct foreign investment were larger than the sum of official grants and loans and private capital invested. This does not, of course, indicate the effect of foreign capital on Latin America's balance of payments, for it does not consider the increases in export earnings and foreign exchange savings (through decreased imports) that the production induced by foreign capital may provide.[7]

Bilateral versus Integration Assistance

As an active supporter of Latin American integration, the United States must make a fundamental reappraisal of its aid policy. Assistance is currently geared to national development, each economy competing individually for U.S. aid. Not only has integration assistance to Latin America been very meager, but national bilateral aid has often worked against integration. In the past, financing has been provided for projects designed only for the national welfare of the recipient, without much regard for a larger, regional efficiency.

A good example is a loan from AID (in combination with U.S. life insurance companies and the World Bank's International Finance Corporation) to Ultrafertil, S.A., for a fertilizer plant in Brazil. Among the persuasive reasons for financing the plant was Ultrafertil's willingness to develop an extensive marketing system throughout southern and central Brazil. But the direct cost of the project over that of importing ammonia

6. OAS, *External Financing for Latin American Development* (Johns Hopkins Press, 1971), p. 46.

7. Some economists take issue with this indirect balance-of-payments accounting; see, for instance, Paul Streeten, "The Contribution of Private Overseas Investment to Development" (paper presented to the Conference on International Economic Development, Columbia University, February 1970).

Table 9. Net Flow of Public and Private Foreign Capital into Latin America, 1967

Millions of dollars

Country	Total foreign capital[a]	Amortization	Interest and profit remittances	Net foreign contribution[b]
LAFTA				
Argentina	383	357	133	−107
Bolivia	61	20	18	22
Brazil	728	638	313	−223
Chile	398	219	214	−35
Colombia	360	225	106	28
Ecuador	59	14	26	19
Mexico	1,177	479	493	205
Paraguay	38	10	6	23
Peru	282	63	149	70
Uruguay	19	47	22	−50
Venezuela	212	62	736	−586
Total	3,717	2,133	2,217	−633
CACM				
Costa Rica	85	32	19	35
El Salvador	37	7	11	20
Guatemala	101	43	23	36
Honduras	39	10	23	6
Nicaragua	47	21	21	5
Total	310	113	96	101
Others				
Dominican Republic	64	20	23	21
Haiti	7	1	3	3
Panama	53	30	16	7
Total Latin America	4,150	2,296	2,354	−501
Total Latin America excluding Venezuela	3,938	2,234	1,618	85

Source: United Nations, Economic Commission for Latin America, *Economic Survey of Latin America, 1968* (1970), pp. 98–99. Figures are rounded and may not add to totals.
a. Including compensatory capital.
b. First column minus second and third columns.

could, with the plant operating at capacity, equal $4.5 million annually, or 8.6 percent of Ultrafertil's total sales volume of $52 million.[8] (Ultrafertil's successful opposition to an ammonia terminal in the port of Santos has given the company a virtual monopoly in Brazil.)

8. Martin Carnoy, *Industrialization in a Latin American Common Market*, an ECIEL study (Brookings Institution, 1971), Chap. 3.

Other aid-giving agencies have also supported national undertakings even though they were not efficient for the region as a whole. A 50,000-metric-ton-per-year ammonia plant near Buenos Aires, financed in part by IDB, is not competitive with projected plants at other Latin American locations, because of both the cost of natural gas in Argentina and the size of the plant. If regional efficiency considerations determined the establishment of petrochemical plants, Argentina could buy fertilizers more cheaply from other Latin American countries than it could produce them nationally.

Although there were no regional alternatives for these national loans, the political pressures to orient loans toward national and autarkic development have pushed regional considerations into the background. The absence of any regional authority concerned with the industrial, transportation, energy, and other Latin Americanwide needs and the inability of national governments to consider the implications of their development plans on regional integration make the task difficult enough.

Foreign aid and investment have often worked to support national shortsightedness, bolstering parallel rather than complementary productive structures. Similar industries have emerged in many countries, generally operating at less than optimum levels because of the limitations of national markets. A regional integration philosophy for foreign assistance would require that official aid and private capital be geared to foster industries producing for multinational rather than limited national markets.

The leverage of aid. One apparent cost of a shift to a regional policy toward Latin American countries is the loss of any political and economic leverage the United States might have over individual countries. Foreign aid might be used to keep a country from turning to extreme political systems, to influence it to side with the United States in international councils, to protect U.S. private economic interests, or to institute internal policies that the United States believed might encourage economic growth.

The influence the United States can exert through such mechanisms, however, is no longer that of an uncontested power in the Western world. Its leverage may still be significant in the smaller Latin American countries or in low-income nations of other continents, but on the whole foreign aid has stopped being a powerful tool of U.S. foreign policy. It has also become a less effective means of pressing for internal reform and improvement.

Contrary to widespread expectations, U.S. aid programs have not fostered democratic regimes in Latin America; there were at least sixteen forceful government changes in the region during the 1960s and five governments have been taken over by the military since the inception of the Alliance for Progress. The U.S. aid mechanism also seems unable to protect private economic interests. In recent interventions in the ownership and operation of private U.S. enterprises, the United States has found it politically unwise to apply full-fledged sanctions: in the 1968 expropriation of the International Petroleum Company as the first act of the military which overthrew the constitutional government of Peru; in the forced renegotiation of a twenty-year contract of the Anaconda Copper Company by the government of Chile, which received the highest per capita aid in Latin America during the 1960s; in nationalization of the Gulf Oil subsidiary by the new Bolivian military government; and in nationalization of the U.S. copper companies by Chile's new socialist regime.

The cost of bilateral aid. Perhaps a case can be made that through program aid—general-purpose loans given for overall balance-of-payments or budgetary support—the United States has been able to influence the recipient countries to adopt economic policies conducive to growth. Representatives of AID have negotiated with government officials of recipient countries on budgetary arrangements, tax legislation and administration, public expenditures and fiscal reforms, monetary and banking measures, foreign exchange regulations, import and export controls, the regulation of private enterprise, and other policies. The AID mission has maintained a constant review of relevant government operations during the administration of its loans. This procedure has probably contributed to the improvement of economic policy in some cases in Latin America: budget deficits have been reduced, the rate of inflation slowed, and foreign trade liberalized.

But program aid may involve substantial political and economic costs.[9] Attempts to change Latin American policies through U.S. aid injunctions can lead to serious political conflicts rather than appropriate solutions. The aid negotiations themselves are irritating, for both the recipient and the donor. By their very existence they imply that the donor has profound knowledge about matters often of a most sensitive nature

9. Albert O. Hirschman and Richard M. Bird, *Foreign Aid—A Critique and a Proposal*, Essays in International Finance, No. 69 (Princeton University, International Finance Section, 1968), particularly pp. 5–13. Although they compare program and project aid, their arguments against program aid are similar to those against bilateral aid made here.

in the recipient country. While the donor may simply seek to improve the recipient's policies, not to interfere in his internal affairs, the recipient may often fail to discern the donor's wisdom in sensitive policy areas. Policy makers and their advisers in many Latin American countries are highly trained, experienced, and sophisticated persons. They are likely to have a better understanding than the outsider of political reality in their country. Often they accept the policy recommendations of the donor for the obvious reason of getting aid and sometimes also as a convenient device to institute unpopular domestic policies that can be blamed on the donor. This apparent meeting of minds, however, frequently backfires because when internal dissensions become great enough to seriously diminish support for the government or threaten its survival, the recipient government may not only renege on its commitments but also turn the popular wrath on the donor country.[10]

The aid relationship is particularly volatile when comparatively low-level officials of the donor act as unsolicited advisers to the minister of finance or president of the central bank of the recipient country, requesting and receiving information that is accessible only to top-level government executives. The public is generally unaware of these relationships; their exposure can cause embarrassment to both governments, do harm to the aid-receiving government and its policies, and rouse strong hostility against the donor. The recipient government may then feel impelled to assert its independence in some conspicuous fashion, by moving away from the donor country in international relations or asserting a rising nationalism in another form.

The consequences of such resentments can reverberate through the donor country, frustrating the purposes of the aid program. The recent loss of support for the foreign aid program in the United States seems to be a reaction of this sort.

The problem of selection of aid recipients. The sensitive problem of which countries to favor and which to neglect in a bilateral aid program becomes acute during periods when foreign aid funds are severely limited. Efficiency considerations dictate that aid be concentrated in a few countries and that only token assistance be given to others. Even the most objective criteria for selecting aid recipients are likely, however, to become

10. The "good" policies may be frustrated by other policies not covered in the "aid bargain." For example, devaluation may lead to a spurt of inflation if the recipient government fails to institute supporting monetary and fiscal measures.

subordinated to political considerations, which tend to perpetuate existing strengths and weaknesses.

The most businesslike criterion for dispensing aid—productivity—points to countries that show the greatest promise for growth and where "self-help" is most developed. Apart from the possibility that self-help means the recipient is willing to accept the donor's policy recommendations (and the consequences of such an intrusion), the countries that show the greatest growth promise in Latin America are likely to be the economically most advanced; they also tend to be the larger countries, because size seems to be an important factor in the economic viability of Latin American nations. The small and least viable countries, which cannot measure up to the standards of efficiency and self-help, will under those criteria receive comparatively little aid; but they are the ones that perhaps need outside help most. Assistance awarded for efficiency and initiative will therefore accentuate the already wide gap between the most backward and the industrially advanced nations in Latin America.

Not only is the selection of bilateral aid recipients an agonizing process for the donor, but it forces the aid candidates to compete, often in a wasteful manner, for the scarce aid resources. The selection process can also have international repercussions, creating dissension among the candidates and resentment among the countries not favored; for the donor an erstwhile "showcase" of aid may turn into an embarrassment if the government of the recipient country becomes more and more repressive toward its own citizens or increasingly hostile to its "benefactor."

Integration Assistance

The most effective contribution the United States can make to Latin American development is aid for regional objectives rather than for national purposes.[11] A little over $30 million annually went to integration projects for all of Latin America during the six-year period 1961–66, according to AID and IDB data. Those projects multinational in scope—such as international roads and integration industries—or devoted to regional export promotion, monetary arrangements, and training and

11. Not only should aid be given to multinational or regional groups, but it should be channeled through multinational institutions.

research institutions received less than 5 percent of "national aid" to the area for that period.

A U.S. program that continues bilateral aid at its present level and integration assistance no higher than the $100 million level proposed in 1967 cannot provide a significant impetus toward integration. It would offer no incentive to Latin American governments to move more boldly toward regional integration. As long as U.S. assistance continues to help Latin American countries individually, they may have more to gain from the United States through autarkically oriented development programs than through regional schemes whose risks the proposed U.S. integration assistance could not begin to cover.[12]

CACM versus LAFTA

More than half of the integration assistance, nearly $17 million annually ($11 million through AID, $6 million through IDB), was granted to Central America, almost all of it to the Central American Bank for Economic Integration (CABEI). Less than $14 million annually went for integration projects outside Central America—largely for roads and promotion of intraregional exports (IDB has financed export projects, as well as a number of integration-oriented research projects).

The United States, when it recognized the Central American Common Market (CACM) as an aid recipient in 1962, established a Regional Office for Central America and Panama (ROCAP) to deal with the common market.[13] All integration aid to Central America is channeled through this AID office. There is no equivalent office for the Latin American Free Trade Association (LAFTA).

Not only has integration aid to Central America been much greater than that to LAFTA ($1.30 per capita compared to $0.07), but, what is more relevant, it has been a far greater share of the total assistance given to member countries. From 1961 through 1965, average annual CACM inte-

12. A case in point is the Latin American chemical fertilizer community that President Johnson proposed in 1965 (see p. 79). The magnitude of the assistance anticipated— a concrete offer was never made public by the United States—was apparently not sufficient to overcome the obstacles perceived by Latin American countries. Moreover, the United States at almost the same time (1966) supported a strictly national fertilizer plant of questionable efficiency for Brazil (see pp. 90–91), which weakened the idea of a region-wide fertilizer community.

13. ROCAP has never dealt with Panama, which is not a member of CACM.

gration loan commitments amounted to approximately 27 percent of total disbursements in the five countries by the U.S. government, IDB, and IBRD. In the LAFTA countries, by contrast, integration aid was less than 2 percent of total aid. If the Central American percentage were applied to Latin America as a whole, it would mean about $225 million annually of integration assistance. This is about twice as much as the past LAFTA average of $14 million plus the $100 million proposed in 1967.

Other factors must be considered in comparing CACM and LAFTA. The countries in CACM are at a lower stage of development than the average LAFTA country and would thus seem to have a greater need for outside assistance.[14] But with respect to economic integration problems, CACM is in a better situation than LAFTA. Differences in levels of development are much less pronounced among the CACM countries. Per capita income in the richest CACM country, Costa Rica, is about twice that of Honduras, at the other extreme, but the LAFTA ratio between the richest, Argentina and Venezuela, and the poorest, Bolivia, is about 5 to 1.[15] If for no other reasons, this disparity makes for greater integration difficulties in LAFTA than in CACM.

Underwriting the Risks of Integration

Because of the lack of homogeneity among LAFTA countries, they would probably not share equally in the benefits of economic union, and some might suffer welfare losses at least temporarily. The less industrialized countries might have to divert their imports from low-cost outside manufacturers to higher cost Latin American producers.[16] Such countries might need balance-of-payments assistance during early stages of the integration process.[17]

An ingenious scheme designed specifically to deal with problems arising from trade diversion proposes that "regional international companies" be set up to provide automatic compensation to countries that must buy

14. Total U.S. aid per capita to CACM countries is not significantly higher than that to LAFTA countries.

15. In a Latin Americanwide common market, CACM countries would presumably be classified among the nations of "lesser development"—a LAFTA category that includes Bolivia, Ecuador, and Paraguay.

16. Some less developed countries might consider lowered rates of industrialization a greater threat of integration than the loss of real resources.

17. See pp. 99–106.

regional products at prices higher than those of outside products.[18] Member countries would be the principal shareholders in a regional company; capital subscriptions would be financed through foreign aid; and all or most profits would be distributed to the participating countries. Other provisions would insure that the host country not benefit unduly, and that the company operate near the minimum cost point and not earn more than a reasonable return. By distributing their profits in proportion to member countries' consumption of company products, and by operating on almost costless aid donations, the regional companies would offer the highest compensation to those countries suffering most from the trade-diversion costs of integration.

In many countries where inefficient industries have been built up behind high levels of protection, adjustment funds would be needed to provide loans to those suffering serious losses in the integration process. Funds might also be needed for retraining labor dislocated because of the formation of the common market. Labor retraining is recognized as "primarily a development measure"; aid to industries, on the other hand, must be selective if it is to be more than a palliative.[19]

Adjustment funds should come from those who benefit from integration as well as from the United States. A $100 million U.S. contribution clearly would not attract contributions from either the less developed candidates for balance-of-payments compensation or the more developed partners needing adjustment assistance for their industries and labor force. In order to determine what would be a reasonable fund, further studies are needed of the size and distribution of expected national welfare losses and the probable industrial damage costs during the transition period.

External financing would continue to be important to many industries in Latin America, and major lenders could thus influence the choice between regionally and nationally oriented industrial development. Regional economic studies should be made to provide development guidance for these lenders.

Integration assistance could facilitate the efficient and equitable geo-

18. I. M. D. Little, "Regional International Companies as an Approach to Economic Integration," *Journal of Common Market Studies*, Vol. 5 (December 1966), pp. 181–86.

19. Paul N. Rosenstein-Rodan, "Multinational Investment in the Framework of Latin American Integration," in Inter-American Development Bank, *Multinational Investment in the Economic Development and Integration of Latin America*, Round Table (IDB [1968]), p. 44.

graphic distribution of integration industries. For instance, if nitrogenous fertilizer industries were established in every would-be producing country in LAFTA by 1975, the region's consumers would pay about $29 million more each year than they would if the industries were concentrated where production, distribution, and transportation costs would be at a minimum.[20] This $29 million difference represents approximately 14 percent of the optimum-location cost. Studies of other industries indicate similarly inflated costs for autarkic development. A regional investment policy could serve as a guide for lending agencies or even as a means of coordinating lending by all agencies. The Inter-American Committee of the Alliance for Progress (CIAP) is making some efforts in this direction:

CIAP has responsibilities for reviewing national programs for economic development and for recommending appropriate policies and actions by the aid-giving agencies. In fulfilling these responsibilities, CIAP can be expected to have a growing concern for programs and projects of regional significance. Multinational projects will need to be incorporated in the national development planning and programming. IDB and CIAP can continue to work closely together to implement multinational investments, and in turn assist the individual countries.[21]

The Case for U.S. Aid for an Intraregional Payments Union

An intraregional monetary arrangement offering temporary financial support to countries adversely affected by trade liberalization has long been considered an important element in Latin American economic integration. The specter of trading deficits deters many Latin American countries from joining wholeheartedly in the integration movement. Practically every LAFTA country fears that its products might not be sufficiently competitive with those of other countries in the bloc, and, therefore, that a speedy reduction in trade barriers might drastically increase its imports during the transition period without expanding its exports correspondingly. A system of intraregional cooperative financial arrangements to tide countries over regional deficits could remove a serious stumbling block on the road to a common market.[22]

20. Carnoy, *Industrialization in a Latin American Common Market*, Chap. 3.

21. Inter-American Development Bank, "Multinational Investment Programs and Latin American Integration" (Development and Resources Corp., 1966; processed), p. 49.

22. "When countries commit themselves to liberalize trade and payments within the region, they are implicitly or explicitly reducing the options open to them to cope with their balance-of-payments difficulties." (Anthony M. Solomon, "The Economic Integration of Latin America," *Department of State Bulletin*, Vol. 57 [Oct. 23, 1967], p. 538.)

Types of payments arrangements. The variety of payments arrangements possible ranges from a simple clearing agreement to a full-fledged monetary union involving significant institutional changes and a sophisticated coordination of monetary and fiscal policies. The basic objective of a clearing arrangement is to facilitate the prompt, inexpensive settlement of claims arising from commercial and financial transactions among the participating countries. Each country's bilateral deficits within the group are balanced against its bilateral surpluses. The Central American Clearing House has proved that a multilateral clearing mechanism results in significant savings on foreign exchange costs; without it each transaction, or at least each bilateral balance, must be settled separately abroad, usually through a New York bank. The simple clearing system also eliminates the need to deposit sizeable funds abroad for settling intra-area claims. Holding international reserves at home instead of dispersing them in numerous foreign accounts increases the power of monetary authorities to handle unexpected balance-of-payments difficulties.

An arrangement to alleviate temporary fluctuations in a country's net balance of receipts from, and payments to, its regional partners would offer more direct support of area trade. Such a payments union could perform a short-term, or even a medium-term, credit function, allowing a deficit country to draw from the system to pay off its negative trade balance with its partners. Funds for such an arrangement would ordinarily be made up from contributions of a certain proportion of each member country's central bank reserves, supplemented by loans or donations from third parties.

A conservative borrowing plan would allow each country to borrow for periods previously agreed upon, up to the amount of its paid-in quota. While this scheme would involve almost no risks, it might not be effective in stimulating economic integration.

More liberal arrangements would enable drawings beyond the paid-in quota, with surplus countries contributing funds beyond their quotas to help finance the temporary deficits of their partners. Credit rights could be automatic, applying whenever certain deficit situations clearly related to intraregional trade liberalization arise. In a less adventurous arrangement, drawings would be discretionary, each case being examined on its merits and taking into consideration the overall balance-of-payments position of the deficit country. Repayments could be made at fixed terms or conditioned upon the subsequent reserve positions of the debtor countries.

The ECLA proposals. In the late fifties many monetary experts agreed that Latin American payments arrangements should comprise both a clearinghouse for settling intraregional net balances and a credit mechanism to ease temporary intraregional trade disequilibria. The principal proponent of a payments union, even before LAFTA was established, was the Economic Commission for Latin America (ECLA). The arguments for a payments union have been stated by UN economists as follows:

If the Latin American countries all had very large reserves of gold and foreign exchange, they could, perhaps, afford to face the prospect of temporary balance of payments deficits arising from liberalisation of imports without undue concern. For their gold and foreign exchange reserves would provide them with the margin of time needed for corrective measures dealing with the basic causes of such deficits to take effect. . . . [If they] are to pay wholly in dollars for their imports from other countries in the area, they may find themselves compelled to maintain restrictions on trade with one another not less severe than the restrictions which they employ in trade with the rest of the world. . . . Given the existing foreign exchange position in Latin America, the conduct of intraregional payments on the basis of complete settlement in gold or dollars would defeat the whole purpose of a common market by making the liberalization of trade impossible, or at least very difficult.[23]

ECLA proposed that countries with deficits in their trade with other member countries receive automatic credits.[24] The United States and the International Monetary Fund (IMF), always opposed to schemes that considered a country's regional rather than its overall balance of payments, saw the proposals as a resurrection of the European Payments Union and a "sheer anachronism in a world that had progressed, in the meantime, from early postwar bilateralism to substantial currency convertibility."[25]

The concentration on regional balances could result in inequities and inefficient diversion of trade. What about the country that might have a deficit with the area but a large surplus in its trade with the rest of the world, and the economically weak country with a favorable trade balance with the area but an enormous deficit with the outside? Should the former's regional

23. United Nations, Economic and Social Council, "The Significance of Recent Common Market Developments in Latin America," E/CN.14/64 (Dec. 2, 1960; processed), p. 76.

24. UN, Economic Commission for Latin America (ECLA), "Multilateral Compensation of International Payments in Latin America," E/CN.12/87 (May 1949; processed).

25. Robert Triffin, "Toward a Latin American Monetary Cooperation," in Miguel S. Wionczek (ed.), *Latin American Economic Integration: Experience and Prospects* (Praeger, 1966), p. 255.

deficit be financed with the latter's regional surplus? Or should they divert their extraregional trade to the area?

No doubt the early ECLA payments union would have affected the flow of trade of Latin American countries and could have led to absurd situations. But the proposals sought to change existing trade patterns. The absurdly low level of trade within the region is very largely the product of an infrastructure—in such fields as transportation, banking, entrepreneurship, capital financing, etc.—historically developed by foreign interests, primarily European and U.S., to promote their own food and raw-material imports from the area and to seek outlets for their own exports. The resulting bias in favor of extra-area trade, and against intra-area trade, was no God-given phenomenon, but a by-product of history, calling for specific policy measures aimed at correcting the lopsidedness and uneconomic character of such a trade pattern.[26]

The IMF, the United States, and potential Latin American creditor countries further objected to ECLA's provision of automatic credits. They feared such a device would hinder progress toward monetary reform in Latin America because debtor countries in balance-of-payments difficulties caused by inflation would automatically receive credits and so have little incentive to take corrective action.

The international banking community was naturally not enthusiastic about an intra-Latin American payments arrangement. Since most external transactions of Latin American countries were settled through foreign banks, regional monetary cooperation would divert business from them. During the 1960s there was a sharp increase in the establishment of branches of U.S. and other foreign banks in Latin America.

The close dependence of the great majority of Latin American countries on outside balance-of-payments and development assistance, the awareness that regional payments schemes were highly unpopular in agencies offering such aid, and the fear prevailing in some central banks of the area that a payments union might force them to finance trade deficits of other LAFTA member countries without any reciprocity largely explain the deadlock reached on this issue when LAFTA was formed.

Alternatives to the ECLA proposals. Among the alternatives to the ECLA proposals were suggestions for establishing better correspondent relationships between U.S. and Latin American banks engaged in LAFTA trade, in order to provide additional liquidity and cut the costs of financing trade. A payments union plan proposed by Robert Triffin, who helped draft

26. *Ibid.*

the Central American payments scheme, called for monthly settlement of member countries' net balances, the clearinghouse providing interim financing for debtors. Residual net credits or debts would be settled once or twice a year.[27]

Credit would be granted only to countries whose overall reserves were decreasing or were well below the members' average in relation to total imports or other relevant criteria. It would almost automatically cover declines in reserves that were clearly seasonal or temporary, but other deficit positions would be scrutinized, particularly those that coincided with domestic inflationary developments. These proposals, though they answer the criticisms of outsiders and the fears of the region's monetary authorities, have not prospered.

CACM and LAFTA arrangements. Shortly after the Managua Treaty establishing the Central American Common Market went into effect, the five republics created the Central American Clearing House, to operate in national currencies. The success of the clearinghouse—its 1968 transactions totaled $223 million, an increase of 23 percent over 1967 and 45 percent over 1966—prompted the member countries to begin moving toward a monetary union. The LAFTA Agreement on Multilateral Clearing and Reciprocal Credits, finally signed in September 1965, stops short of a simple multilateral clearing system, although it has some of the operational characteristics of the Central American Clearing House. It does not use national currencies for intraregional payments and its interim finance arrangements for the settlement of accounts are bilateral rather than collective.[28]

At the end of 1969 LAFTA began to move toward balance-of-payments relief. The central banks of the LAFTA countries agreed to establish a modest emergency fund in 1970, with an initial subscription of $30 million, to be used to assist countries with overall balance-of-payments deficits and with either increasing regional deficits or decreasing regional surpluses that were caused by integration. Loans and repayments would be in dol-

27. Robert Triffin, "International Monetary Arrangements, Capital Markets and Economic Integration in Latin America," *Journal of Common Market Studies*, Vol. 4 (October 1965), pp. 70–104.

28. There are over thirty reciprocal agreements for settling bilateral net balances and credits within LAFTA. The Central Bank of Peru has been designated as the fiscal agent for the system (see Centro de Estudios Monetarios Latinoamericanos [CEMLA], *El progreso de la integración latinoamericana, 1966–67*, Sixth Meeting of Latin American Central Bank Governors, at Alta Gracia [April 1968], p. 16).

lars.[29] At about the same time, the CACM central banks agreed to create a $20 million Central American Fund for Monetary Stabilization, dramatizing the greater integration progress of their countries (a LAFTA fund of about $500 million would be proportionally equivalent to the CACM fund in terms of gross domestic product).[30] The Central American fund is made up of paid-in cash, the LAFTA fund of credit commitments. Both funds are divorced from their respective regional clearinghouse schemes, apparently to avoid the impression that the automaticity inherent in clearing agreements applies to balance-of-payments adjustment funds.

The discrepancies between the monetary arrangements of the two common markets reflect fundamental differences in monetary conditions in the two areas and in the complexity of their multilateral problems. While the CACM countries have always enjoyed greater monetary stability than the LAFTA countries and their clearinghouse could not be translated to a Latin Americawide scale, there is no reason why their system for settling net balances in national currencies up to a certain limit, beyond which hard currencies are used, would not be workable in a Latin American common market. Fear that their scarce hard-currency reserves may be depleted is, of course, common among less developed countries. The Central American Clearing House has so diminished the need for hard currency that "the use of dollars has been reduced to less than one-fifth of the total amount of transactions compensated."[31]

Currency overvaluation quite often compounds less developed countries' trading weaknesses, so that obliging them to settle accounts among themselves in hard currency increases their disadvantages. A payments union could overcome the obstacles of overvaluation to intraregional trade.[32]

29. Acuerdo de Santo Domingo (Acuerdo multilateral de apoyo para atenuar deficiencias transitorias de liquidez), Asociacion Latinoamericana de Libre Comercio (ALALC), Fifth Meeting of the Financial and Monetary Policy Council, at Santo Domingo, Sept. 24–26, 1969. In addition the LAFTA central banks agreed to create a market for long-term bank acceptances.

30. Central American Monetary Council, "Acuerdo del Fondo Centroamericano de Estabilización Monetaria" (San José, Costa Rica: Consejo Monetario Centroamericano, 1969; processed).

31. González del Valle, "Monetary Arrangements in LAFTA" (Inter-American Development Bank, 1967; processed), p. 9.

32. Jaroslav Vanek, "Payments Unions Among the Less Developed Countries and Their Economic Integration," *Journal of Common Market Studies*, Vol. 5 (December 1966), pp. 187–91.

Needs. Obviously a payments union would have to be more than a clearinghouse in order to combat the fear of trade liberalization. It would have to offer credit in order to encourage countries facing a scarcity of foreign exchange and loss of reserves to lower trade barriers and risk temporary balance-of-payments deficits. A credit scheme would facilitate the expansion not only of intraregional trade but of trade with the rest of the world: a country having a transitional deficit within the area could finance it without cutting into the reserves available for its extraregional trade.[33] Conceivably a payments union could, by stimulating trade among members, help reduce the extraregional deficits of Latin American countries or at least make more dollars available to finance such deficits. Of course, no payments union is designed to cover the chronic deficits of participating countries, and safeguards might be necessary to prevent such situations.

While coordination of the monetary policies of the member countries of a payments union is not a possibility at this time, their commitment to monetary cooperation is a necessity. In a payments institution based largely on capital subscriptions by member countries, national monetary authorities would be brought closer together and their vested interest in a mutually beneficial arrangement would assure its continuation. Participating nations could not afford to follow completely autonomous monetary policies that were likely to destroy the union. Once the institutional framework of a payments compact existed, more elaborate methods of monetary cooperation would probably evolve naturally. Some economists believe that a payments union is of such importance that "considerable benefits can be derived by the less developed countries, even in the absence of other accompanying forms of economic integration."[34]

It is doubtful whether an effective Latin American payments union could be established without a specific contribution by the United States. While a clearinghouse needs only small resources of its own and therefore can be established without any outside assistance, a more comprehensive scheme involving credits to ease temporary balance-of-payments disequilibria would need external financing if for no other reason than to get started. Of course, in order to make a union operate efficiently, the member countries themselves would have to subscribe a part of their own reserves.

33. Although trade among Latin American countries has been a small fraction of their total trade, intraregional trade balances might be a much higher percentage of total balances.
34. *Ibid.*, p. 187.

The United States in 1967 promised "a substantial contribution to a fund that will help ease the transition into an integrated regional economy."[35] The purpose of that adjustment or "buffer" fund was "to contribute to the solution of problems in connection with the balance of payments, industrial readjustments, and retraining of the labor force."[36] The U.S. commitment to provide balance-of-payments support could easily be translated into support for a Latin American payments arrangement. The benefits resulting from a relatively small commitment—the U.S. contribution to the European Payments Union did not exceed $350 million —could be very high.

The payments schemes that have been initiated in the region can be used to test the strength of the Latin American integration movement. The United States could offer to match contributions substantially in excess of the $50 million already committed by the area's central banks ($30 million in LAFTA plus $20 million in CACM) as an inducement to Latin American countries to raise their own contributions.

Summary

Multinational projects eligible for aid would include roads, communications networks, and other infrastructure works and industrial undertakings involving two or more countries. Assistance could be given by the United States directly to a multinational scheme; it might be more desirable, however, to pass funds through such regional agencies as the Inter-American Development Bank and the Central American Bank for Economic Integration that are better suited to handling multinational undertakings.

Assistance to regional institutions responsible for coordinating integration programs may be even more important than project aid. It would consist of contributions to special regional funds for balance-of-payments assistance for countries that suffer transitory foreign-exchange difficulties due to their lowering of trade barriers, industrial reorganization loans for industries gravely affected by international competition that need help to

35. President Johnson's speech at the inter-American summit meeting in Punta del Este on April 13, 1967 (*Weekly Compilation of Presidential Documents*, Vol. 3 [1967], p. 637).
36. Declaration of the Presidents of America (see Appendix D, pp. 187–88).

change into other lines or activities, and loans for the retraining and up-grading of labor displaced in the reallocation of resources provoked by rising regional competition. The primary recipients of such U.S. aid ought to be regional institutions initiated and controlled by the Latin American countries. Institutions designed for these purposes have already been established: contributions for balance-of-payments adjustment can be given to the Central American Fund for Monetary Stabilization and to the balance-of-payments emergency fund for LAFTA countries; con-tributions for industrial reorganization assistance and labor force retrain-ing can be given to the Inter-American Development Bank and the Andean Development Corporation.

Some aid, of course, may not be fully used at first, for Latin American countries may not respond efficiently to a radical shift in U.S. policy from national to regional aid. Such a shift may even provoke resentment in countries that have been major aid recipients and are cool to regional integration efforts.

Regional integration can be an essential ingredient in the acceleration of Latin American economic growth. Any efforts to help overcome the obstacles to integration will benefit Latin American development, one of the important objectives of U.S. foreign policy. Foreign assistance for multinational projects and for an insurance scheme to protect countries from foreign exchange losses and business and labor from bankruptcy and unemployment can provide powerful incentives to the public and private sectors in Latin America for moving more rapidly toward economic co-operation. While external integration assistance can only supplement or stimulate regional efforts, its benefits may well be quite out of proportion to its size.

CHAPTER SIX

Private Participation

THE UNITED STATES HAS always been concerned about and given support to U.S. private interests operating within Latin America. Proponents of this U.S. policy have argued that it serves the Latin American interest by contributing to regional growth. President Kennedy argued in its defense:

The effective participation of an enlightened U.S. businessman, especially in partnership with private interests in the developing country, brings not only his investment, but his technological and management skills into the process of development. His successful participation in turn helps create that climate of confidence which is so critical in attracting and holding vital external and internal capital.[1]

The U.S. view is not shared by all Latin Americans, on either economic or political grounds. Many Latin American governments are willing to sacrifice some national economic growth and restrict foreign capital in order to assert greater control over their own affairs. Past experience and present nationalism have prompted the Latin American republics in their search for foreign private investment to accept it only on their own terms.

1. *Congressional Record*, April 2, 1963, p. 5128.

Foreign Private Investment

Most U.S. investors see in a Latin American common market the possibility of a large growth in the region's production. Both investors and exporters therefore endorse U.S. support for a common market that is "commercially outward looking and receptive to foreign investment on reasonable terms."[2] Latin American businessmen and nationalist-minded groups on the other hand demand that the market benefit Latin Americans primarily and that regional industrialization be controlled by local interests. Foreign enterprises, and particularly large multinational corporations with a worldwide network of subsidiaries and affiliates, often excite strong nationalist sentiment as well as raising economic conflicts in their host countries.[3] Thus, whatever the potential benefits of U.S. private investment may be for developing countries, policy makers must weigh them against the inevitable political friction engendered by foreign controlled enterprises.

Growth in Foreign Private Capital

After the Spanish-American War, U.S. privately owned assets in Latin America increased substantially, rising from some $300 million in 1897 to $1.6 billion by 1914.[4] Primarily U.S. investments went into tropical agriculture and raw-material development (sugar, bananas, and mining), although there were important U.S.-controlled public utility and railroad ventures in

2. *Latin American Summit Conference*, Hearings before the Senate Committee on Foreign Relations, 90 Cong. 1 sess. (1967), p. 28.

3. In a series of confrontations with the United States, Latin American governments have on several occasions revoked contractual concessions, special privileges, and agreements entered into with U.S. firms. The U.S. government often has acted on behalf of U.S. business, recent outstanding examples being the disputes between the Brazilian government and the International Telephone and Telegraph Corporation (ITT) in 1962 and the American and Foreign Power Company (AMFORP) in 1963, and between the Peruvian government and the International Petroleum Company (IPC) during the 1960s. In the ITT case the U.S. government played a critical role primarily through the introduction of the Hickenlooper amendment, in the AMFORP and IPC cases primarily through withholding of foreign aid.

4. Data on private investments from U.S. Department of Commerce, *Survey of Current Business*, various issues, and *Balance of Payments; Statistical Supplement* (Washington, 1963); J. Grunwald, "Change Does *Not* Spell the End of Profits," *Challenge*, June 1964, pp. 34–37.

Table 10. Book Value of U.S. Direct Private Investment in Selected Latin American Countries, 1950, 1960, 1965, and 1967

Country	Amount (millions of dollars)				As percent of Latin American total			
	1950	1960	1965	1967ᵃ	1950	1960	1965	1967ᵃ
Argentina	356	472	992	1,080	9	6	11	11
Brazil	644	953	1,074	1,326	17	13	11	13
Chile	540	738	829	878	14	10	9	9
Colombia	193	424	526	610	5	6	6	6
Mexico	415	795	1,182	1,342	11	11	13	13
Peru	145	446	515	605	4	6	6	6
Venezuela	993	2,569	2,705	2,553	26	35	29	25
Others	517	1,035	1,568	1,817	14	14	17	18
Total	3,803	7,431	9,391	10,213	100	100	100	100

Source: Organization of American States (OAS), *External Financing for Latin American Development* (Johns Hopkins Press, 1971), p. 65. Figures are rounded and may not add to totals.
a. Preliminary.

Cuba, Mexico, and Central America, as well as substantial portfolio investments.

European investments in Latin America, concentrated in railroads and government bonds, were progressively liquidated during the First World War. U.S. holdings in turn increased sharply,[5] and by 1929 the book value of U.S. private investment in Latin America surpassed the $5 billion mark, accounting for about one-third of total U.S. investment abroad. Portfolio investments continued to be important, but 70 percent of U.S. holdings consisted of direct investments. Foreign private funds, which had disappeared during the Great Depression and then returned with the outbreak of the Second World War, came almost solely from the United States from 1940 until the mid-fifties. Over three-fourths of all U.S. private investment in the region went to Brazil, Chile, Cuba, Mexico, and Venezuela, by far the largest share going into petroleum exploitation in Venezuela (see Tables 10 and 11). By 1960 the book value of direct foreign investment in Latin America had risen to an estimated $13 billion, and about $7.4 billion of that was U.S. capital.[6]

5. The magnitude of U.S. investments today cannot match the British investments of almost one billion pounds sterling at the end of 1913 (J. Fred Rippy, "British Investments in Latin America, End of 1913," *Inter-American Economic Affairs*, Vol. 5 [Autumn 1951], p. 91).

6. Much of the increase in U.S. direct investment from $3.5 billion in 1929 reflected the revaluation of assets under inflationary conditions.

Table 11. Book Value of U.S. Direct Private Investment in Latin America, by Economic Sector, 1929, 1950, 1960, 1965, and 1967

Economic sector	Amount in millions of dollars and as percent of total investment									
	1929		1950		1960		1965		1967[a]	
Mining and refineries	732	21	628	17	1,153	16	1,114	12	1,218	12
Petroleum	617	18	1,213	32	2,740	37	3,034	32	2,917	29
Manufacturing	231	7	726	19	1,499	20	2,745	29	3,301	32
Public utilities	887	25	656	17	820	11	596	6	614	6
Trade	119	3	221	6	674	9	1,041	11	1,207	12
Others	933	27	367	10	546	7	861	9	956	9
Total	3,519	100	3,803	100	7,431	100	9,391	100	10,213	100

Source: OAS, *External Financing for Latin American Development*, p. 67. Figures are rounded and may not add to totals.
a. Preliminary.

Petroleum, mining, and smelting continued to be the chief attraction for U.S. investors. About 90 percent of all new U.S. investment in Chile and 65 percent in Peru went into mining and smelting during the 1950s. Of the $2.6 billion book value of U.S. direct private investment in Venezuela in 1960, about $2.0 billion was in the oil industry.[7] Only in the public utilities sector did U.S. capital show a significant decline as Latin American governments nationalized many foreign-owned utilities (see Table 11).

Current Role of Foreign Capital

For generations, foreign capital contributed to Latin American growth only in the export sector. Foreign enterprises were liable for few local taxes or government fees, the major part of their earnings was held abroad, and their ties with local economies were weak. Foreign firms bought most of their supplies and equipment abroad, hired a very small percentage of the country's total labor force, and processed little of the output of their mines and plantations locally. Furthermore, they made little effort to train local personnel for managerial, supervisory, and technical positions, but imported most of their skilled employees.

Outside investments can be expected to supply greater benefits today. The failure of foreign firms to transfer technological knowledge or to train

7. Mining, including petroleum, employs about 1 percent of the total labor force and contributes about 4 percent to Latin America's gross domestic product, but it has the highest productivity of any economic sector in the region (see Appendix Table A-2).

managerial and technical personnel and their propensity to corrupt officials or to intervene directly in national politics have largely disappeared. Foreign capital is now taxed much more heavily, more foreign earnings are returned to the host country, foreign firms buy more from and sell more to domestic producers, and know-how is being transferred in the industrialization process.

Yet the conspicuous cases of unbridled exploitation in the past overshadow the performance of foreign capital today. The United States continues to be accused of economic domination, political intervention, and perversion of Latin American values through its investments. The chronic Latin American fear of foreign exploitation of the region's natural resources now extends to its industrial and banking sectors.

Evidence of the economic power of large international corporations in Europe and elsewhere and a conviction that foreign policies are heavily influenced by foreign nationals' business operations compound Latin American fears. The belief that U.S. aid and trade policies are designed to further the business interests of U.S. citizens is reinforced by such instances as the withholding of aid from Peru during its dispute with U.S. oil companies in the early 1960s, and the subsequent Hickenlooper amendments. International strategic considerations are also accused of turning foreign policy against Latin American interests. For example, the United States with little regard for Chilean interest has in wartime controlled the price of Chile's copper, "partly through tariffs, partly through direct price and production controls or stimuli, and partly through the operation of a strategic stockpile of copper."[8] U.S. companies, producing most of Chile's copper, have implemented U.S. policy, thus contributing to the hostility against foreign capital.

The ownership and operation of natural resource industries have been regarded as national patrimony in most developing countries. Natural resources are a particularly sensitive area because the great economic and political power vested in their control still brings the policies of foreign companies into conflict with those of host countries.[9] Since the Second World War, however, foreign operations in the natural resource and utility sectors

8. Joseph Grunwald and Philip Musgrove, *Natural Resources in Latin American Development* (Johns Hopkins Press for Resources for the Future, 1970), p. 160.

9. John E. Tilton, "The Choice of Trading Partners: An Analysis of International Trade in Aluminum, Bauxite, Copper, Lead, Manganese, Tin, and Zinc," *Yale Economic Essays*, Vol. 6 (Fall 1966), pp. 419–74.

have been increasingly restricted and controlled by Latin American governments. Latin American policies, together with the discovery of alternative sources of supply in Africa and elsewhere, have turned the flow of foreign private capital from extractive activities to manufacturing, commerce, and financial services in Latin America.[10] From 1960 to 1967, for example, net U.S. direct investment in Latin American mining, smelting, and petroleum activities was negligible, but in manufacturing amounted to almost $2 billion. The book value of U.S. capital in the extractive sectors of Latin America declined from about 53 percent of the value of all U.S. direct investment in Latin America in 1960 to 40 percent in 1967. During the same period the share of manufacturing investment rose from 20 to over 32 percent (see Table 11).[11]

National governments have been substantial investors in Latin America, important not only in natural-resource exploitation (particularly oil) and utilities development (communications and energy), but recently also in banking and manufacturing, especially steel production and other heavy industries. The fields in which public enterprises are the predominant investors will become more restrictive to foreign capital than economic activities in which foreign investors compete with existing or potential local private capital.

Investment in Manufacturing and Services

The shift of U.S. investments in Latin America to manufacturing and services has led to new difficulties, especially in those countries with important domestic manufacturing sectors. Domestic manufacturers often view foreign firms as "unfair" competitors because of their vast technological superiority and the ease with which they can cover losses or meet needs for additional working capital through access to funds from their home offices.

Foreign investment, Albert Hirschman believes, "can be at its creative

10. See *The Investment of U.S. Private Enterprise in Developing Countries*, Report of Subcommittee on Foreign Economic Policy of the House Committee on Foreign Affairs, 90 Cong. 2 sess. (1968), pp. 38–39.

11. In other less developed areas, the bulk of U.S. capital continues to flow into the extractive industries, petroleum investment alone accounting for about 60 percent of such investments during 1960–66. Since 1966 U.S. plant and equipment expenditures in Latin American metal mining and smelting have increased, primarily as a consequence of an accord between the Chilean government and the U.S. copper companies to expand production greatly (*Survey of Current Business*, recent issues).

best by bringing in 'missing' factors of production, complementary to those available locally, in the early stages of development of a poor country." It may play a stunting role "later on, when the poor country has begun to generate ... its own entrepreneurs, technicians, and savers and could now do even more along these lines if it were not for the institutional inertia that makes for a continued importing of so-called scarce factors of production."[12] Most Latin American countries have reached this stage of development; foreign firms therefore tend to compete with rather than complement domestic enterprise. Their contributions vanish when foreigners buy out solvent local businesses.

Furthermore, if a large portion of the more dynamic new industries is in foreign hands, industrialists cannot constitute an effective interest group for modernization. Guests tend to act with great caution and restraint, not as a pressure group for the reform of domestic policies. On the other hand, policy makers cannot afford to make decisions whose fruits "would accrue to non-nationals and would strengthen their position."[13] Thus many policies, because they are aimed to "squeeze" the foreigner, may prove irrational from an economic development point of view.

Latin Americans argue that the net flow of foreign private capital to the region is now so small that it may not be an important contributor to growth. The flow of U.S. direct private investment, net of amortization, but including reinvested earnings, ranged between $400 million and almost $600 million during the 1960s, and other direct foreign investment was at most one-half that of U.S. investment. Thus private direct foreign investment totaled between $600 million and $900 million annually, or about 3–4 percent of total annual Latin American domestic investment during that period.[14] If interest and profit remittances are taken into consideration, the final net flow is much lower.[15]

12. Albert O. Hirschman, *How to Divest in Latin America and Why*, Essays in International Finance, No. 76 (Princeton University, International Finance Section, 1969), p. 6. Hirschman's views are shared by many Latin Americans.

13. *Ibid.*, p. 7.

14. Penelope Roper, *Investment in Latin America*, QER Special No. 6 (London: The Economist Intelligence Unit, April 1970), pp. 7 and 8.

15. The United Nations Economic Commission for Latin America (ECLA) calculates a net outflow of capital if all official and private capital movements are added together (see Table 9). This is not an unusual situation after an initially high inflow of capital that has generated high amortization, interest, and profit payments just when the size of new foreign investment is diminishing.

Capital investment does not, of course, always lead to economic development. Capital allocated to highly protected inefficient industries can lead to a decrease in welfare. And foreign capital for such industries adds a further burden to the economy: interest and profit remittances must be paid for by additional exports that the industries cannot provide. Foreign companies can do further harm as preferred customers of Latin American banks by diverting scarce credit from local entrepreneurs.[16]

Foreign Investment in a Common Market

The conflict between Latin American governments and foreign investors in manufacturing and sophisticated service industries could be particularly acute in a regional common market. Foreign firms stand to benefit most from the reduction of trade barriers: those with branches in a number of countries can comparatively easily expand the marketing of their products throughout the region; furthermore, they are likely to have access to lower cost capital in developed countries. Large foreign firms have, in fact, been the first to build their own multination complementarity arrangements under the Latin American Free Trade Association (LAFTA) agreement.

A substantial part of foreign investment in Central America during past years went into the purchase of existing local firms, which then expanded as the common market grew. This type of investment frequently fails to bring with it the traditional benefits of new capital or technology, and it may stifle local enterprise.

Because of Latin American fears that within a common market foreign investment might run rampant, rules governing foreign investment are apt to be tougher under regional integration arrangements than under individual countries. Restrictions and controls on operation of foreign private capital vary widely from country to country in Latin America, and within countries from one manufacturing activity to another.[17] The less developed

16. Miguel S. Wionczek, *La banca extranjera en América Latina* (Centro de Estudios Monetarios Latinoamericanos [CEMLA], 1971). If the rate of interest is below the rate of inflation, foreigners will benefit at the expense of the local population.

17. Foreign private capital is restricted in the following fields in LAFTA countries: in Argentina, petroleum; in Brazil, petroleum, mass communications media, and banking; in Chile, petroleum, mining, shipping, insurance, and banking; in Mexico, petroleum, mining, public utilities, fisheries, forestry, heavy petrochemicals, banking, insurance, radio, and motion pictures; in Paraguay, petroleum and public utilities; and in Peru, petroleum, banking, insurance, air transport, and mass communications media.

countries would probably benefit from a continuation of present treatment. The more developed LAFTA members are unwilling to open their borders unconditionally to products of the less developed, partly for fear they might offer foreign capital extremely broad concessions that would endanger domestically owned firms in the advanced LAFTA countries.

The most successful attempt so far to establish a common foreign investment code was made by the Commission of the Cartagena Agreement, the governing instrument of the five Andean common market nations (Bolivia, Chile, Colombia, Ecuador, and Peru); they agreed in December 1970 on common rules for foreign investors, giving special consideration to Bolivia and Ecuador, the two least developed countries. Economic activities reserved for local capital only include public utilities (water and sewage, electric light and power, telephone, telecommunications, and so forth), inland transport, insurance, commercial banks and other financial institutions, advertising, and news media (commercial radio, television, newspapers, and magazines). Foreign companies operating in these fields must transfer 80 percent of their capital to local investors within three years. A debilitating escape clause provides that each member country may vary the rules from the common policy if circumstances justify such action; exempted activities will be excluded from the benefits of the duty-reduction program as well.

Mining, petroleum and gas (including oil and gas pipelines), and forestry products are specifically exempted from the investment rules. During the first ten years of the agreement, foreign companies may be granted concessions not to exceed twenty years. No depletion allowance is available, but foreign companies may earn preferences by doing business in association with state enterprises.

In other activities—primarily manufacturing—foreign companies must pledge to convert to national or joint enterprises within fifteen years in Chile, Colombia, and Peru and twenty years in Bolivia and Ecuador if they wish to have access to the subregional common market. The agreement defines a foreign company as an enterprise with 51 percent or more foreign ownership, or one whose technical, administrative, and commercial management is controlled by aliens; a domestic company as one in which at least 80 percent of the capital (and management) is held by entities

---

Only in a few republics, notably Colombia, Ecuador, and Venezuela, can a prospective foreign investor still find great freedom of operation. Further restrictions were introduced in the Andean Group in mid-1971.

(including the state) or persons from any of the member countries of the Andean Development Corporation (to which Venezuela also belongs); and a joint enterprise as one that falls between the 51 and 80 percent limitations. Foreign investors may buy into domestic enterprises only when their doing so would prevent the bankruptcy of the local company. Profit remittances abroad are limited to an annual rate of 14 percent (the level now existing in Colombia). The agreement also covers rules on the transfer of technological knowledge.

While the Andean common market ostensibly welcomes foreign private enterprise, its rules are probably more restrictive than those of any single Latin American country except Chile and Peru. On the other hand the Andean agreement can provide the clarity and stability in regulations that are so badly needed for the making of investment decisions. If the "rules of the game" are spelled out and are likely to last, they may, despite their severity, provide greater incentives for foreign investors than the ever-changing and vague regulations of individual weak countries with apparently more favorable "investment climates." Confronted with a firm set of rules, the foreign investor can decide more easily whether to "take it or leave it."

Despite tougher rules, foreign investment flows will continue if there is dynamic economic growth. In general, the degree of control reflects the development of domestic industry and the rate of growth of the economy; the higher the growth rate, the greater the power of the host government to restrict foreign capital without inhibiting its flow. Indeed, the scant evidence available indicates that neither government controls nor social unrest, short of wholesale nationalization or suspension of currency convertibility, are important determinants of the rate of U.S. direct foreign investment in a country.[18] There is little doubt that the most favorable investment climate is afforded by a rapidly growing economy. Creation of the Latin American common market would accelerate the growth rate of the region, attracting foreign private investment on a much larger scale than before.[19]

Specially designed investment incentives, applying to both foreign and

18. Samuel Armstrong Morley, "American Corporate Investment Abroad Since 1919" (Ph.D. dissertation, University of California, Berkeley, 1965), p. 135.

19. Paradoxically, the largest increases might be in the countries that currently regulate foreign capital most strictly—Argentina, Brazil, Chile, and Mexico—because the development of manufacturing industry is expected to be greatest there. About 80 percent of the book value of U.S. investment in manufacturing and 45 percent of total U.S. investment in Latin America is in these four countries (see Table 10).

domestic capital, can have a very important role in a Latin American common market. They could help orient the nature of investment as well as its location, increasing the benefits to both the investor and the less developed areas within a country or region. Investment incentives have been used extensively within the Central American Common Market (CACM) and in parts of LAFTA—particularly in the northeastern part of Brazil. Their effectiveness is, of course, limited by the investor's calculation of profits he can expect, which in turn depends upon the economic dynamism of the area.

Tax incentives have been used most often in Latin America to attract investment in physical capital. But capital-intensive industries, which usually require highly skilled labor, are not what is needed in economies where capital and skills are scarce. Emphasis should rather be on subsidizing the use of labor.[20]

Regional Investment and the Multinational Corporation

The main effort of the first stage of Latin American integration is to increase regional investment; trade is expected to follow capital expansion. The distribution of benefits from investments in a regional market is a matter of great concern. In a free market situation, it is feared, investments would tend to be made in the largest and more industrialized nations, to the detriment of the smaller and economically weaker countries.[21] In Europe the question of whether and how much to plan the nature and location of investment has been answered by "indicative" planning and flexible coordination for a "concerted" economy.[22] A supranational planning authority would be as unrealistic to propose for Latin America as for Europe. But in order to stimulate investment, some regional policy making is neces-

20. U.S. private investment per person employed was $7,900 in Latin America in 1957 compared to about $3,800 in Europe. Even excluding petroleum and mining investment, capital intensity was higher in Latin America (over $4,500). (See Organization of American States [OAS], *External Financing for Latin American Development* [Johns Hopkins Press, 1971], p. 78.)

21. Market considerations were the paramount motive for the location of foreign firms in Europe, and lower labor costs were relatively unimportant (Pierre Uri, "Foreign Investment: The European Experience," in Inter-American Development Bank, *Multinational Investment, Public and Private, in the Economic Development and Integration of Latin America* [IDB (1968)], Round Table, pp. 259–60).

22. Albert Coppé, "The European Experience," in IDB, Round Table, p. 235.

sary, and it can be designed to protect the national interest of the partners without sacrificing the benefits of economic efficiency. In Europe, where the entrepreneur was primed to perceive new markets and investment opportunities and the general conditions for integration through trade liberalization were much more favorable than in Latin America, the European Coal and Steel Community (ECSC) led the way in investment expansion and allocation (it got started with the help of a $100 million loan from the United States). While the ECSC has not assigned productive activities within the member countries, it has reviewed investment projects above a certain size, providing strong "moral suasion" and orientation on private investment needs and for potential sources of financing.

A Regional Investment-Promotion Agency

A mechanism like the ECSC might be appropriate for Latin America. Many countries in the region have had national investment promotion agencies for some time and more recently have experimented with national development planning. Such planning has improved since the early days of the Alliance for Progress, when plan-making was often a paper exercise performed only to satisfy the requirements of aid-giving agencies. Regional planning for infrastructure projects can in large part be undertaken as national planning, without major international bargaining machinery. Obviously each country sharing an international highway could be responsible for planning the section within its own borders, and its portion of the total investment would be included in its national plan. The international production and distribution of electric power would be somewhat more complex; however, if it were clearly in the interest of two or more countries, they could negotiate the sharing of the investment burden without too much difficulty.[23] International maritime and air transportation and communications projects, on the other hand, could not be handled adequately by national agencies. Regional operation of such projects would result in con-

---

23. The first truly multinational electric power development project in Latin America, the Acaray River Hydroelectric Station in Paraguay, was designed to supply surplus power to large areas in Brazil and Argentina. The $30 million financing for the project from the Inter-American Development Bank would have constituted an intolerable burden on Paraguay had it not been planned that surplus power would be exported to neighboring markets. (José C. Cárdenas, "Latin American Experience in the Multinational Investment Field," in IDB, Round Table, p. 350.)

siderable economies. Their economic integration, as well as that of regional industrial projects, would require multinational organization.

The major task in planning investments for Latin American integration is to combine maximum regional efficiency with equitable national distribution of the gains from integration. The wide range of options for efficient allocation of productive activities within the region makes political negotiations feasible.[24]

The first aim of a regional investment-promotion agency—either an independent entity or an arm of an existing regional institution—would be to increase capital formation in the region. Its second aim would be to promote an equitable distribution of integration benefits within the region.[25] Established industries that could not survive intraregional competition when trade barriers were eliminated present a problem, for no country would choose to destroy its important industries, if only because of the decline in employment.

Economic integration can be a less painful process if countries specialize within industrial sectors rather than in entire industries. Politically the process may be facilitated if industrial sectors are integrated one at a time until most important industries are covered. Though integration within sectors implies a greater welfare loss to consumers than integration across the whole gamut of industries, Latin Americans may be willing to pay the price in order to attain a high degree of industrial diversification within each nation.

Intraindustry agreements could provide for plants in the various member countries to specialize in particular products within an industry or—what requires more coordination—in different components of given products. Such complementarity arrangements would safeguard the interests of participating nations in a customs union and at the same time promote a better

24. See Martin Carnoy, *Industrialization in a Latin American Common Market*, an ECIEL study (Brookings Institution, 1971). In any case, concessions to their poorer trading partners would not impose an intolerable burden on the richer Latin American countries; the less developed countries (Central America, Haiti, the Dominican Republic, Bolivia, Ecuador, and Paraguay) have not much more than 14 percent of the total population and less than 5 percent of the total income of Latin America.

25. Both objectives would be considered in the identification and promotion of new investments. An investment-promotion agency could identify the comparative production advantages of member countries, make information available on technological advances in the various fields, and possibly undertake industrial research and feasibility studies.

division of labor in the region. Since integration in Latin America aims at a massive expansion of the industrial sector as well as efficient production, complementarity agreements could be used as a means of establishing new industries. They would be especially important in developing such heavy industries as chemicals, petrochemicals, steel, and heavy machinery and equipment.[26]

Each agreement could be administered by a commission consisting of representatives of the member countries, eliminating the need for a supranational authority. The commission would operate under a definite time schedule for eliminating intraregional trade barriers and establishing a common external tariff. If several complementarity arrangements were negotiated simultaneously, the bargaining process among member countries would be opened up and integration gains could be more widely distributed.

The Multinational Corporation

Probably the most efficient vehicle for implementing the complementarity principle without supranational planning is the multinational corporation. A corporation that operates in several national markets avoids a great deal of duplication of overhead capital, realizes economies of scale in its operation, and centralizes decision making on multinational matters. Such an en-

26. At the end of 1970 sixteen complementarity agreements were in effect and some twenty under negotiation within LAFTA. Six of them covered four or more countries: (1) statistical and calculating machines, among Argentina, Brazil, Chile, and Uruguay (1962); (2) electronic tubes, Argentina, Brazil, Chile, Mexico, and Uruguay (1964); (3) chemical industry, Argentina, Brazil, Colombia, Chile, Mexico, Peru, Uruguay, and Venezuela (1967); (4) petrochemical industry, Bolivia, Colombia, Chile, and Peru (1968); (5) phonographic equipment, Argentina, Brazil, Mexico, and Venezuela (1970); (6) petrochemical products, Argentina, Brazil, Mexico, and Venezuela (1970). Three countries— Argentina, Brazil, and Mexico—have signed two agreements on office machines (1970; Chile is to join one of these agreements) and an agreement on pharmaceutical products (1970). The remaining agreements are between two countries: electrical machinery and household appliances, and communications equipment, Brazil and Uruguay (1966); household equipment, Argentina and Uruguay (1968); glass industry, Argentina and Mexico (1969); electric energy generation and transmission, Brazil and Mexico (1969); electronic and electrical communications, and refrigeration, airconditioning, and electrical domestic appliances, Brazil and Mexico (1970). (Asociacion Latino-americano de Libre Comercio [ALALC], *Actualización de los acuerdos de complementación suscritos y de los proyectos*, CEP/Repartido 1074/Rev. 10, Sept. 3, 1970; and *LAFTA's Newsletter*, No. 4 [December 1970].)

terprise is concerned with the actions of all of its subsidiaries and would tend to prevent profit-seeking by one at the expense of another. It thus would lend itself to the coordination of regional investments, thus obviating an elaborate regional planning institution.

A multinational corporation could be private or public and could operate infrastructure works as well as manufacturing and distribution enterprises. The public corporation would be particularly suitable for international air and maritime transportation and communications, as the Scandinavian Airlines System (SAS), which combines the airlines of Denmark, Norway, and Sweden, has proven. The more modest Flota Grancolombiana has successfully merged the merchant shipping fleets of Colombia and Ecuador; in the mid-sixties it carried an average of 11 percent of the total imports and 14 percent of the export cargo of the two countries. Its success is based on modern and efficient operations, not the protection and subsidies that its competitors in many developed countries depend upon.

Existing companies in Latin American countries could join together to form multinational enterprises. The pooling of technical, managerial, and financial resources and production at high enough output levels to yield economies of scale would strengthen Latin American enterprises, making them more competitive with extraregional corporations. A stronger competitive position should remove much of the fear of integration that private enterprise has exhibited.

Regional companies owned by member governments would be especially appropriate in circumstances where economic union is apt to cause some countries to suffer losses. The profits of such multinational corporations, in which the participating countries would hold shares proportional to their consumption of the company's output, would compensate weaker countries for the higher prices they might pay in switching to regional products and the loss of industrialization they might sustain in giving up an independent policy of protection. With the help of foreign aid, such multinational enterprises could be made clearly beneficial to all parties.

At present Latin America is not well equipped for the establishment of truly regional firms. Legislation on the formation of enterprises in most countries governs national or foreign companies that operate exclusively within the frontiers of the country. Without laws providing for the needs of transnational enterprises—such as the elimination of double taxation—and permitting escape from purely national regulations, multinational corporations in Latin America are likely to be foreign and have their decision centers outside the region.[27]

Since multinational investments in Latin America can, at present, best be made by foreign capital, complications arise. Many Latin American businessmen, intellectuals, and public officials recognize the need for foreign investment and appreciate the importance of the large international corporation in the transmission of technological know-how, external resources, and managerial capabilities but they fear that an integrated Latin America may become merely a market arrangement for the convenience of a small number of huge foreign enterprises. Even in Europe, with a relatively well-developed capital market, mobility, and entrepreneurship, the indigenous corporation did not prosper as much during the first decade of economic integration as did the U.S. international enterprise with its great technological, financial, and managerial superiority. The gaps in capability between the United States and Europe may be large, but they are several times larger between the United States and Latin America. These facts underline the need for common foreign investment rules and regional planning and promotion as a part of an effort toward economic integration.

Regional Communications and Transportation Systems

Latin American trade patterns have to a large extent been determined by foreign investors and entrepreneurs who developed the region's natural resources and financed its transportation systems and other infrastructure primarily to encourage exports of primary products. High trade barriers designed to protect national import-substituting industrialization and bilateral relations with the United States have contributed to the bias toward extra-area trade. Regional integration could correct this bias, but only if the mountains and deserts can be bridged and the jungles penetrated. In order to make intra-area trade more efficient, artificial trade restrictions must be removed and great emphasis given to the development of a regional communications network, including maritime transportation.

27. Peru in 1968 enacted legislation that exempts multinational companies from Peruvian taxes on their regional operations and gives them other privileges; the ADELA Investment Company in July 1969 qualified as the first firm under this new law (Atlantic Community Development Group for Latin America [ADELA], "Monthly Bulletin," July 1969).

The United States has been aware for some time that its attitude toward development of a regional infrastructure can have a profound effect on the speed with which the economies of Latin America integrate. The Charter of Punta del Este calls for special attention to financing multinational projects, and President Johnson obligated the United States to contribute to a "fund for preparing multinational projects."[28]

U.S. aid affects primarily telecommunications, road projects, and port development, which are in public hands. While ocean transport is in private hands, the U.S. government can affect shipping policies; thus special attention ought to be given to maritime shipping.

Telecommunications

Extremely poor telecommunications within Latin America and to the outside have been detrimental to the development of the region. The difficulties of calling by telephone between cities only a short distance apart (Buenos Aires to Montevideo, Rio de Janeiro to São Paulo, Quito to Guayaquil) have hindered business operations in Latin America. It is far easier, for example, to telephone from Rio de Janeiro to New York or London than to Buenos Aires. The first communications satellite for Latin America was launched in 1968. The satellite system, financed by the United States and the Inter-American Development Bank, is expected to improve telephone service radically between major cities in the hemisphere. Better communications should bring direct and significant benefits for the area's development.

Overland Transport

The United States, in keeping with its own history of transcontinental transport, has always supported overland transport projects in Latin America. Almost one hundred years after the first transcontinental railroad was completed in the United States, only one overland route connects the coast of Brazil with Peru, and South and Central America remain inaccessible to

28. *Public Papers of the Presidents of the United States: Lyndon B. Johnson, 1965*, Bk. 2, p. 887. Multinational infrastructure was the subject of a chapter of the Action Program of the 1967 Punta del Este summit conference; it was also the principal point in President Johnson's remarks at the signing of the Organization of American States Charter amendment in Washington on April 23, 1968.

each other except by ship. Even in the last century, some people in the United States saw South America as a single geographical area that could reap the same economic rewards from transcontinental railroads that North America had won. A proposal for a Pan American railway stretching from New York to Buenos Aires was officially approved by the participants in the First International Conference of American States in 1889–90. The United States gave its support in part as a means of moving closer to the Latin American economies whose trade was oriented primarily toward Europe. The U.S. Congress appropriated funds to survey the proposed railway, but the project was never undertaken because it entailed very high costs and the route would have had to run parallel to ocean routes.[29]

The Pan American Highway, which was approved at the Fifth International Conference of American States in 1923, is now almost complete. The United States has strongly supported the system and has helped finance the section passing through the Central American countries; it has contributed little to the system in Mexico and South America.[30] The highway, several times the distance from the East to the West Coast in the United States, is used most intensively for commerce within the individual countries. The traffic across national boundaries is confined to those areas where frontier regions of adjoining countries have developed considerable commerce.

Since the Second World War the United States has been active in financing roads to the interior of the continent, as has the Inter-American Development Bank, almost half of whose credits for integration have gone for roads. Both highway and railroad use should increase greatly with a Latin American common market. There is evidence, for instance, that between São Paulo and Santiago, machinery, tractors, and automobiles can be shipped overland much more cheaply than by ocean, once duties and the administrative obstacles that currently exist at international borders are eliminated.[31]

Bureaucratic roadblocks, such as the need to transship freight at national borders from the trucks of one country to those of the other, are often

29. Robert T. Brown, *Transport and the Economic Integration of South America* (Brookings Institution, 1966), pp. 188–90.

30. *Ibid.*, pp. 194–99. By 1966 the United States had spent more than $135 million on the Central American section.

31. Carnoy, *Industrialization in a Latin American Common Market*; see particularly Chaps. 5 and 6 on tractors and lathes.

greater obstacles to land transport than are poor roads. These difficulties, however, can be overcome rather easily, as Central America demonstrated in eliminating such obstacles over a relatively brief period. It seems reasonable to assume that between Ecuador and Colombia, Colombia and Venezuela, and Mexico and Central America shipment of many products would also be more efficient by land.[32]

Since the expansion of land transport and communications appears to offer long-run benefits for Latin America (although in the short run the benefit-cost ratio may be low compared to other investments) and does not adversely affect U.S. private interests, U.S. policy has been singularly progressive in promoting international road building in the area. The need for a communications network was stressed at the 1967 meeting in Punta del Este. The Action Program adopted there concentrates on overland transport and communications, especially the construction of highways. The Pan American Highway, Bolivarian Highway (Carretera Marginal de la Selva), and Trans-Chaco Highway are specifically mentioned (see Appendix D).

The expansion of overland facilities, which would greatly promote integration in the long run, would be very expensive. Other multinational projects might yield much higher benefit-cost ratios, both because of their lower costs and because of their higher benefits in the short run. Certainly the most important of these is ocean shipping, a seriously neglected sector. At the present time, ocean shipping arrangements are the most likely area of conflict between the United States and Latin America.

Ocean Transport

Latin American attempts to build a larger merchant marine and to re-draft shipping conventions in the region's favor have foundered on intense national jealousies within the region and opposition from the international shipping conferences. U.S. shipping lines, which the government directly subsidizes, will not tolerate the "cargo reserves" recommended in the 1964 draft of the LAFTA shipping convention,[33] "even though these would not

32. A significant part of intra-Latin American trade in high-value commodities is carried by airplane.

33. Bilateral cargo reserves restrict the shipment of goods to vessels of the two trading countries, multilateral reserves to the ships of a group of trading countries (Brown, *Transport and Economic Integration*, p. 109).

directly affect trade between the United States and Latin America. Under strong pressure from the U.S. shipping lines which operate routes to Latin America, the Federal Maritime Commission announced that if U.S. ships were excluded from carrying cargo from one Latin American country to another, the United States would not permit ships of one Latin American nation to carry goods between the United States and another Latin American country."[34]

In 1966 LAFTA's eleven member countries signed a Water Transport Agreement giving members preference over outsiders in ocean shipment of goods within LAFTA. Cargo reserves would be progressively increased so that eventually all shipments within the area would be reserved for area lines. Such cargo as LAFTA lines could not handle would be left for foreign flag lines, with traditional or scheduled lines getting preference over tramp lines.[35]

Latin America's objectives are an independent merchant marine and possibly a regional shipbuilding industry, and lower freight rates between Latin American ports. Freight rates between most Latin American ports are now as low or lower than those between U.S. and Latin American ports. However, shipping rates are set by conferences; rates between ports belonging to different conferences are much higher than the average. If Latin America formed its own conference, average rates might possibly rise faster than they have in the past—as the United States has argued—but rates between ill-served or cross-conference ports would fall.[36]

34. *Ibid.*, p. 111. The Maritime Commission has also made clear that it opposes establishment of a LAFTA shipping line that would restrict the use of extraregional vessels; it wishes to promote the freest possible flow of goods. "In the light of the practices in force in the U.S. shipping industry, as well as in world shipping, a considerable degree of ingenuity would be needed to accept in this particular field an elaborate line of reasoning hostile to Latin American ocean transport cooperation constructed around the argument that 'the American economy was built on competition.'" (Miguel S. Wionczek, "Latin American Integration and U.S. Economic Policies," in Robert W. Gregg [ed.], *International Organization in the Western Hemisphere* [Syracuse University Press, 1968].)

35. "Convenio de Transporte por Agua" (Montevideo: ALALC, Sept. 30, 1966; processed). In 1968 its implementation was approved by LAFTA countries with the conspicuous exceptions of Argentina, Brazil, and Uruguay. In 1967 LAFTA countries (excepting Bolivia) paid $2.4 billion in ocean freight charges, of which LAFTA flag ships received $338 million or 14 percent (ECLA, *Economic Survey of Latin America, 1969*, E/CN.12/AC.62/Add.2, March 1970, Tables III-68 and III-69, pp. III-230 and III-231).

36. Brown, *Transport and Economic Integration*, pp. 134–49.

The expected cost of a Latin American merchant marine can only be equitably judged against the cost of shipping under the existing conference system. Free competition on the seas does not exist; within shipping conferences, charges are fixed. At present four Latin American shipping lines belong to such conferences. Unless they are now more heavily subsidized than their foreign competitors, it is reasonable to assume that Latin America could run its own conference at existing rates. Total shipping costs of course include much more than freight rates. Many Latin American ports are notorious for long turn-around time, high in-port costs, and poor service; lowering of these costs could be an important stimulus to trade in the area.

It is neither high port costs nor freight rates that have roused U.S. opposition, but measures that would discriminate against U.S. shipping between Latin American ports—specifically the reservation-of-cargo clause of the Water Transport Agreement. Yet reservation of cargo has been U.S. policy on nonmilitary shipments of government-owned goods since 1954.[37]

[It seems clear that for LAFTA] the principle of multilateral reserves and the formation of shipping conferences to establish rates and to assure regular, frequent, and stable liner services could be beneficial. For this to be possible, it would be necessary for the LAFTA nations to delegate regulatory powers over maritime transport within the LAFTA area to an international regulatory commission. If the LAFTA members are not yet prepared for this type of political innovation, neither are they in a position to benefit from the proposed cargo reserves.[38]

Since Latin American cargo reserves would not apply to the area's trade with the United States, they would affect only those U.S. carriers that operate between Latin American ports—relatively, a very small part of U.S. trade (it amounted to $2.8 million in 1962). Should Latin America choose to develop a regional merchant marine without cargo reserves, direct subsidies might serve efficiently to control rates and service. Even such subsidies have been vehemently opposed by the United States and other developed countries.

37. "Continuing pressure has also been applied to increase routing of government-sponsored cargoes via U.S. flag beyond the 50 percent minimum prescribed in the statute. Agency practice has varied greatly, ranging from minimum compliance in the case of the Department of Agriculture to the use of American vessels whenever possible in post-1961 AID shipments out of the continental United States." (Samuel A. Lawrence, *United States Merchant Shipping Policies and Politics* [Brookings Institution, 1966], p. 174.)

38. Brown, *Transport and Economic Integration*, pp. 156 and 160–61.

Strong protests were made by the governments of Belgium, Britain, Italy, Norway, and Sweden against a decree by the government of Uruguay in June 1963 under which partial exemption from certain import charges was granted in respect of merchandise imported in Uruguayan ships; and in September 1964 the United States announced its intention of levying an equalization fee on goods exported to Uruguay in the ships of that country.[39]

But as a Uruguayan newspaper noted, "the Uruguayan decree was . . . in the spirit of the United States shipping legislation of 1935 and 1954, and of the energetic programme of cargo preference and subsidies developed under that legislation."[40]

The focus on overland transport and telecommunications by both Latin Americans and the United States has left the problem of ocean shipping in Latin America to be settled among the world's shipowners. Policy making should be taken out of the shipowners' hands and shipping should be considered in the context of the overall development of the region and the public interest. The United States, which until now has defended the tenuous status quo, could initiate a change by supporting a vigorous program to lower port costs and by working to open Latin American shipping to greater participation by regional companies.

Conclusions

Nationalism, so important a factor in Latin American economic life and particularly where foreign investment is concerned, seems readily to transcend country boundaries and to become Latin Americanism. Nationalist views might adapt to a common market, for they are not confined to any special economic or political group but are found in most countries of the region and from one extreme of the political spectrum to the other.

Measuring the economic costs and benefits of nationalism, weighing the short- against the long-run benefits, assigning economic costs to noneconomic objectives, and finally calculating their combined values is not feasible. Nationalism usually involves some economic costs, but for Latin American policy makers its noneconomic benefits often far outweigh any such costs. Many governments realize, for instance, that favorable tax treat-

39. Sidney Dell, *A Latin American Common Market?* (Oxford University Press, 1966), p. 106.
40. *Ibid.*, p. 107.

ment and liberal repatriation of capital and profits for foreign companies could increase mineral investment and output. Both the national economy and the foreign investors might gain. But for internal political reasons such policies most often cannot be adopted. Those sacrifices of economic welfare that a country chooses to make could be viewed as the price it pays for greater control over its own affairs.

Moreover, there may be some long-run benefits in restricting foreign investments. Local interests may be moved to explore opportunities and increase investment and production. Though domestic efforts, public and private, may initially be more wasteful and less efficient than foreign operations, the cost of the learning process might be a wise investment in the long run.

Since few Latin American countries are in a position to develop without private foreign investment, and since multinational investment is recognized as an important factor in integration, Latin America is now searching for means of attracting external capital without offering itself for corporate penetration from the United States and other developed countries. One of the most important and also the most difficult problems of developing countries is the acquisition of technological know-how. Patents on modern techniques and scientific advances could be purchased, but technological knowledge is continually advancing. Until "research and development" becomes an integral part of industrialization in Latin America, foreign capital will be the principal instrument for keeping the region abreast of the most recent technological progress.

Foreign capital investments in Latin American manufacturing have contributed significantly to import substitution endeavors. Foreign firms producing for domestic markets have demanded and received tariff and other protection from host governments, and external capital has helped finance autarkically oriented business enterprises. In this manner outside investment and enterprise have helped to fragment the Latin American economy, promoting inefficient use of resources.[41] Foreign investment during the import-replacement stage was subordinated to the needs of the national economy in which it operated and could therefore be fairly well controlled, particularly in the larger countries. Foreign capital, for example, played an important role in the formation of basic industries during the administra-

41. Foreign investment in natural resources has not behaved this way and has usually been export-oriented.

tions of Presidents Juscelino Kubitschek in Brazil and Arturo Frondizi in Argentina, yet the national character of development was preserved in these countries.

Foreign corporations would have a different role in regional economic integration. Unfettered operation of international corporations could have many ill effects. The strategic production and investment decisions of the international corporations, because they are made abroad (usually in the United States) and are based on a multitude of considerations, may not be related to Latin American needs. Exports of the subsidiaries might be restricted, either by the cartel-like policies of the parent company or by the foreign policy of the country in which its home office is located.[42]

Foreign businesses tend to stifle indigenous enterprise. The foreign subsidiary has the advantage of much greater technical and administrative know-how and access to external resources; it does not have to worry about foreign-exchange reserves and working capital because it can always get help from home and it can obtain supplies and equipment on favorable terms from sources that are not available to domestic enterprise. On the other hand, it does little in generating technological developments and therefore can contribute little to Latin America's scientific advancement.

Huge international firms can threaten host countries' control over their own economic policies. The proper relationship between government and private business—always a matter of concern—is delicate between the government of a poor country and a large private enterprise; it is particularly difficult when the enterprise is foreign, has attractive international alternatives, and can elude the pressures of the host country's economic measures.[43]

On the other hand, it may be healthier to resolve the conflicts generated by nationalism within a regional than a national context. The inherent imbalance between individual weak Latin American nations and the United States creates resentment in these countries and thus provokes contentiousness. Conflicts are apt to be less serious as the weak nations gain confidence through regional union in dealing with outside powers.

Joint ventures by foreign capital and Latin American enterprise seem to

42. For instance, the United States may have an embargo on sales to Cuba, which could be in conflict with the commercial policies of the host country.
43. Presumably, sensitivity toward the international corporation would be reduced if its decision center were located in a small, politically unimportant country and not in the United States.

hold great promise. Such an association might assure the flow of technological know-how; it would also respond to regional needs, aiding in the development of local entrepreneurship, training of local personnel, and preparation of local staff for top management positions.

Another scheme would anticipate sale of private foreign interests to host-country businessmen (or to the government) after a certain period of time. Thus foreign investment might be viewed as a revolving fund that would supplement temporarily, over periods of varying lengths depending on the kind of investment, the scarce technical and financial resources of local enterprise. According to this view, the foreign investor should always be ready to transfer majority interest in the firm to local investors and seek other investment opportunities in those activities where technological contributions continue to be of fundamental importance.[44]

Although foreign investors might not readily accept this approach, it may be the most appropriate to modern nationalism and the development goals of low-income countries. It is the approach adopted in the Andean common market foreign investment code that entered into force in mid-1971.

The less developed countries in Latin America could probably benefit considerably by instituting legislation to promote the organization of regional multinational firms. Such legislation (on taxation, mobility of human and financial resources, bureaucratic formalities, and so forth) would greatly increase the possibility of their attracting capital and technical and managerial resources, thus lessening income inequality among Latin American countries, while at the same time giving multinational enterprises a Latin American character.

Obviously, regional integration would appeal more to Latin American businessmen if the major investors were domestic rather than foreign firms. Latin American entrepreneurs invested willingly during the period of easy import substitution, when the potential demand was obvious and import restrictions gave strong protection. Now that import substitution of consumer goods has just about been completed in the more developed countries of the region, Latin American businessmen do not foresee an expansion in national demand beyond that caused by the population increase. Economic integration, by providing a huge protected regional market, should be a powerful stimulant for new investment. However, it may be

44. IDB, Round Table, p. 8, and a nearly identical statement on p. 15.

overwhelmed by the Latin American private sector's dread of foreign enterprises.

At present, apprehension about the private international corporation presents a serious obstacle to the formation of a common market in Latin America. It can be overcome by measures that involve local capital and entrepreneurship in the integration process and that dramatize the fact that the gains of integration will accrue to local interests.

As long as the nation-state system is maintained in the world, controls on foreign investment are inevitable. If this were not so, a country's entire capital stock could conceivably pass into the hands of foreigners. U.S. business and U.S. foreign policy makers should recognize that Latin American regulation of foreign capital is not only inevitable but also desirable; there can be no Latin American entrepreneurship without Latin American capital and entrepreneurs. The United States can exert influence on the private U.S. investor to arrive at a new modus vivendi with Latin American governments and business. In addition, the United States would do well to follow its precedent in the case of the European Coal and Steel Community and offer to support a Latin American development—or investment-promotion —agency dedicated to fostering industrialization on a regional scale.

The United States should divorce its long-run national interest as much as possible from U.S. private business interests. An overemphasis on U.S. private investment—particularly if public assistance to the developing countries is reduced—will tend to confirm the impression that U.S. foreign policy is linked to U.S. business interests. Enlightened U.S. policies would contribute to allaying Latin American suspicions that the immediate interests of large U.S. corporations lurk behind the United States' recent interest in the region's integration.

CHAPTER SEVEN

Effects on U.S. Trade

THE ISSUES SURROUNDING trading arrangements between the United States and Latin America are enormously complex because of concurrent pressures for change in world trade. The United Nations Conference on Trade and Development (UNCTAD), institutionalized at Geneva in 1964, has become the agent in the less developed countries' battle to alter the General Agreement on Tariffs and Trade (GATT), which they believe is biased against their trade and in favor of that of the developed countries.

The United States has only recently relaxed its free trade objectives enough to respond to demands for change. Criticized at the 1964 meeting of UNCTAD for its apparent inflexibility, the United States was finally induced to abandon its strictly nondiscriminatory position on world trade. Not only has the United States recognized that a common market arrangement among less developed countries can significantly reduce the cost of import-substituting industrialization, but in 1967 President Johnson stated the country's readiness "to explore with other industrialized countries—and with our own people—the possibility of temporary preferential tariff advantages for all developing countries in the markets of all the industrialized countries."[1]

1. "Remarks in Punta del Este at the Public Session of the Meeting of American Chiefs of State," *Public Papers of the Presidents of the United States: Lyndon B. Johnson, 1967*, Bk. 1, p. 447. An even stronger statement in favor of trade preferences was made by President Nixon; see "Inter-American Press Association: The President's Remarks

In deciding whether to support a Latin American common market and whether to give preferences to developing countries—two different but related issues—it is important for the United States to know how these actions would affect its balance of trade. Although trade with Latin America now accounts for less than 15 percent of total U.S. trade, an important change in exports to or imports from the region could significantly affect the U.S. balance of payments (see Tables 12 and 13). In addition, particular industries in the United States might be hurt by a decrease in exports or a lowering of U.S. tariffs on imports.

U.S. Exports and a Latin American Common Market

The level of the common external tariffs around a Latin American common market and the rate of growth generated by union would determine the market's effect on U.S. exports. An acceleration in economic development is widely expected to benefit the United States:

It is . . . likely that many [U.S.] industries, and indeed firms, which lose markets because of Latin American industrialization will frequently also be the ones that gain new markets; this pattern of interdependence and shifting specialization characteristic of modern industry becomes clearer perhaps by recalling that many multiproduct firms within a given industry find their best customers within the same industry. Thus the growth of the Latin American machinery and chemicals industries, for instance, should mean more rather than fewer sales of U.S. machinery and chemicals to Latin America.

The fundamental consideration, however, is the likelihood that more rapid growth of production and exports fostered by a common market will bring about a greater rather than a lesser volume of imports into the area. This has indeed been the case with respect to U.S. exports to the European Economic Community (EEC) and the Central American Common Market (CACM).[2]

After formation of the Central American Common Market, U.S. exports to the area increased from an annual average of $208 million in 1960–61 to $360 million in 1966–67. Imports from CACM in the same period did not increase as rapidly, rising from about $190 million to $305 million. While

at the Association's Annual Meeting in Washington," *Weekly Compilation of Presidential Documents*, Vol. 5 (1969), pp. 1528–35.

2. Assistant Secretary of State Anthony M. Solomon, in *Latin American Development and Western Hemisphere Trade*, Hearings before the Subcommittee on Inter-American Economic Relationships of the Joint Economic Committee, 89 Cong. 1 sess. (1965), p. 176.

Table 12. Latin American Share of Total U.S. Exports, 1963, 1966, and 1968

Type of goods[a]	Total U.S. exports (millions of dollars)			Exports to Latin America					
				Millions of dollars			As percent of total U.S. exports		
	1963	1966	1968	1963	1966	1968	1963	1966	1968
Food, beverages, and tobacco (0, 1)	4,100	5,190	4,540	375	425	445	9.2	8.2	9.8
Crude materials (except fuels), oils and fats (2, 4)	2,800	3,430	3,770	145	225	235	5.2	6.6	6.2
Mineral fuels and related materials (3)	950	980	1,060	93	135	150	9.8	13.8	14.2
Chemicals (5)	1,990	1,680	3,290	395	540	620	19.9	32.2	18.8
Machinery and transport equipment (7)	8,270	11,160	14,460	1,390	1,870	2,210	16.8	16.8	15.3
Other manufactured goods (6, 8)	4,390	5,430	5,900	620	850	860	14.1	15.7	14.6
Total[b]	23,100	30,000	34,230	3,240	4,170	4,660	14.0	13.9	13.6

Source: United Nations, *Monthly Bulletin of Statistics*, Vols. 23 and 24 (March 1969 and 1970), pp. xviii–xxxi. Figures are for f.o.b. cost of exports.
a. Numbers in parentheses refer to Standard International Trade Classification (SITC) categories.
b. Includes SITC items not classed by kind.

Table 13. Latin American Share of Total U.S. Imports, 1963, 1966, and 1968

| Type of goods[a] | Total U.S. imports (millions of dollars) | | | Imports from Latin America | | | | | |
| | | | | Millions of dollars | | | As percent of total U.S. imports | | |
	1963	1966	1968	1963	1966	1968	1963	1966	1968
Food, beverages, and tobacco (0, 1)	3,730	4,360	4,960	1,630	1,740	1,950	43.7	39.9	39.3
Crude materials (except fuels), oils and fats (2, 4)	2,890	3,260	3,310	485	570	460	16.8	17.5	13.9
Mineral fuels and related materials (3)	1,770	2,240	2,490	850	970	910	48.0	43.3	36.5
Chemicals (5)	510	850	1,030	48	74	62	9.4	8.7	6.0
Machinery and transport equipment (7)	2,010	5,010	8,380	6	12	50	0.3	0.2	0.6
Other manufactured goods (6, 8)	5,550	8,740	11,520	350	510	530	6.3	5.8	4.6
Total[b]	16,580	24,640	31,950	3,380	3,890	3,970	20.4	15.8	12.4

Source: United Nations, *Monthly Bulletin of Statistics*, Vols. 23 and 24 (March 1969 and 1970), pp. xviii–xxxi. Figures are drawn from f.o.b. cost of exports of trading partners of the United States.

a. Goods are grouped by Standard International Trade Classification (SITC) categories.
b. Includes SITC items not classed by kind.

the United States continued to import coffee and bananas almost exclusively, its exports to CACM expanded greatly in chemicals, machinery and transport equipment, and manufactured goods.[3] Even though market conditions in the United States for Central America's crops were favorable during this expansion period, the area's rise in imports from the United States was greater than its rise in exports; the U.S. trade surplus with the region more than doubled during the period.

Possible Trade Effects of Integration

Expansion of U.S. trade in a Latin American common market will depend to a large extent on the growth of the major economies in the region—in particular, of Argentina and Brazil. Brazil presently receives about one-third of its imports from the United States, Argentina considerably less. Their highly developed industrial structures and the proximity of the two countries should be mutually beneficial to their economic growth in a common market. Their rapid economic expansion would significantly increase third-country trade and would therefore be highly favorable for U.S. exports. The same should be true of Mexico and Venezuela, the major trading partners of the United States during the last few decades, accounting for over two-fifths of U.S. exports to the region; however, these two countries have had the highest economic growth rates in Latin America since the Second World War and it may be difficult to raise them further. (See Appendix Table A-4 for data on trade between individual Latin American countries and the United States.)

U.S. exports due to accelerated growth. At the historical rate of economic growth in Latin America, the area's imports would increase by about 70 percent in a ten-year period; they would increase an additional 20 percent if the growth rate were accelerated through reasonable increases in savings and in exports and economies of import substitution.[4] If the accelerated growth were assumed to result from the formation of a common market, imports of Latin American countries could be expected to

3. U.S. Bureau of the Census, *Foreign Commerce and Navigation of the United States, 1946–1963* (1965), p. 251, and *U.S. Exports, Commodity by Country*, Report FT 410, December issues 1963, 1965, 1967, 1968 (title varies slightly).

4. Estimates based on Hollis B. Chenery and Peter Eckstein, "Development Alternatives for Latin America," *Journal of Political Economy*, Vol. 78 (Supplement to July/August 1970), pp. 966–1006.

almost double during this period. U.S. exports should increase apace if the U.S. share of the Latin American market remains stable. Immediately after the Second World War, imports from the United States accounted for almost 60 percent of Latin America's total imports. This share fell rather steadily as Europe recovered and the region returned to its traditional sources of supply there. New suppliers, such as Japan, also detracted from U.S. sales. Since the mid-1960s, however, the U.S. share has stabilized at about 40 percent and is not expected to decline further.[5]

U.S. exports and the establishment of a common external tariff. If the growth rate and consequent import demand are assumed to remain at their historical level, the quantity of goods imported could change only as the result of a change in relative price levels. U.S. exports to Latin America might decrease because they would have become relatively dearer. The principal reasons for such a change would be the establishment of a Latin American common external tariff and the diversion of imports to Latin American sources as tariffs were eliminated or reduced among common market countries.

Trade diversion would tend to reduce U.S. exports because the elimination of tariffs between common market members would cause their prices to fall relative to those of the United States. At the same time, however, consumer real income in the area would increase, and so would trade, which would tend to increase imports from the United States. The height of the common external tariff is the important variable in these two opposing effects; the lower the tariff, the more favorable the effects on U.S. exports.

It is difficult to estimate the magnitude of the effects. Methodologies devised to estimate these effects for the European Common Market and the European Free Trade Association do not seem relevant to developing areas. Because of low production levels of goods that can be traded within the region and the initially low supply elasticity in Latin America, even an exorbitantly high common external tariff, say, 100 percent, is not in fact expected to affect U.S. exports significantly. On the other hand, with a more realistic tariff of, say, 50 percent, U.S. exports would increase greatly.

The initial effect of the move to a common external tariff is likely to be more serious than the trade creation and trade diversion effects (see Appen-

5. While Latin American imports expanded significantly during the period 1948–65, U.S. exports to the region remained fairly stable, fluctuating between $2.8 billion (in 1950) and $4.1 billion (in 1958) and averaging about $3.6 billion.

dix B for a calculation of the effect). If the common external tariff were set at 101 percent—the unweighted arithmetic mean of tariffs in the early 1960s (see Table 14)—U.S. exports would not vary greatly. The United States could expect to share in the rising level of Latin American imports stemming from the accelerated income growth associated with economic integration. But if the common external tariff were set at one-half the mean of the early 1960s tariffs, or 50 percent, U.S. exports to Latin America would be considerably larger than under actual tariffs, even without considering the increase due to accelerated income growth.

For example, if total Latin American imports are assumed to rise in accordance with historic income growth, or by about 70 percent, from $10 billion in 1967 to $17 billion in 1977, U.S. exports, assuming continuation of the 1967 share of 42 percent of the market, would rise from $4.2 billion to $7.1 billion. With a common market, however, if the additional 20 percent accelerated growth is realized, Latin American imports could be expected to double from $10 billion in 1967 to $20 billion in 1977. Even with a common external tariff of 101 percent, U.S. exports would rise more (to $8.4 billion in 1977) than they would without a common market because of the higher total level of imports associated with faster growth.

Table 14. Unweighted Averages of Nominal Duties and Other Charges by Seven Latin American Countries, Early 1960s

Percentages

	Average duty						
Type of goods	*Argen-tina*	*Brazil*	*Chile*	*Colom-bia*	*Ecuador*	*Mex-ico*	*Peru*	*Seven coun-tries*
Intermediate I[a]	75	93	104	42	50	33	22	60
Intermediate II[b]	163	244	239	154	76	117	98	156
Consumer goods[c]	229	304	263	234	112	128	36	186
Investment goods[d]	98	84	45	18	27	14	16	43
All commodities[e]	131	168	138	112	62	61	34	101

Source: Santiago Macario, "Protectionism and Industrialization in Latin America," *Economic Bulletin for Latin America*, Vol. 9 (March 1964), p. 75. Quantitative restrictions on imports are not included (see *ibid.*, pp. 61–102).

a. Industrial raw materials and semimanufactured goods (including fuels) other than products of traditional industries.

b. Current consumer manufactures other than processed foods (including semiprocessed products of traditional industries).

c. Processed foods and durable consumer goods.

d. Capital goods.

e. Includes some commodities not included in the categories above.

If an external tariff of 50 percent is assumed, U.S. exports could rise even more sharply, perhaps to as much as $9.7 billion by 1977 (see Appendix B).

These estimates are of course intended to indicate only general orders of magnitude, not exact amounts; they depend upon certain assumed elasticities of supply and demand (see Appendix B); and they do not consider trade creation and trade diversion effects. They do show, however, that even under an extremely high common external tariff, U.S. exports to a common market in Latin America would probably increase significantly. If the external tariff were fixed at a reasonably low level, Latin American trade would grow more rapidly, as would U.S. exports to the region, possibly more than doubling within a decade (or becoming over one-third higher than without a common market).

Average tariff levels have gone down markedly in Latin America since 1963. Argentina and Brazil, which were high-tariff countries, have adopted a significant trade liberalization policy in recent years. Therefore, the average tariff level in Latin America in 1970 would be far below 101 percent, or the seven-country average of the early 1960s tariff, shown in Table 14.[6] A 101 percent average common external tariff would be highly unlikely; the actual tariff may be well below 50 percent and thus more advantageous to U.S. exports than the favorable alternative shown here.

The Common External Tariff and Industrialization

If increasing the rate of growth were the sole objective of Latin American development policy, it would probably be in the interest of Latin Americans themselves to set the common external tariff at a level lower than the current arithmetic mean. Unusually high tariff walls are generally agreed to have been detrimental to economic growth in Argentina, Brazil, and Chile. Secretary of State Rusk warned of the possibly deleterious effect of a high common external tariff on Latin American development without mentioning the U.S. self-interest in the question:

Latin America's economic development will in large part depend on its ability to export a diversified range of products competitively to world markets. This will be possible only if the common market is not built up behind an unreasonably high protective wall and is not based on cartels or national monopolies.

The Guidelines agreed on at the 11th Meeting of Foreign Ministers make it clear that a common external tariff (CXT) in Latin America should be at "levels

6. Furthermore, the tariff levels of the countries not shown in this table are much below the seven-country average.

that will promote efficiency and productivity." Forthcoming inter-American meetings will give us many opportunities to encourage the Latin American governments to decide in favor of a reasonable CXT as consistent with these guidelines and in the area's own long-term best interests. . . .

We would not only wish to see a low initial CXT but would want to be able to negotiate further reductions in trade barriers.[7]

But increased industrialization—even if it would lower the overall rate of growth in the short run—is also a goal of development in Latin America. An important economic rationale for a common market is that it would permit industrial expansion to continue in the region but at a much lower welfare cost to Latin American consumers than in the past. The common external tariff would provide protection to "infant industries." The protected market, however, would be much larger than the individual national markets. Production costs would decrease in the area because of economies from increases in the scale of production, increased competition within the region, better allocation of resources, and the side effects of industrialization (improved transportation and communication, a more competent and more mobile labor force, greater mobility of capital, and all the other benefits derived from external economies, stronger linkages, and modernization). These side effects are difficult to evaluate but they are the principal dynamic element in industrialization. Conceivably most industries in a Latin American common market could become competitive with those in the United States and Europe if they were afforded protection until their production costs were lowered through the economies of industrialization. The problem of how long and how much to protect will continue to be the main point of contention between Latin American protectionists and U.S. and Latin American free traders.

Latin American Exports to Developed Countries

The United States at the 1967 summit meeting indicated its readiness to make significant concessions to Latin American countries. The U.S. trade policy showed the United States' willingness to work for the reduction of barriers to less developed countries' goods in world markets, and to grant trade preferences for their manufactured products; to undertake intergovernmental consultations to assure that the donation and sale of U.S.

7. Dean Rusk, in *Latin American Summit Conference*, Hearings before the Senate Committee on Foreign Relations, 90 Cong. 1 sess. (1967), pp. 28–29.

agricultural surpluses would take into account Latin American interests; to strengthen the international coffee agreement; and to promote Latin American exports by helping to make them more competitive and to improve their marketing.[8]

Import-substituting industrialization has sharply increased the need for imports of capital and intermediate goods rather than alleviating national balance-of-payments problems. Even a Latin American common market cannot be expected during its early stages to provide enough additional foreign exchange for the area's industrialization through the export of manufactures. Until the region's industrial structure becomes efficient enough to permit exports of manufactures, industrialization must rely for financing primarily on earnings from the sale abroad of the region's agricultural and mineral raw materials.[9]

Agricultural Protectionism

The possibilities of increasing traditional exports to industrial countries depend upon those countries eliminating certain obstacles. The industrial nations protect their own production of agricultural products and some minerals through domestic subsidies and through restrictions against imports from developing and developed countries. Less developed countries could increase their annual earnings by $2 billion, it is estimated, if agricultural protection in developed countries were completely eliminated.[10] The increase is equal to approximately one-eighth of the total agricultural exports of the developing countries.[11] About 40 percent of the foodstuffs and agricultural raw materials exported from less developed to developed countries come from Latin America.[12] The region's annual earnings would

8. See Appendix D, pp. 190–91.

9. Intraregional trade in raw materials will undoubtedly expand also because industrialization will require increased amounts of primary goods as inputs into the production process.

10. Harry G. Johnson, *Economic Policies Toward Less Developed Countries* (Brookings Institution, 1967), p. 94.

11. The average annual exports of agricultural raw materials were $4.7 billion during 1963–65 and the exports of food and beverage items, $11.3 billion. Thus, a total of $16 billion of food and nonfood agricultural products exports came from the developing countries. (United Nations Conference on Trade and Development, "UNCTAD Commodity Survey, 1967," TD/B/C.1/46 [January 1968; processed], Pts. 1, 2, pp. 23 and 31).

12. UNCTAD, *Handbook of International Trade Statistics*, E/Conf. 46/12/Add. 1 (Feb. 28, 1964).

increase by about $800 million if it benefited proportionally from the removal of agricultural protectionism in developed countries.[13] About 36 percent of Latin American food exports went to the United States in 1967, and on that basis about $300 million of the region's benefit would come from elimination of U.S. restrictions.

Need for Trade Preferences

Trade preferences for less developed countries' manufactures would be more effective the higher the trade barriers that protect developed-country markets. Developing countries have been accused of exaggerating the potential importance of preferences, for where existing tariff levels of the developed countries are already low, the gain from any trade preferences to Latin America and other less developed countries will be small. As the U.S. assistant secretary of state put it in 1964:

[Given a 10 percent tariff level on the average], the questions we have asked ourselves are these: Are there many manufacturing enterprises in the developing countries, excluding those like textiles which are quite competitive already and need no preferential advantage, that could break into industrial markets against established developed country suppliers on the basis of a 10-percent margin on the average? . . .

. . . It is difficult to believe that the trade and investment effect of a 10-percent preferential margin would be more than marginal. If so, the breach in the most-favored-nation principle would add little to economic growth in the underdeveloped world but it might at the same time create resistance to further multilateral tariff reductions because such reductions would narrow the scope for preference margins for the low-income countries.[14]

Tariff averages, however, "conceal the fact that tariff rates on manufac-

13. A large part of that would result from removal of tariffs and excise taxes on sugar. Latin American sugar exporters enjoy a premium price in the protected U.S. market, which is limited by well-regulated quotas. Under free market conditions they might receive a lower equilibrium price that would be more than offset by increased exports. Several Latin American countries have a comparative advantage in the production of sugar. Johnson estimates that freeing trade in sugar would result in an increase of $675 million in annual trade by exporters to seven major sugar protectionist countries ($251 million to the United States) (*Economic Policies Toward Less Developed Countries*, p. 264). Should Latin America's share of the additional trade in sugar equal its 18 percent share of world exports to developed countries and 43 percent share of U.S. imports in 1965, it would gain an increase of over $120 million in foreign exchange annually ($110 million from U.S. trade).

14. Anthony M. Solomon, in *Latin American Development and Western Hemisphere Trade*, Hearings, p. 157.

tures in which the less developed countries are particularly interested are relatively high, running from 20 up to 40 percent or more."[15] "Tariff structures of the U.S.A. and U.K. discriminate particularly severely against imports of the sort of processed product that Latin America has begun to export in the past few years . . . refined petroleum, refined non-ferrous metals (especially copper), pig-iron, vegetable oil, and cotton and leather products."[16] Furthermore, nominal tariff rates on manufactures are misleading indicators of the amount of protection actually offered developed-country industries. The "effective" rate of protection—that on the value added in the production process itself—is considered to reflect more accurately the degree of protection on manufactured goods.[17] For example, if 40 percent of the cost of a manufactured product is for raw materials and if they bear no tariff, any tariff on the product applies only to the processing of those inputs—to the value added—or 60 percent of the total cost; the effective protection is therefore two-thirds above the nominal tariff protection (in the case of a 10 percent nominal tariff, the effective rate is 10/60 or 16.7 percent).

From effective rates of protection in developed countries and 1967 trade data, it is possible to estimate an increase of about $135 million annually in Latin American exports to developed countries if tariffs on the less developed countries' manufactured goods were eliminated and Latin America maintained its share of exports of those goods (see Appendix C).

15. Johnson, *Economic Policies Toward Less Developed Countries*, p. 96.

16. David Wall, "Latin America in an Atlantic Free Trade Area," *Bank of London and South America Review*, Vol. 2 (April 1968), p. 189. Latin America apparently gained little in the short term from the Kennedy Round of tariff reductions concluded in Geneva in 1967 after four years of negotiations. The members of the European Economic Community (EEC) did not grant most-favored-nation treatment for any concessions in tropical products (presumably wishing to preserve preferential trading arrangements with their associated overseas territories). "After the tariff reductions negotiated in the Kennedy Round have been implemented, the group of commodities left with the greatest degree of protection in the developed countries' markets will be the labour-intensive processed goods and manufactured products in which the less developed countries have an undoubted comparative advantage and which are consequently of greatest current or potential export interest to them" (*ibid.*, p. 186). Bela Balassa also points to "the continuation of a tendency for tariffs on goods which are traded chiefly among industrial countries to be reduced more than tariffs on imports from developing areas" (UNCTAD, *Trends and Problems in World Trade and Development*, TD-69, Feb. 1, 1968, p. 4).

17. See Johnson, *Economic Policies Toward Less Developed Countries*, pp. 94–104, and Bela Balassa, "Tariff Protection in Industrial Countries: An Evaluation," *Journal of Political Economy*, Vol. 73 (December 1965), pp. 573–94.

While the $135 million represents about 1 percent of total Latin American exports in 1967, it is a third more than the level of annual direct assistance for integration proposed by the United States just before the 1967 summit meeting.[18]

For the United States, eliminating barriers to less developed countries' manufactures would mean an increase in imports of less than $450 million annually. Although it may be difficult to reconcile the U.S. business community to the fact that some domestic producers might incur losses from the lowering of trade barriers at the same time that Latin American producers were given protection against competition from the United States, these possible losses should be more than offset by the benefits of increased exports of sophisticated capital goods to the region as it indusdustrializes.[19]

The increased exports of less developed countries would at first constitute a very small proportion of the total of goods available in the importing developed countries, and therefore the effects on consumer prices would be negligible. As the quantities imported became larger, constituting a significant part of the supply of certain consumer goods in the United States, the benefits of lower prices would accrue to U.S. consumers.[20] Thus in the long run the increase in U.S. imports from less developed countries could be offset by the freeing of domestic resources for more efficient uses, by lower consumer prices, and by an increase in exports to the less developed countries if their economic growth accelerates because of preferences.

18. In order to estimate the net increase in foreign exchange earnings to Latin America, the import content of the export expansion would have to be deducted; in technologically complicated manufactures, imported inputs may account for a high proportion of the value of the product.

19. Preferential access to developed-country markets could permit developing nations to concentrate on the production of certain manufactures for exports. To make such an industrial expansion possible, they would have to purchase heavy machinery and technologically advanced capital and intermediate goods from the developed countries. (Alfred Maizels, assisted by L. F. Campbell-Boross and P. B. W. Rayment, *Exports and Economic Growth of Developing Countries* [London: Cambridge University Press, 1968], particularly pp. 22 and 275.)

20. Some preference-receiving countries might have a monopoly in certain products and choose not to sell more goods at a lower price but to take the "economic rent" provided by the preference. In that case, the prices in the United States would not fall and there would be no benefits to consumers or losses to producers, even in the long run. The only result would be that tariff revenue previously accruing to the U.S. Treasury would go instead to the countries receiving the preferences.

The goal of trade preferences and of a Latin American common market is to foster industrialization. It is not clear, however, whether the methods are entirely compatible. Preferences for manufactured goods could well delay the development of a common infrastructure for the Latin American countries, which is considered an important objective of the integration process. They could weaken the need for tariff reduction among Latin American countries, perpetuating the small intraregional trade in manufactures and allowing parallel national industrialization policies with all of their inefficiencies to continue.[21]

Nevertheless, trade preferences in developed-country markets, together with regional integration, are likely to accelerate Latin American industrialization more than would either of the two measures alone. While preferences would increase access for the region's manufactures to extraregional markets, an external tariff around a regional common market would give the same commodities a relative price advantage in Latin American markets. The two policies would reinforce each other's positive effects on investments and therefore on economic growth. For some investors in the Latin American area, trade preferences in developed-country markets would provide the main stimulus for industrial expansion; for others, the principal incentive for investment would come from a Latin American common market. The magnitude of trade preferences could be made contingent on the degree of intraregional trade liberalization, so that the greater the tariff reductions among Latin American countries, the greater those granted in the U.S. market. Preferences could be keyed to the countries' degree of industrial development. For example, the big three— Argentina, Brazil, and Mexico, which at present have the most to gain from developed-country trade preferences for manufactured goods—might be required to reduce intraregional tariffs to a greater extent than the other Latin American countries to receive the same level of tariff concessions; or favored treatment might be offered the least developed coun-

---

21. Manufactured goods have constituted an increasing proportion of intra-Latin American trade; they still account for only about 30 percent of the total (see Donald W. Baerresen, Martin Carnoy, and Joseph Grunwald, *Latin American Trade Patterns* [Brookings Institution, 1965], p. 313, for 1959–63 figures). Intraregional exports constituted slightly more than 10 percent of Latin American exports to all countries in 1967; thus intra-LAFTA manufactured exports were not much more than 4 percent of total LAFTA exports. Latin American manufactured exports to Latin America equal approximately 80 percent of those to the United States, and one-quarter of those to all countries.

tries in the region—Bolivia, Ecuador, Paraguay, and the Central American republics. In this manner trade preferences would constitute an incentive for trade liberalization and so stimulate the integration process.[22] In view of the fact that trade preferences are nonreciprocal—there is no direct quid pro quo for the developed countries—it would be difficult to argue that the tying to integration constitutes intervention.

22. Although such a scheme would be most feasible between the United States and Latin America, it could be worldwide: developed countries would grant greater trade preferences to those developing countries that reduce trade barriers to other developing countries.

CHAPTER EIGHT

Outlook

DIFFICULTIES IN INCREASING or even maintaining their rates of growth and industrialization have forced Latin American countries during the last decade to turn from inward-looking industrialization toward international trade as a vehicle for development. In focusing their attention once again on exports, Latin Americans are not contemplating a return to the international trade patterns that existed before the Second World War; they are concerned not only with exporting traditional primary commodities but increasingly with producing manufactures for sale abroad. This stems from a recognition that the slow growth of national markets limits the expansion of industry and that industrialization cannot be efficient unless it is based at least in part on production for export.

Present Status and Future Outlook

In trying to implement this mixture of an inward- and outward-oriented strategy, Latin Americans have found an inhospitable climate in the world around them. Trade prospects for traditional products are not encouraging, trade blocs restraining imports have emerged, trade barriers in developed countries discriminate against goods from the region, and no financial or other commercial incentives are offered for their exports. To overcome these obstacles Latin American countries have concentrated their efforts on three objectives: (1) to improve the conditions of world trade in pri-

149

mary products, (2) to obtain preferential access to developed-country markets for their industrial commodities, and (3) to band together and to begin opening up their economies to one another in a process of integration.

Integration efforts in Latin America have already been successful enough to produce the Latin American Free Trade Association (LAFTA), encompassing Mexico and all of South America except the Guianas; and the Central American Common Market (CACM), including all but one of the countries of Central America. Partly because the latter group were at a much lower level of development and therefore had fewer vested interests to defend, partly because the area is smaller and the countries geographically closer together, partly because of a more favorable demand for their products within their market, and especially because the area received greater financial support from the United States, CACM has made more progress than LAFTA since the groups were established in 1960.

The movement toward integration in LAFTA slowed down significantly in the second half of the 1960s. Formation of the group, after decades of failure and frustration, had been an enormous achievement. Prior to the 1950s, Latin American economic integration was a very remote idea. The signing of the Montevideo Treaty in 1960—unexpected by many people— unleashed grandiose anticipations that were patently unrealistic. The exaggerated hopes of the early LAFTA years have been replaced by an equally exaggerated disillusionment with regional integration. The euphoria fed by the easy success of the first rounds of tariff negotiations has disappeared with the need to make hard decisions. Had early expectations been more realistic, the later disappointment would not have been so deep. Latin American policy makers have yet to show whether they are willing or able to take the politically difficult steps that are needed to accelerate the advance toward a common market. An encouraging portent is the Andean Subregional Integration Agreement signed in 1969. If this venture prospers, the major countries on the outside cannot easily remain aloof from the integration movement.

Changes Needed

Further steps toward Latin American integration would be in the best interests of the United States. However, the threat of deleterious effects on U.S. interests and the dillydallying of Latin American governments still hamper U.S. policy moves. Although the United States can hardly be blamed for the difficulties encountered in the economic integration effort since 1960, its bilateral relations with individual Latin American governments have impeded regional integration efforts. Despite its acknowledgment that regional integration may contribute substantially to increasing growth rates in Latin America, the United States has offered only verbal support for LAFTA since its inception. (In Central America it has moved from verbal to active support and become an important factor in the region's progress toward a common market.)

The United States is in a position to facilitate the difficult transition from the current malfunctioning integration machinery to a Latin American common market. Its success in doing so will depend not only on its specific policy measures but also on a broad understanding of its economic relations with the region. The regional integration process for a group of developing countries must be accepted as different from that of advanced economies. Furthermore, it must be understood that U.S.–Latin American cooperation in implementing the 1967 Punta del Este commitments will be very difficult politically, given the highly nationalist attitudes in the region and the deep fear of domination of a future Latin American common market by powerful U.S. business interests.

External Assistance

Even though the 1967 summit meeting appeared to give Latin American integration top priority in hemispheric economic relations, both the United States and Latin America continue to be committed to, and conditioned by, bilateral trade relations and a bilateral aid program. The success of Latin American integration may depend upon Latin American actions, but bilateralism is an obstacle to regional cooperation because it encourages most Latin American republics to work for a "special relationship" with the hemisphere's superpower.

The United States can alter this detrimental proclivity by making changes in its policy toward Latin America as profound, and sometimes painful, as those Latin Americans must make in forming a common market. Increased regional aid by the United States could expedite the formation of the market and permit a reduction in bilateral aid less traumatic than it might otherwise be. Countries that have come to expect aid will very likely resent the change.

The United States should reappraise and revise its aid policy in Latin

America, increasing its aid for integration purposes even if this means sacrificing most aid to individual countries. If integration aid is small in relation to bilateral aid, it can provide no incentive for Latin American governments to move more boldly toward economic union. Latin America needs external assistance to provide safeguards against potential losses from integration and to offer possibilities of immediate benefits for the least developed countries of the region; aid for integration would have to be geared to the general objective of assuring gains to all participants in a common market.

The success of new aid policies would depend not only on the amount of integration-supporting aid, but on the commitment of continuing aid for the entire period of transition toward a regional common market, such aid to be administered by institutions in which Latin Americans would have a strong voice. Furthermore, official aid activities must be co-ordinated with the flow of international and private financial resources to the area; otherwise the effort of one agency to aid integration might be offset by another's aid for strictly national development, or an increase in aid might be offset by an increase in trade restrictions in the developed countries.[1]

Multinational aid—whether from the United States, other donor countries, or international agencies—should be channeled through regional institutions. Certain of the objectives of integration assistance would be dissipated unless its recipients were multinational. However, multinational recipients cannot be expected to develop if bilateral aid for national development continues on its past scale. Latin American countries, beset by short-term problems, can hardly be expected to put integration assistance ahead of their immediate national interests unless they are convinced that the United States is determined to put into effect a new policy of regional aid and unless the importance of bilateral assistance declines sharply. Meetings during 1967 and 1968 on regional financial mechanisms for integration made it clear that the absence of enthusiasm for such mechanisms, especially in the larger countries, is dictated by a fear of loss of bilateral aid. Each country sees not a long-run gain to the area as a whole but a potential immediate loss to itself. If the United States should offer concrete and long-term commitments in favor of regional integration, Latin

1. *Partners in Development*, Report of the Commission on International Development, Lester B. Pearson, Chairman (Praeger, 1969), argues strongly for the harmonization of aid, trade, and investment policies.

American attitudes might change. Latin American countries would be induced to move further in establishing regionwide mechanisms to receive and administer aid for regional integration. The United States can afford through its superior power to set an example in suppressing short-run in favor of long-run considerations, a responsibility that weaker nations find very difficult to assume.

The resources needed for regional integration—especially during the transition period—are too great for less developed countries to muster by themselves. External aid could help overcome parochial nationalism and the resistance of vested interests inside and outside the region. Direct assistance would provide funds for balance-of-payments adjustments, infrastructure works and other regional investments, industrial reorganization, and labor force retraining; it would also include technical assistance in preparing multinational projects, in establishing and operating enterprises, and in upgrading the labor force.

Indirect external aid would also be needed for the promotion of Latin American trade with the rest of the world. Such assistance would require the advanced countries to eliminate the most onerous restrictions against exports of the region and to facilitate access of goods to the developed-country markets by granting trade preferences. Even if the direct economic gains accruing to Latin America from such external cooperation were comparatively small, the psychological and other noneconomic effects would be positive and large.

Just as the European countries in a drive to regain their self-confidence clamored for "trade not aid" after the first few years of the Marshall Plan, so now Latin Americans tend to emphasize more favorable trade conditions from the developed countries (particularly since U.S. foreign aid is declining). A general improvement in world trade conditions might help to foster integration possibilities in Latin America, as was the case in Europe during the 1950s. Integration while Latin America's international trade is stagnating would be politically difficult if not impossible.

The major role for the United States in the formation of a Latin American common market lies in the areas of direct and indirect assistance, but fulfillment of this role requires an understanding of the nature of the problems of Latin American economic development and integration. The institutions for Latin American economic integration must be created by Latin Americans. Except in Central America, there are at present few regional organizations equipped to receive external assistance and to implement the integration process. The need for a regional development corporation could be filled either by a new organization or by a subsidiary of an existing one, such as the Inter-American Development Bank. Formation of such an institution is not likely to come about spontaneously in Latin America, but will depend on the commitment of substantial, long-term external assistance for regional integration.

If increasing the pace and soundness of Latin American economic growth is a major concern of the United States, then U.S. foreign policy, including the orientation of foreign assistance, should be geared to facilitate the regional integration process. The public U.S. resources available for foreign aid have been sharply cut and any massive expansion in the aid to low-income countries in general, and to Latin America in particular, is unlikely in the foreseeable future. The vital concern of U.S. policy makers should therefore be to get maximum productivity out of the small amount of aid funds available. Reducing bilateral assistance and concentrating aid for regional integration purposes could do this.

The U.S. bilateral aid program for Latin America at the beginning of the 1970s is about half the 1960–67 average, and the real resource flow is less than half the official average. No substantial results can be obtained from bilateral aid even if it is concentrated in only a few countries of the region. Little would be lost by giving up the present system but much could be gained by rationalizing it and focusing it on regional integration.

Immediately after the institution of a new U.S. policy, the region may not be prepared to take full advantage of integration aid. But when Latin American governments realize that the days of bilateral aid and special relationships with Washington are gone, they may be induced to adjust existing mechanisms and create new ones equipped to absorb integration aid efficiently.

Improved Integration Machinery

Among the measures necessary to improve the existing integration machinery in Latin America are across-the-board and automatic reductions in intraregional tariffs and nontariff barriers, establishment of a common external tariff, coordination of industrialization and investment programs, and harmonization of national economic policies, particularly those related to foreign investment rules, taxes, subsidies, and monetary management. Latin American countries are not prepared to plunge into such commitments[2] until safeguards can be established to protect their payments balances and their industries. It would be unrealistic to expect harmonization of national economic policies within the next few years. On the other hand, tariff-cutting measures alone are not enough to achieve Latin American objectives.

Most countries in the region fear the adverse effects of economic integration on their balance of payments. With the exception of Mexico and Venezuela—the former blessed with high foreign-exchange revenues from tourism, the latter from petroleum exports—Latin American nations have suffered chronic balance-of-payments difficulties since World War II. A commitment to lower their trade barriers against one another would make their external economic relations more vulnerable; such a move would not only produce uncertainty, but would also eliminate one of the means of protecting themselves against losses of foreign exchange.

A payments union, supported by contributions from the participating countries and the United States, could provide temporary credits to attenuate balance-of-payments deficits arising from the integration process. It should go beyond the clearinghouse stage and be designed to encourage countries facing a scarcity of foreign exchange to accelerate trade liberalization.

A customs union could also offer help against the hazards of competition. The more industrialized Latin American nations are wary of exposing their industries to competition from each other and to the allegedly low labor costs of their poorer neighbors. The vested interests in the semi-industrialized countries that have prospered behind high national trade barriers are not eager to open up their secure national markets to the unknown strength of their existing and potential competitors. Where entrepreneurship is strong, national industries could be expected to grasp the advantages of economies of scale and try to produce for export. But sophisticated risk-taking is rare in less developed countries. A customs union could provide adjustment funds to help insecure industries reorganize within the same or other lines of production.

All schemes designed to compensate for the negative effects of integration—buffer funds for the balance of payments, for industrial adjustment, and for labor force retraining and relocation—are essentially insurance policies to help overcome the obstacles to a common market. They might

2. The Andean common market countries have entered such commitments; it remains to be seen whether they can be implemented without foreign assistance.

never be used in actual practice, but their availability would be important. Much of the resistance to economic integration derives from fear of its possible short-run costs. Commitments to an untried scheme appear to Latin American entrepreneurs to involve serious risks. The various adjustment funds would reduce the risk associated with increased investment in a common market.

The objective of an equitable distribution of costs and benefits within an economic grouping again demands foreign aid. Thus, buffer funds could be applied to so distribute gains from integration that weaker countries would benefit more than wealthier. Supplementary or full financing of such funds from the outside would be similar to the U.S. contribution to the Social Progress Trust Fund and the Fund for Special Operations—the grant and soft loan "windows"—of the Inter-American Development Bank. Or foreign aid might supply the capital to establish regional international companies designed to compensate countries disadvantaged by the integration process.

Trade Concessions Tied to Integration

Some larger Latin American countries would prefer to expand exports through developed-country concessions rather than through economic union with other Latin American countries. If the choice must be between extra- and intra-regional concessions, economic union would probably provide more long-run gains for Latin America than would selected, non-reciprocal tariff reductions by the developed countries. A combination of the two would, however, reinforce the positive effects of each on the economic growth of Latin America.

As a means of encouraging trade liberalization among developing countries, developed countries might consider tying their trade concessions to regional integration schemes. The high-income countries could lower their tariffs on the goods of those developing countries that reduced trade barriers among themselves. Such a policy would be in line with the long-run objectives of trade liberalization and would stimulate less developed countries and regions to move in that direction in a world threatened by rising protectionist sentiment.

If the formation of a common market is part of a trade liberalization movement, provisions should be made for a progressive lowering of tariffs against third countries. Preferential access to the markets of developed countries would create propitious conditions for setting the external tariff of the common market at reasonable levels. The more industrialized Latin American countries have begun to recognize that the usefulness of preferential treatment for their manufactures in the economically advanced countries will depend to a considerable extent on the adjustment of tariffs on the imports they need in order to produce exportable goods. Latin American republics individually and as a group might reconsider their autarkic policies if they could be assured, first, that the developed countries would renounce the use of the weapons of quota restrictions and other trade barriers and, second, that their access to the high-income markets would be facilitated through the granting of temporary tariff preferences.

Granting trade concessions would involve only a small direct cost to the industrial countries, while potentially yielding great benefits to them as well as to the developing countries. As a rough order of magnitude, the abandonment of agricultural protectionism by the developed nations—an action that would not entail special preferences for the less developed countries—could increase annual Latin American export earnings by about $800 million, perhaps some $300 million from the United States. Elimination of tariffs on less developed countries' manufactured goods could increase Latin America's share of the gains from those exports to the developed countries by over $130 million annually (see Appendix C).

The United States would gain, on the other hand, from the elimination of protection for agricultural goods, from the granting of tariff preferences for less developed countries' manufactures, and from Latin American economic integration. The first two actions, even if they were unilateral, would tend to increase U.S. welfare by freeing domestic resources for more efficient uses and lowering domestic prices. If they contributed to economic development in the less developed countries, they would be likely to have beneficial effects on U.S. export trade. The accelerated growth that might result from a Latin American common market should significantly increase the regional demand for imports from the United States.

The Role of Private Foreign Investment

Latin Americans fear that U.S. investors might dominate the new markets resulting from economic union. When in 1966 the United States opted to support the formation of a Latin American common market, it became clear that, whatever the original motivation, U.S. policy makers would support integration efforts only under certain conditions. Among them were Latin American guarantees not to discriminate against U.S. investments. Such guarantees conflict directly with the nationalist attitudes that permeate Latin America today. By asking for them, the United States heightened Latin American suspicions that U.S. businesses had spurred U.S. interest in the common market.

It is doubtful that U.S. government action on behalf of U.S. business operations in Latin America would greatly affect the amount of U.S. foreign investment flowing to the region, but it could evoke serious adverse political reactions there. Economic growth rates and development prospects of capital-receiving countries appear to determine the flow of foreign investment much more than do their tax or specific foreign investment policies (short of expropriation or nationalization). It is likely, therefore, that an increase in demand for goods as a result of the elimination of tariffs within Latin America would increase foreign investment flows into the region. Members of a Latin American common market, needing capital and technological aid, would probably develop investment policies consistent with their domestic and regional goals. Those policies would tend to be somewhat restrictive of, but not necessarily hostile to, foreign capital. Beyond stating its views clearly so that they can be given fair consideration, it would be unwise for the United States to interfere with the making and implementation of these policies. Protection of U.S. business interests should be subordinate to the U.S. objective of promoting regional development and economic autonomy consistent with its long-term interests.[3] Such a policy was successful in postwar Western Europe and on balance appears to have benefited U.S. interests.

Although capital from outside the region seems to be best adapted to undertaking multinational investments (as it has in Europe), the unrestricted operation of foreign-controlled multinational enterprises in a Latin American common market would be unacceptable to the region. Joint ventures might appropriately combine the benefits of the international firm with the objective of Latin American participation and possible control. A regional development corporation dedicated to industrial promotion on a regional scale could mobilize foreign and Latin American capital to undertake joint ventures that would produce for a regional market. Special em-

3. Repeal of the Hickenlooper amendment, a step in this direction, would be of great symbolic importance in Latin America. Under a regional aid program the amendment would be useless as an instrument for retaliating against national governments.

phasis could be given to the industrialization of the least developed members of the economic union. The joint ventures might involve capital and management participation of several developed countries as well as of Latin American countries. Under one suggested contractual relationship, foreign capital would help establish multinational enterprises and after a specified term of years pull out of the developing area, or perhaps go into other lines of endeavor where their contributions would still be needed.[4] This would deflate the specter of huge U.S. corporations engulfing the common market.

Perspective

The vital requirements of a Latin American customs union are: (1) the elimination or reduction of institutional barriers to the movement of goods, capital, and people within the region, and the imposition of a common external tariff; (2) the building of a transportation and communications network in order to overcome physical barriers; (3) multinational investments in order to build a diversified industrial structure in the region; and (4) external assistance.

The first three of these elements would require some coordination and planning because of the underdevelopment of entrepreneurship, lack of social and economic mobility, and other deficiencies in the social structure of developing nations, and because of the important political aim of an equitable distribution of gains from integration among the countries of the region. Since a supranational authority is not a realistic possibility, regional planning would consist essentially of covenants among the partner countries, covering such aspects as intra-area payments agreements, the administration of integration adjustment assistance, the preparation of regional infrastructure projects, the promotion and orientation of regional complementarity arrangements, and multinational investment programs.

Two questions might be asked about external aid: Why should the United States now concentrate on assisting a Latin American effort in which important Latin American countries seem to have lost interest during the last few years? And, would not this change in U.S. aid policy signify intervention on the part of the United States in the internal affairs of the region?

During the late 1960s Latin American concerns appear to have shifted

4. This is the principle of the Andean common market foreign investment rules.

from regional economic cooperation to extraregional trade. But nothing happened during that period to make regional integration a less urgent matter than it was before. The economic viability of many Latin American nations is still highly questionable. And for all of them the prospects for rapid economic expansion are still circumscribed by their overall export possibilities. Regional integration offers the best immediate hope for Latin American countries to put their economic development on a sounder footing by permitting them to open themselves gradually to international trade without sacrificing their infant industries.

Appearances to the contrary, Latin American interest in regional integration is not dead. While little concrete progress toward a common market was made in the late 1960s, the movement toward cooperation is continuing. Even the big three—Argentina, Brazil, and Mexico, who seem to have been sitting on the sidelines—have joined all other Latin American countries in forming CECLA, the Special Coordinating Commission for Latin America, which in 1969 produced the Consensus of Viña del Mar (see Appendix E). But even more important than CECLA and the consensus, which was primarily addressed to the United States, are several steps concretely related to the integration process that were taken during 1969. The Latin American central banks created an emergency balance-of-payments assistance fund. A special committee convoked by the LAFTA members to make specific recommendations for the future evaluated LAFTA's recent progress. Several industrial complementarity agreements were signed. And, most important, the Andean common market and its agent the Andean Development Corporation were formed.

A shift in U.S. aid policy could indeed be regarded by Latin Americans as intervention. But the United States looms so large in the continent that any U.S. policy, whether of action or inaction, can be broadly conceived of as "intervention" and will certainly affect the course of Latin American events. The bilateral U.S. aid program has signified indirect interference in the domestic policies of the recipient countries; because the political nature of bilateral aid cannot be eliminated, such aid has often boomeranged. On the other hand, integration assistance can avoid most of the sensitive areas of internal national policies, so that the opportunities for outside interference are less.

Above all, U.S. policy in favor of Latin American integration should be expressed only in terms of offers of assistance that can be taken up or rejected by Latin Americans. No political or economic pressures, apart from aid offers, should force the region in the direction of a common market. Trade preferences could, however, be logically tied to regional economic integration efforts; industrial countries could encourage economic cooperation within low-income areas by extending special preferences, beyond those granted generally to the less developed nations, to those countries that are prepared to lower trade barriers to other low-income countries.

U.S. assistance for integration may strengthen the integration forces in Latin America. While at present there may not be any large groups in the region with strong commitments to further economic union, significant foreign support for integration purposes only is likely to stimulate greater local support for regional projects and economic cooperation, particularly if aid is oriented to reducing the risks of and compensating the losses from integration. Such incentives should make the potential benefits from integration much more visible to private and public local investors, thus hopefully promoting interest groups with a stake in greater regional economic cooperation.

The renewed concern in Latin America for its independence from the outside world can perhaps best be relieved by regional economic integration. Latin American nations must choose whether to make some sacrifices for more serious regional cooperation or, following the line of least resistance, to continue the autarkic policies that limit their development and deepen their dependence on developed countries. The United States can help in making a positive Latin American choice more feasible. Its offer of integration assistance, on a take-it-or-leave-it basis, will bring into the open Latin American development alternatives. If Latin American mistrust of U.S. motivations is so deep-seated that U.S. integration aid cannot be accepted, perhaps the mere offer of such concrete aid will stimulate Latin American governments to cooperate more closely among themselves. Trying to help Latin America to help itself is the only sound relationship between the region and its northern developed neighbor.

Integration support may help create not only an economically stronger but also a socially and politically more viable Latin America, one better equipped to assume the responsibilities and reap the benefits of an effective development policy. In giving this support, the United States would be showing statesmanship at its best, helping to shape an international environment conducive to peaceful economic and social evolution rather than, as it has so often in the past, reacting to crises that could have been avoided.

APPENDIX A

Statistical Tables

Table A-1. Latin American and U.S. Welfare Indicators, Mid-1960s

Country	Illiteracy (percent of population)[a]	Rural population, 1965 (percent of total)	Life expectancy at birth (years)[b]	Domestic consumption of newsprint, 1966 (kilograms per capita)	Energy consumption, 1966 (kilograms of coal equivalent per capita)	Passenger cars, 1966 (per 1,000 population)
LAFTA						
Argentina	8.6	24.7	67	10.6	1,378	40.8[c]
Bolivia	67.9	67.5	51	0.9	228	4.6
Brazil	39.0	55.7	57	2.1[c]	389	16.1
Chile	16.4	32.7	61	6.2	1,113	12.4
Colombia	27.1	48.7	60	2.8	534	7.3
Ecuador	32.5	57.5	54	2.3	215	3.6
Mexico	22.5	42.0	63	3.0	997	18.4
Paraguay	25.7	68.1	59	0.5	117	2.3[d]
Peru	38.9	55.9	55	3.7	625	14.8
Uruguay	9.7	23.6	71	7.5	843	41.5
Venezuela	23.8	32.3	66	6.2	2,469	43.1
CACM						
Costa Rica	15.6	67.6	65	5.1	312	18.3
El Salvador	51.0	65.7	52	3.3	183	9.1
Guatemala	62.1	71.5	49[e]	0.7	213	7.3
Honduras	55.0	76.0	49	0.7[c]	172	5.0
Nicaragua	50.2	63.5	69	2.2	266	7.6
Others						
Cuba	n.a.	41.3	n.a.	4.2[d]	977	n.a.
Dominican Republic	35.5	66.5	52	1.1[d]	201	8.4
Haiti	89.5	85.3	47	0.1[c]	33	1.1
Panama	23.3	53.6	65	3.3	1,143	25.2

Total Latin America	...	49.1	...	70	...	717	17.2
United States	2.2	30.1[f]	...	41.9	...	9,595	395.9

Sources: Inter-American Development Bank, *Socio-Economic Progress in Latin America*, Social Progress Trust Fund Eighth Annual Report, 1968 (IDB, 1969), pp. 49–314; United Nations, Economic Commission for Latin America (ECLA), *Economic Survey of Latin America, 1968*, E/CN.12/825/Rev. 1 (1970), pp. 39–40; U.S. Bureau of the Census, *Statistical Abstract of the United States, 1968*, pp. 16, 53, 844; United Nations, *Statistical Yearbook, 1967*, Tables 17, 142, 152, 173.

n.a. Not available.

a. Measured in various years during the 1960s, except for Bolivia and Haiti, 1950, and the United States, 1959.

b. Measured in various years during the 1960s.

c. 1965.

d. 1964.

e. Estimated.

f. 1960.

Table A-2. Latin American Gross Domestic Product and Labor Force, by Economic Sector, 1967

Economic sector	Gross domestic product (GDP)		Labor force		Value of GDP per labor-force unit	
	Billions of dollars	*Percent of total*	*Millions of persons*	*Percent of total*	*Dollars*	*As percent of average output*
Agriculture	24.7	20.5	34.3	43.3	722	47
Mining	5.3	4.4	0.8	1.0	6,789	446
Manufacturing	29.1	24.1	11.0	13.9	2,645	174
Construction	4.0	3.3	3.4	4.2	1,184	78
Commerce and finance	22.7	18.8	7.8	9.8	2,913	191
Other services	34.9	28.9	22.0	27.8	1,585	104
Total	120.7	100.0	79.2	100.0	1,523[a]	100[a]

Source: UN, ECLA, *Economic Survey of Latin America, 1968*, Tables 5, 12, 21. Figures are rounded and may not add to totals.

a. Average.

Table A-3. International Trade of Latin America, by Product Group, 1955 and 1967

Millions of dollars

Latin American trade with	Food (0, 1) 1955	Food (0, 1) 1967	Raw materials (2, 4) 1955	Raw materials (2, 4) 1967	Fuels (3) 1955	Fuels (3) 1967	Chemical products (5) 1955	Chemical products (5) 1967	Machinery (7) 1955	Machinery (7) 1967	Other manufactures (6, 8) 1955	Other manufactures (6, 8) 1967	Total (0–9) 1955	Total (0–9) 1967
Developed regions[b]														
Exports	3,230	3,840	1,300	1,780	970	1,770	65	115	4	40	580	1,100	6,170	8,650
Imports[c]	510	710	280	355	155	150	600	1,140	2,150	3,740	1,760	1,950	5,530	8,190
Balance	2,720	3,130	1,020	1,425	815	1,620	−535	−1,025	−2,146	−3,700	−1,180	−850	640	460
United States														
Exports	1,920	1,750	500	490	690	970	35	72	3	25	345	450	3,510	3,770
Imports[c]	345	425	145	220	145	135	365	530	1,320	1,900	790	770	3,300	4,080
Balance	1,575	1,325	355	270	545	835	−330	−458	−1,317	−1,875	−445	−320	210	−310
Western Europe														
Exports	1,190	1,950	610	840	235	495	25	38	2	14	225	600	2,290	3,940
Imports[c]	115	185	105	69	9	12	210	570	800	1,500	750	860	2,000	3,220
Balance	1,075	1,765	505	771	226	483	−185	−532	−798	−1,486	−525	−260	290	720
Developing regions[d]														
Exports	435	485	155	245	940	1,090	14	95	5	73	66	275	1,620	2,270
Imports[c]	375	385	265	225	460	425	14	94	6	77	125	325	1,250	1,530
Balance	60	100	−110	20	480	665	—	1	−1	−4	−59	−50	370	740
Latin America														
Balance[e]	365	360	145	180	175	245	14	85	5	70	63	265	760	1,210
Other[f]														
Exports	70	124	10	62	765	852	—	10	1	3	3	9	860[e]	1,053
Imports[c]	10	22	120	43	285	183	—	9	1	6	62	57	490[e]	321
Balance	60	102	−110	19	480	669	—	1	−1	−3	−59	−48	370[e]	732
Communist countries[g]														
Exports	90	652	83	117	—	—	7	15	—	—	—	5	181	800
Imports[c]	5	168	10	84	23	90	6	55	34	297	52	182	142	880
Balance	85	484	73	33	−23	−90	1	−40	−34	−297	−52	−177	39	−80
Total[h]														
Exports	3,760	4,970	1,540	2,140	1,900	2,860	85	235	10	115	640	1,380	7,980	11,700
Imports[c]	890	1,260	550	660	640	660	620	1,280	2,190	4,120	1,930	2,460	6,920	10,600
Balance	2,870	3,710	990	1,480	1,260	2,200	−535	−1,045	−2,180	−4,005	−1,290	−1,080	1,060	1,100

Sources: United Nations, *Monthly Bulletin of Statistics*, Vol. 15 (March 1961), Special Table E, Tables II and III, pp. XVIII–XXXI, and Vol. 23 (March 1969), Special Table E and Tables II and III, pp. XVIII–XXXI; ECLA, *Economic Survey of Latin America, 1968*, Table 32. Discrepancies between totals in Tables A-3 and A-4 arise mainly from differences in defining imports and in reporting trade with communist countries.

− Nil or negligible.

a. Numbers in parentheses following product group refer to Standard International Trade Classification (SITC) categories.

b. Includes North America, Western Europe, South Africa, Japan, Australia, and New Zealand.

c. "Imports" are exports of trading partners to the area or country concerned.

d. Includes Latin America, developing Africa, developing Asia, and the Middle East and all other developing countries.

e. Exports equal imports.

f. 1955 figures estimated.

g. Includes USSR, Albania, Bulgaria, Czechoslovakia, East Germany, Hungary, Poland, Rumania, Mainland China, Mongolia, North Korea, and North Vietnam.

h. Includes special category exports, ships stores, bunkers, and so forth, whose destination could not be determined. U.S. special category exports are included in total exports by destination, and by commodity class to world as a whole, but are excluded from the detailed commodity class by destination data. Figures are rounded and may not add to totals. Latin American exports were 8.6 percent of total world exports in 1955 and 5.5 percent of total world exports in 1967. Latin American imports fell from 7.5 percent of total world imports in 1955 to 5.0 percent in 1967.

Table A-4. International Trade of Latin America, by Country, 1950 and 1967

Millions of dollars

	LAFTA countries											
	Argentina		Bolivia		Brazil		Chile		Colombia		Ecuador	
Trade with	1950[b]	1967	1950	1967	1950	1967	1950	1967	1950	1967	1950	1967[b]
Developed regions[c]												
Exports	919	1,080	91	156	1,193	1,343	225	795	368	442	52	227
Imports	558	768	33	128	809	1,196	187	580	337	429	39	192
Balance	361	312	58	28	384	147	38	215	31	13	13	35
United States												
Exports	206	124	63	67	734	548	153	177	326	222	39	101
Imports	142	243	24	62	379	572	119	273	255	225	28	99
Balance	64	-119	39	5	355	-24	34	-96	71	-3	11	2
Western Europe												
Exports	670	916	28	85	414	711	71	464	33	207	13	107
Imports	381	454	10	44	412	538	65	262	70	169	10	76
Balance	289	462	18	41	2	173	6	202	-37	38	3	31
Developing regions[d]												
Exports	157	316	3	14	130	215	67	80	27	52	16	14
Imports	149	306	23	21	272	394	60	172	26	57	2	28
Balance	8	10	-20	-7	-142	-179	7	-92	1	-5	14	-14
Latin America												
Balance	43	28	-17	-5	-44	-67	-5	-88	-16	-20	20	-7
Other												
Exports	7	30	—	—	22	51	18	1	24	22	1	—
Imports	42	49	3	2	120	163	16	5	6	7	—	7
Balance	-35	-19	-3	-2	-98	-112	12	-4	18	15	1	-7
Communist countries[e]												
Exports	29	70	—	—	23	97	1	—	—	16	—	—
Imports	19	22	—	2	17	80	1	—	2	10	—	—
Balance	10	48	—	-2	6	17	—	—	-2	6	—	—
Total												
Exports	1,105	1,465	94	171	1,347	1,655	294	875	396	510	69	242
Imports	725	1,096	56	151	1,098	1,670	248	752	365	497	42	220
Balance	380	369	38	20	249	-15	46	123	31	13	27	22

LAFTA countries

Trade with	Mexico 1950	Mexico 1967	Paraguay 1950b	Paraguay 1967	Peru 1950	Peru 1967	Uruguay 1950	Uruguay 1967	Venezuela 1950b	Venezuela 1967	Total LAFTA 1950	Total LAFTA 1967
Developed regionsᶜ												
Exports	468	866	20	29	124	705	241	122	532	1,791	4,233	7,556
Imports	499	1,680	11	34	168	682	147	90	506	1,267	3,294	7,046
Balance	−31	−814	9	−5	−44	23	94	32	26	524	939	510
United States												
Exports	433	621	6	12	51	328	130	12	324	972	2,465	3,184
Imports	430	1,102	3	11	99	299	39	24	368	662	1,886	3,572
Balance	3	−481	3	1	−48	29	91	−12	−44	310	579	−388
Western Europe												
Exports	26	162	14	17	68	271	102	107	128	537	1,567	3,584
Imports	52	446	7	23	59	280	104	59	114	454	1,284	2,805
Balance	−26	−284	7	−6	9	−9	−2	48	14	83	283	779
Developing regionsᵈ												
Exports	32	109	5	14	69	49	11	25	45	1,079	562	1,967
Imports	9	64	1	16	19	128	50	77	28	66	639	1,329
Balance	23	45	4	−2	50	−79	−39	−52	17	1,013	−77	638
Latin America												
Balance	13	37	4	1	46	−63	−32	−30	6	168	18	−46
Other												
Exports	8	27	—	—	8	9	3	8	20	871ᶠ	111	1,019
Imports	4	18	—	—	4	25	10	28	10	28	205	332
Balance	4	9	—	—	4	−16	−7	−20	10	843	−94	687
Communist countriesᵉ												
Exports	2	9	—	—	—	19	2	12	1	—	58	223
Imports	1	5	—	—	1	3	4	6	2	9	47	137
Balance	1	4	—	—	−1	16	−2	6	−1	−9	11	86
Total												
Exports	502	1,143	26	48	194	774	254	159	578	2,870	4,859	9,912
Imports	509	1,748	12	58	187	813	202	172	537	1,343	3,981	8,520
Balance	−7	−605	14	−10	7	−39	52	−13	41	1,527	878	1,392

See notes at end of table.

169

Table A-4. (continued)

| | CACM countries | | | | | | | | | | | |
| | Costa Rica | | El Salvador | | Guatemala | | Honduras | | Nicaragua | | Total CACM | |
Trade with	1950	1967	1950	1967	1950	1967	1950	1967	1950	1967	1950	1967
Developed regions[a]												
Exports	53	105	65	126	67	134	16	128	31	126	232	619
Imports	41	140	41	150	59	187	28	116	22	143	191	736
Balance	12	−35	24	−24	8	−53	−12	12	9	−17	41	−117
United States												
Exports	43	68	60	55	60	62	15	69	24	42	202	296
Imports	31	74	32	70	49	101	26	79	20	88	158	412
Balance	12	−6	28	−15	11	−39	−11	−10	4	−46	44	−116
Western Europe												
Exports	6	32	5	54	6	54	1	54	6	36	24	230
Imports	7	45	8	59	9	61	2	28	2	40	28	233
Balance	−1	−13	−3	−5	−3	−7	−1	26	4	−4	−4	−3
Developing regions[d]												
Exports	4	38	4	81	—	64	6	28	3	24	17	235
Imports	5	49	6	74	11	60	6	48	2	60	30	291
Balance	−1	−11	−2	7	−11	4	—	−20	1	−36	−13	−56
Latin America												
Balance	—	−13	−2	11	−4	3	2	−20	1	−40	−6	−59
Other												
Exports	—	6	1	1	—	5	—	5	1	4	2	21
Imports	1	4	1	6	4	4	2	6	1	2	9	22
Balance	−1	2	—	−5	−4	1	−2	−1	0	2	−7	−1
Communist countries[e]												
Exports	—	—	—	—	—	—	—	—	—	2	—	2
Imports	—	—	—	—	1	—	1	1	—	—	1	1
Balance	—	—	—	—	−1	—	−1	−1	—	2	−1	1
Total												
Exports	56	143	70	207	68	197	23	156	35	152	252	855
Imports	46	189	47	224	71	248	34	165	25	204	223	1,030
Balance	10	−46	23	−17	−3	−51	−11	−9	10	−52	29	−175

170

| | Other countries | | | | | | | | Total Latin America^f | |
| | Cuba | | Dominican Republic | | Haiti | | Panama | | | |
Trade with	1950	1967b	1950	1967	1950	1967b	1950	1967	1950	1967
Developed regions^c										
Exports	595	122	82	152	38	40	9	74	4,594	8,441
Imports	464	235	38	154	36	37	53	142	3,612	8,115
Balance	131	-113	44	-2	2	3	-44	-68	982	326
United States										
Exports	380	—	37	136	23	21	9	65	2,736	3,702
Imports	408	—	32	96	28	25	44	91	2,148	4,196
Balance	-28	—	5	40	-5	-4	-35	-26	588	-494
Western Europe										
Exports	200	93	45	16	15	16	—	3	1,651	3,849
Imports	40	184	4	41	5	9	6	34	1,327	3,122
Balance	160	-91	41	-25	10	7	-6	-31	324	727
Developing regions^d										
Exports	46	30	4	4	1	1	1	10	585	2,216
Imports	50	22	5	21	1	1	14	58	689	1,700
Balance	-4	8	-1	-17	—	-1	-13	-48	-104	516
Latin America										
Balance	-1	-7	0	4	—	-1	-8	-52	14	-162
Other										
Exports	31	30	3	3	1	—	—	7	117	1,050
Imports	34	15	4	16	1	—	5	5	224	375
Balance	-3	15	-1	-13	—	—	-5	2	-107	675
Communist countries^e										
Exports	2	n.a.	—	—	—	—	—	—	58	225
Imports	1	n.a.	—	—	—	—	—	—	48	138
Balance	1	n.a.	—	—	—	—	—	—	10	87
Total										
Exports	642	152	87	156	39	40	11	84	5,248	11,047
Imports	515	257	44	175	38	38	67	227	4,353	9,990
Balance	127	-105	43	-19	1	2	-56	-143	895	1,057

Sources: United Nations, International Monetary Fund (IMF) and International Bank for Reconstruction and Development (IBRD), *Direction of International Trade*, Statistical Papers, Series T, Vol. 5, No. 8 (1954), and IMF, IBRD, *Direction of Trade: Annual 1963–67*. Discrepancies between totals in Tables A-3 and A-4 arise mainly from differences in defining imports and in reporting trade with communist countries.

n.a. Not available
— Nil or negligible
a. Excluding Cuba.
b. Derived from trading partner returns.
c. United States, Canada, Western Europe, South Africa, Japan, Australia, and New Zealand.
d. Latin America, developing Africa, developing Asia, and the Middle East and other developing countries.
e. Includes USSR, Albania, Bulgaria, Czechoslovakia, East Germany, Hungary, Poland, Rumania, Mainland China, Mongolia, North Korea, and North Vietnam.
f. Figure includes Netherlands Antilles and Trinidad and Tobago.

Table A-5. Shares, by Country, of Latin American International Trade, 1950 and 1967

Percent of total

Country	Total exports 1950	Total exports 1967	Total imports 1950	Total imports 1967	Exports to United States 1950	Exports to United States 1967	Imports from United States 1950	Imports from United States 1967	Exports to Latin America 1950	Exports to Latin America 1967
LAFTA										
Argentina	21	13	17	11	19	8	20	22	14	19
Bolivia	2	2	1	2	67	39	43	41	3	8
Brazil	26	15	25	17	54	33	35	34	8	10
Chile	6	8	6	8	52	20	48	36	17	9
Colombia	8	5	8	5	82	44	70	45	1	6
Ecuador	1	2	1	2	57	42	67	45	20	6
Mexico	10	10	12	18	86	54	84	63	5	7
Paraguay	a	a	a	1	23	25	25	19	19	29
Peru	4	7	4	8	26	42	53	37	31	5
Uruguay	5	1	5	2	51	8	19	14	3	11
Venezuela	11	26	12	13	56	34	69	49	4	7
Total	93	90	91	85	51	32	47	42	9	10
CACM										
Costa Rica	1	1	1	2	77	48	67	39	7	22
El Salvador	1	2	1	2	86	27	68	31	4	38
Guatemala	1	2	2	3	88	31	69	41	—	30
Honduras	1	1	1	2	65	44	76	48	26	15
Nicaragua	1	1	1	2	69	28	80	43	6	13
Total	5	8	5	10	80	35	71	40	6	25
Others										
Dominican Republic	2	1	1	2	43	87	73	55	1	a
Haiti	1	a	1	a	59	53	74	66	a	a
Panama	a	1	2	2	82	77	66	40	9	2
Latin America	100	100	100	100	52	34	49	42	9	11

Source: Table A-4. Figures are rounded and may not add to totals.   a. Less than 0.5 percent.

Table A-6. Intra-Latin American Trade, by Country and Region, 1967

Millions of dollars

| | Importer: LAFTA | | | | | | | | | | | |
Exporter	Argentina	Bolivia	Brazil	Chile	Colombia	Ecuador	Mexico	Paraguay	Peru	Uruguay	Venezuela	Total
LAFTA												
Argentina	—	8	101	75	8	2	10	14	52	10	4	284
Bolivia	9	—	2	1	—	—	—	—	2	—	—	14
Brazil	98	4	—	22	2	—	7	4	4	18	3	162
Chile	34	1	14	—	3	3	9	—	10	4	2	79
Colombia	4	3	1	2	—	4	—	1	6	—	3	24
Ecuador	3	—	—	—	5	—	1	—	4	—	—	13
Mexico	9	—	12	14	4	1	—	—	6	2	9	57
Paraguay	11	—	—	—	—	—	—	—	—	3	—	14
Peru	9	—	5	8	6	—	6	—	—	1	4	39
Uruguay	3	—	5	2	—	—	—	—	3	—	4	17
Venezuela	29	—	43	27	5	10	2	—	9	4	—	129
Total	209	15	183	151	33	20	35	19	96	42	29	832
CACM												
Costa Rica	—	—	—	—	—	—	—	—	1	—	—	1
El Salvador	—	—	—	—	—	—	—	—	—	—	—	—
Guatemala	—	—	—	—	—	—	—	—	—	—	—	—
Honduras	—	—	—	—	—	—	—	—	—	—	—	—
Nicaragua	—	—	—	—	—	—	—	—	—	—	—	—
Total	—	—	—	—	—	—	—	—	1	—	—	1
Others												
Dominican Rep.	—	—	—	—	—	—	—	—	—	—	1	1
Haiti	—	—	—	—	—	—	—	—	—	—	—	—
Panama	—	—	—	—	—	—	—	—	—	—	—	—
Total Latin Am.[a]	209	15	183	151	33	20	35	19	97	42	30	834

See notes at end of table.

Table A-6. (continued)

Exporter	Importer: CACM						Importer: Others			Importer: Total Latin America
	Costa Rica	El Salvador	Guate-mala	Hon-duras	Nica-ragua	Total	Dominican Republic	Haiti	Panama	
LAFTA										
Argentina	—	—	—	—	—	—	—	—	1	285
Bolivia	—	—	—	—	—	—	—	—	—	14
Brazil	—	—	—	—	—	—	—	—	1	163
Chile	1	—	—	—	—	—	—	—	—	79
Colombia	—	—	—	—	1	2	—	—	3	30
Ecuador	—	—	—	—	—	—	—	—	—	14
Mexico	3	3	6	1	3	16	—	—	7	82
Paraguay	—	—	—	—	—	—	—	—	—	14
Peru	—	—	—	—	—	—	—	—	—	40
Uruguay	—	—	—	—	—	—	—	—	—	17
Venezuela	4	8	13	—	6	31	2	—	41	206
Total	8	11	19	1	10	49	2	—	53	944
CACM										
Costa Rica	—	6	6	4	11	27	—	—	4	32
El Salvador	13	—	33	20	14	79	—	—	—	79
Guatemala	9	29	—	9	11	58	—	—	—	59
Honduras	3	11	6	—	2	22	—	—	1	23
Nicaragua	7	5	2	4	—	18	—	—	1	19
Total	32	51	47	37	38	204	—	—	5	212
Others										
Dominican Republic	—	—	—	—	—	—	—	—	—	1
Haiti	—	—	—	—	—	—	—	—	—	—
Panama	1	—	—	—	—	1	—	—	—	2
Total Latin America[a]	41	62	66	38	48	254	2	—	58	1,158

Source: IMF, IBRD, *Direction of Trade: Annual 1963–67*. a. May not agree with totals in Table A-4 because data are from individual country accounts.
— No trade or not applicable.

Estimated Effect of Possible Latin American Common External Tariffs on U.S. Exports to Latin America

TWO ALTERNATIVE ESTIMATES of average common external tariff levels for a Latin American common market are used to calculate the effect of the establishment of a common tariff on U.S. exports. One assumes an average tariff equal to 101 percent, or the average level of seven countries' individual tariffs in the early 1960s. That average is based on the un-weighted arithmetic mean of estimated nominal tariffs of seven countries that accounted for about two-thirds of Latin American imports from the United States in the mid-1960s (Venezuela is the only major importer for which tariff data are not available). The other estimate assumes an average tariff level equal to 50 percent or half the unweighted arithmetic mean of the individual country tariffs in the early 1960s (see Table 14).

The estimates are derived from the percentage difference between a country's existing tariff and the common external tariff multiplied by the sum of the average demand and supply elasticities[1] for the economy; the sum of the elasticities is weighted by an indicator that measures the production of the economy in relation to imports from the United States. Because of the assumed elasticities, a downward adjustment of tariffs would result in an increase in consumption of imports (the magnitude is determined

1. The demand elasticity measures the percentage change in the quantity of goods used or consumed as a ratio to the percentage change in price (since these changes are generally in opposite directions the elasticity will be negative). The supply elasticity measures the percentage change in quantities produced as a ratio to the percentage change in price.

by the demand elasticity) and a decrease in domestic production of imports (determined by the elasticity of supply), and the effect of a tariff adjustment would be greater the lower the importance of imports in the economy.

The percentage change in imports from the United States can be expressed as:

$$(1) \qquad \frac{dM_i}{M_i} = \frac{t_i - t_x}{1 + t_i}(\eta + \epsilon)\frac{P_i}{M_i}c$$

where M_i are imports of country i from the United States, t_x is the common external tariff, t_i is the average existing tariff in country i, η is the average demand elasticity (assumed to be equal for all countries), ϵ is the average supply elasticity (assumed to be equal for all countries), P_i is the value added for the production sectors of gross domestic product (agriculture, manufacturing, mining, and construction, that is, the part of GDP that potentially can be traded and therefore excludes services) in country i, and c is a constant.[2]

The average demand elasticity η is assumed to be -0.8 and the average supply elasticity ϵ is assumed to be 0.2.[3] Both are assumed to be short-run values. The coefficient c is based upon the relation of the seven countries' total imports from the United States to their total "production GDP," $\Sigma M_i / \Sigma P_i$, and is equal to 0.07.

Because the interest here centers on the effects of a Latin American common market on U.S. exports, the calculations are applied only to that country. However, on a more general level the formulation can be applied to all extraregional imports.

2. This formulation can be taken as a gross simplification of the Balassa-Johnson formulation to estimate the effect of duties on the imports of a commodity. The Balassa-Johnson formulation expresses the relative change in imports both as a function of the demand elasticities in the importing country weighted by the ratio of consumption to imports and multiplied by the nominal tariff rates, and the supply elasticities (in the individual processes) in the importing country weighted by the ratios of value added in the country to imports and multiplied by the effective rates of protection to value added. (Bela Balassa, "Tariff Protection in Industrialized Countries: An Evaluation," *Journal of Political Economy*, Vol. 73 [December 1965], pp. 573–94.)

3. The demand elasticity is somewhat higher and the supply elasticity is lower than the average of the values assumed by Balassa for industrial countries (*ibid.*, p. 592). The reason for the former is that prices in effect for many goods in Latin America tend to be higher, and for the latter, that factor mobility and efficiency in resource allocation are lower.

The calculations are based on the tariffs for the seven countries given in Table 14 (Argentina, Brazil, Chile, Colombia, Ecuador, Mexico, and Peru) and on 1967 trade data. The results are summarized in Tables B-1 and B-2. Table B-1 shows that under the first assumption, a common external tariff averaged at the arithmetic mean of tariffs in the early 1960s (101 percent), U.S. exports to the seven countries would increase slightly, by $34 million. Applying the result to total Latin American imports from the United States gives an increase of about $51 million, based on 1967 imports. (See Appendix A, Table A-4 for 1967 trade figures by country.) This is an insignificant percentage change in U.S. exports (about 1 percent).

Table B-1. Effect of 101 Percent Average Common External Tariff on Imports from the United States by Seven Latin American Countries

| Country | Estimated change in imports[a] | |
	Percent	Millions of dollars
Argentina	24	55
Brazil	21	113
Chile	6	16
Colombia	3	6
Ecuador	−6	−6
Mexico	−9	−111
Peru	−15	−39
Total	1.2[b]	34

a. Based on 1967 export figures.
b. Weighted average.

Table B-2. Effect of 50 Percent Average Common External Tariff on Imports from the United States by Seven Latin American Countries

| Country | Estimated change in imports[a] | |
	Percent	Millions of dollars
Argentina	66	149
Brazil	38	200
Chile	15	36
Colombia	16	35
Ecuador	2	2
Mexico	3	30
Peru	−4	−9
Total	16[b]	443

a. Based on 1967 export figures.
b. Weighted average.

Under the second assumption, that the common external tariff is set at 50 percent, Table B-2 shows that U.S. exports to the seven countries would increase by $443 million, or 16 percent of the total imports of those countries from the United States in 1967. This would imply an increase of $664 million in total U.S. exports to Latin America.

These figures are given only to illustrate the rough order of magnitude of changes likely to come about through the averaging of individual country tariffs to the common external tariff. Even so, they must be interpreted with caution. For example, the tariffs shown for Mexico in Table 14 do not reflect the degree of protection enjoyed by Mexican industry. Macario points out that his estimates of Mexican protection are probably low because of the preference in that country for import licensing.[4] If this is true, U.S. exports to Mexico would not decrease as much as estimated here as a result of Mexico's raising its tariff to meet the average common tariff. Since Mexico received over a fourth of U.S. exports to Latin America in 1967 (see Appendix A, Table A-4), a significant error in the Mexican estimate (Table B-1) is likely to increase total U.S. exports to the region considerably. A further cause of possible underestimate of the positive effect of an average common tariff based on tariff levels in the early 1960s is that tariff rates have diminished in most Latin American countries since that date. Thus a common external tariff set at the mean of 1969 tariffs would be considerably lower than 101 percent.

On the other hand, it is important to note that the average nominal tariff for the seven countries is high relative to the existing tariffs for many other countries that were not included in this calculation for lack of tariff data. Thus, these countries would be averaging their tariffs in an upward direction which would normally lead to some fall in imports from outside the area including the United States.

Finally, if the estimated common tariff "overprotects" Latin industries— is higher than the percentage difference between the domestic price and the c.i.f. world price of goods—the lowering of the tariff in Argentina and Brazil will not increase imports from the United States as much as shown in Tables B-1 and B-2.

The balance of these different factors is not determinate and the estimates given here should be considered only as a range of possible effects.

4. Santiago Macario, "Protectionism and Industrialization in Latin America," *Economic Bulletin for Latin America*, Vol. 9 (March 1964), p. 68.

Estimated Effect of Removal of Tariff Protection in Developed Countries on Imports of Manufactured Goods from Latin America

THE CHANGE IN THE LESS developed countries' share in developed-country import markets can be measured by the share elasticity times the effective tariff in the developed country.[1] The implicit assumptions are a perfectly elastic demand for imports in the developed countries and an elastic supply of those manufactured goods at present exported by developing countries.

Balassa has determined that the effective tariff (weighted average) in 1962 for the United States was 20 percent, for the United Kingdom 27.8 percent, for the European Economic Community (EEC) 18.6 percent, and for Japan 29.5 percent.[2] These countries account for about 94 percent of the total imports of manufactured goods[3] from Latin America into developed countries. In 1967 the United States imported $264 million in manufac-

---

1. Using effective tariffs assumes that tariffs are reduced only on finished manufactures. The share elasticity equals the percent change in the proportion of total imports coming from a given area due to a percent change of relative prices of imports from that area.

2. Bela Balassa, "Tariff Protection in Industrial Countries: An Evaluation," *Journal of Political Economy*, Vol. 73 (December 1965), p. 591.

3. Manufactured goods are defined throughout this appendix as chemicals, basic manufactures, machinery and transport equipment, and other manufactured goods (Standard International Trade Classification [SITC] categories 5, 6, 7, and 8) minus nonferrous metals (SITC 68) which are imported by developed countries from Latin America mainly in an unwrought state.

tured goods from Latin America, the United Kingdom $24 million, the EEC $71 million, and Japan $40 million.[4]

Assuming a share elasticity of 1.5,[5] multiplying it by the effective tariff, and applying the product to these figures yields the following increases in imports of manufactured goods from Latin America in 1967: United States $79 million, United Kingdom $10 million, EEC $20 million, and Japan $18 million. The total increase—$127 million—represents a 32 percent rise in these developed countries' imports of manufactures from Latin America in 1967 (assuming that they are a constant share of total imports of manufactures into developed countries from less developed countries). As these countries took 94 percent of imports of manufactures from Latin America, the total increase allowing for the remaining 6 percent would be $135 million.[6] This increase, small in relation to total Latin American exports in 1967, is larger than total 1963 intra-LAFTA trade in manufactures.

The effect of preferences on U.S. imports is relatively small. In 1967 U.S. imports of manufactured goods from less developed countries were as follows: Africa $40 million, Asia $1,110 million, Latin America $264 million, and others $81 million, for a total of $1,495 million.[7] Applying the effective tariff times the assumed share elasticity to these figures results in an increase in imports of manufactures from all less developed countries into the United States of $449 million in 1965.[8] This figure represents only 3 percent of total imports of manufactures into the United States and less than 2 percent of all U.S. imports in 1967.

4. United Nations, Department of Economic and Social Affairs, *Commodity Trade Statistics, 1968*, Statistical Papers, Series D, issues for these countries.

5. P. J. Verdoorn calculated the share elasticity to be 2.0 based on Benelux experience (Tibor Scitovsky, *Economic Theory and Western European Integration* [London: Allen & Unwin, 1958], p. 64). The elasticity would be lower for less developed areas such as Latin America: preferences for imports from given suppliers are likely to be less flexible, consumption habits more fixed than in developed countries. For this reason the share elasticity was assumed to be three-fourths of the European value.

6. This increase would be more than twice as great if nonferrous metals (SITC 68) were included in the definition of "manufactures" and a much higher multiple if processed foods were included.

7. *Commodity Trade Statistics, 1968*, Vol. 18, No. 1–8 (1969).

8. No correction is made for the cotton textiles arrangements. All estimates must be regarded as short-term approximations. Since manufactured imports from less developed countries are a small percentage of total manufactured imports, it is assumed that the income effect of the fall in import prices is negligible.

Declaration
of the
Presidents of America

THE PRESIDENTS OF THE AMERICAN STATES AND THE PRIME MINISTER OF TRINIDAD AND TOBAGO MEETING IN PUNTA DEL ESTE, URUGUAY,[1]

RESOLVED to give more dynamic and concrete expression to the ideals of Latin American unity and of solidarity among the peoples of America, which inspired the founders of their countries;

DETERMINED to make this goal a reality within their own generation, in keeping with the economic, social and cultural aspirations of their peoples;

INSPIRED by the principles underlying the inter-American system, especially those contained in the Charter of Punta del Este, the Economic and Social Act of Rio de Janeiro, and the Protocol of Buenos Aires amending the Charter of the Organization of American States;

CONSCIOUS that the attainment of national and regional development objectives in Latin America is based essentially on self-help;

CONVINCED, however, that the achievement of those objectives requires determined collaboration by all their countries, complementary support through mutual aid, and expansion of external cooperation;

PLEDGED to give vigorous impetus to the Alliance for Progress and to emphasize its multilateral character, with a view to encouraging balanced development of the region at a pace substantially faster than attained thus far;

UNITED in the intent to strengthen democratic institutions, to raise the living standards of their peoples and to assure their increased participation in the development process, creating for these purposes suitable conditions in the political, economic and social as well as labor fields;

1. Meeting held April 12–14, 1967. Only the first three of the six chapters of the Action Program are reproduced here.

RESOLVED to maintain a harmony of fraternal relations in the Americas, in which racial equality must be effective;

PROCLAIM

The solidarity of the countries they represent and their decision to achieve to the fullest measure the free, just, and democratic social order demanded by the peoples of the Hemisphere.

I

Latin America will create a common market.

THE PRESIDENTS OF THE LATIN AMERICAN REPUBLICS resolve to create progressively, beginning in 1970, the Latin American Common Market, which shall be substantially in operation in a period of no more than fifteen years. The Latin American Common Market will be based on the complete development and progressive convergence of the Latin American Free Trade Association and of the Central American Common Market, taking into account the interests of the Latin American countries not yet affiliated with these systems. This great task will reinforce historic bonds, will promote industrial development and the strengthening of Latin American industrial enterprises, as well as more efficient production and new opportunities for employment, and will permit the region to play its deservedly significant role in world affairs. The ties of friendship among the peoples of the Continent will thus be strengthened.

THE PRESIDENT OF THE UNITED STATES OF AMERICA, for his part, declares his firm support for this promising Latin American initiative.

THE UNDERSIGNED PRESIDENTS AFFIRM THAT:

We will lay the physical foundations for Latin American economic integration through multinational projects.

Economic integration demands a major sustained effort to build a land transportation network and to improve transportation systems of all kinds so as to open the way for the movement of both people and goods throughout the Continent; to establish an adequate and efficient telecommunications system; to install inter-connected power systems; and to develop jointly international river basins, frontier regions, and economic areas which include the territory of two or more countries.

We will join in efforts to increase substantially Latin American foreign-trade earnings.

To increase substantially Latin American foreign-trade earnings, individual and joint efforts shall be directed toward facilitating non-discriminatory access of Latin American products in world markets, toward increasing Latin American earnings from traditional exports, toward avoiding frequent fluctuations in income from such commodities, and, finally, toward adopting measures that will stimulate exports of Latin American manufactured products.

We will modernize the living conditions of our rural populations, raise agricultural productivity in general, and increase food production for the benefit of both Latin America and the rest of the world.

The living conditions of the rural workers and farmers of Latin America will be transformed, to guarantee their full participation in economic and social progress. For that purpose, integrated programs of modernization, land settlement, and agrarian reform will be carried out as the countries so require. Similarly, productivity will be improved and agricultural production diversified. Furthermore, recognizing that the Continent's capacity for food production entails a dual responsibility, a special effort will be made to produce sufficient food for the growing needs of their own peoples and to contribute toward feeding the peoples of other regions.

We will vigorously promote education for development.

To give a decisive impetus to education for development, literacy campaigns will be intensified, education at all levels will be greatly expanded, and its quality improved so that the rich human potential of their peoples may make their maximum contribution to the economic, social, and cultural development of Latin America. Educational systems will be modernized taking full advantage of educational innovations, and exchanges of teachers and students will be increased.

We will harness science and technology for the service of our peoples.

Latin America will share in the benefits of current scientific and technological progress so as to reduce the widening gap between it and the highly industrialized nations in the areas of production techniques and of living conditions. National scientific and technological programs will be developed and strengthened and a regional program will be started; multinational institutes for advanced training and research will be established; existing institutes of this kind in Latin America will at the same time be strengthened and contributions will be made to the exchange and advancement of technological knowledge.

We will expand programs for improving the health of the American peoples.

The fundamental role of health in the economic and social development of Latin America demands that the prevention and control of communicable diseases be intensified and that measures be taken to eradicate those which can be completely eliminated by existing techniques. Also programs to supply drinking water and other services essential to urban and rural environmental sanitation will be speeded up.

Latin America will eliminate unnecessary military expenditures.

THE PRESIDENTS OF THE LATIN AMERICAN REPUBLICS, conscious of the importance of armed forces to the maintenance of security, recognize at the same time that the demands of economic development and social progress make it necessary to devote to those purposes the maximum resources available in Latin America.

Therefore, they express their intention to limit military expenditures in proportion to the actual demands of national security in accordance with each country's constitutional provisions, avoiding those expenditures that are not indispensable for the performance of the specific duties of the armed forces and, where pertinent, of international commitments that obligate their respective governments. With regard to the Treaty on the Banning of Nuclear Arms in

Latin America, they express the hope that it may enter into force as soon as possible, once the requirements established by the Treaty are fulfilled.

IN FACING THE PROBLEMS CONSIDERED IN THIS MEETING, which constitute a challenge to the will of the American governments* and peoples, the Presidents proclaim their faith in the basic purpose of the inter-American system: to promote in the Americas free and democratic societies, existing under the rule of law, whose dynamic economies, reinforced by growing technological capabilities, will allow them to serve with ever-increasing effectiveness the peoples of the Continent, to whom they announce the following program.

II

Action Program

CHAPTER I

LATIN AMERICAN ECONOMIC INTEGRATION AND INDUSTRIAL DEVELOPMENT

1. *Principles, objectives, and goals*

Economic integration is a collective instrument for accelerating Latin American development and should constitute one of the policy goals of each of the countries of the region. The greatest possible efforts should be made to bring it about, as a necessary complement to national development plans.

At the same time, the different levels of development and economic and market conditions of the various Latin American countries must be borne in mind, in order that the integration process may promote their harmonious and balanced growth. In this respect, the countries of relatively less economic development, and, to the extent required, those of insufficient market, will have preferential treatment in matters of trade and of technical and financial cooperation.

Integration must be fully at the service of Latin America. This requires the strengthening of Latin American enterprise through vigorous financial and technical support that will permit it to develop and supply the regional market efficiently. Foreign private enterprise will be able to fill an important function in assuring achievement of the objectives of integration within the pertinent policies of each of the countries of Latin America.

Adequate financing is required to facilitate the economic restructuring and adjustments called for by the urgent need to accelerate integration.

* When the term "Latin America" is used in this text, it is to be understood that it includes all the member states of the Organization of American States, except the United States of America. The term "Presidents" includes the Prime Minister of Trinidad and Tobago. The term "Continent" comprises both the continental and insular areas.

It is necessary to adopt all measures that will lead to the completion of Latin American integration, above all those that will bring about, in the shortest time possible, monetary stability and the elimination of all restrictions, including administrative, financial, and exchange restrictions, that obstruct the trade of the products of the area.

To these ends, the Latin American Presidents agree to take action on the following points:

a. Beginning in 1970, to establish progressively the Latin American Common Market, which should be substantially in operation within a period of no more than fifteen years.

b. The Latin American Common Market will be based on the improvement of the two existing integration systems: the Latin American Free Trade Association (LAFTA) and the Central American Common Market (CACM). The two systems will initiate simultaneously a process of convergence by stages of cooperation, closer ties, and integration, taking into account the interest of the Latin American countries not yet associated with these systems, in order to provide their access to one of them.

c. To encourage the incorporation of other countries of the Latin American region into the existing integration systems.

2. *Measures with regard to the Latin American Free Trade Association (LAFTA)*

The Presidents of the member states of LAFTA instruct their respective Ministers of Foreign Affairs, who will participate in the next meeting of the Council of Ministers of LAFTA, to be held in 1967, to adopt the measures necessary to implement the following decisions:

a. To accelerate the process of converting LAFTA into a common market. To this end, starting in 1970, and to be completed in a period of not more than fifteen years, LAFTA will put into effect a system of programmed elimination of duties and all other nontariff restrictions, and also a system of tariff harmonization, in order to establish progressively a common external tariff at levels that will promote efficiency and productivity, as well as the expansion of trade.

b. To coordinate progressively economic policies and instruments and to harmonize national laws to the extent required for integration. These measures will be adopted simultaneously with the improvement of the integration process.

c. To promote the conclusion of sectoral agreements for industrial complementation, endeavoring to obtain the participation of the countries of relatively less economic development.

d. To promote the conclusion of temporary subregional agreements, with provision for reducing tariffs within the subregions and harmonizing treatments toward third nations more rapidly than in the general agreements, in keeping with the objectives of regional integration. Subregional tariff reductions will not be extended to countries that are not parties to the subregional agreement, nor will they create special obligations for them.

Participation of the countries of relatively less economic development in all stages of the integration process and in the formation of the Latin American

Common Market will be based on the provisions of the Treaty of Montevideo and its complementary resolutions, and these countries will be given the greatest possible advantages, so that balanced development of the region may be achieved.

To this same end, they have decided to promote immediate action to facilitate free access of products of the LAFTA member countries of relatively less economic development to the market of the other LAFTA countries, and to promote the installation and financing in the former countries of industries intended for the enlarged market.

The countries of relatively less economic development will have the right to participate and to obtain preferential conditions in the subregional agreements in which they have an interest.

The situation of countries characterized as being of insufficient market shall be taken into account in temporary preferential treatments established, to the extent necessary to achieve a harmonious development in the integration process.

It is understood that all the provisions set forth in this section fall within or are based upon the Treaty of Montevideo.

3. *Measures with regard to the Central American economic integration program*
The Presidents of the member states of the Central American Common Market commit themselves:

a. To carry out an action program that will include the following measures, among others:

(1) Improvement of the customs union and establishment of a Central American monetary union;

(2) Completion of the regional network of infrastructure;

(3) Promotion of a common foreign-trade policy;

(4) Improvement of the common market in agricultural products and implementation of a joint, coordinated industrial policy;

(5) Acceleration of the process of free movement of manpower and capital within the area;

(6) Harmonization of the basic legislation required for economic integration.

b. To apply, in the implementation of the foregoing measures, and when pertinent, the temporary preferential treatment already established or that may be established, in accordance with the principle of balanced development among countries.

c. To foster closer ties between Panama and the Central American Common Market, as well as rapid expansion of trade and investment relations with neighboring countries of the Central American and Caribbean region, taking advantage, to this end, of their geographic proximity and of the possibilities for economic complementation; also, to seek conclusion of subregional agreements and agreements of industrial complementation between Central America and other Latin American countries.

4. *Measures common to Latin American countries*
The Latin American Presidents commit themselves:

a. Not to establish new restrictions on trade among Latin American countries, except in special cases, such as those arising from equalization of tariffs and other instruments of trade policy, as well as from the need to assure the initiation or expansion of certain productive activities in countries of relatively less economic development.

b. To establish, by a tariff cut or other equivalent measures, a margin of preference within the region for all products originating in Latin American countries, taking into account the different degrees of development of the countries.

c. To have the measures in the two preceding paragraphs applied immediately among the member countries of LAFTA, in harmony with the other measures referring to this organization contained in the present chapter and, insofar as possible, to extend them to nonmember countries in a manner compatible with existing international commitments, inviting the latter countries to extend similar preferences to the members of LAFTA, with the same qualification.

d. To ensure that application of the foregoing measures shall not hinder internal readjustments designed to rationalize the instruments of trade policy made necessary in order to carry out national development plans and to achieve the goals of integration.

e. To promote acceleration of the studies already initiated regarding preferences that LAFTA countries might grant to imports from the Latin American countries that are not members of the Association.

f. To have studies made of the possibility of concluding agreements of industrial complementation in which all Latin American countries may participate, as well as temporary subregional economic integration agreements between the CACM and member countries of LAFTA.

g. To have a committee established composed of the executive organs of LAFTA and the CACM to coordinate implementation of the foregoing points. To this end, the committee will encourage meetings at the ministerial level, in order to ensure that Latin American integration will proceed as rapidly as possible, and, in due course, initiate negotiation of a general treaty or the protocols required to create the Latin American Common Market. Latin American countries that are not members shall be invited to send representatives to these meetings and to those of the committee of the executive organs of LAFTA and the CACM.

h. To give special attention to industrial development within integration, and particularly to the strengthening of Latin American industrial firms. In this regard, we reiterate that development must be balanced between investments for economic ends and investments for social ends.

5. *Measures common to member countries of the Organization of American States (OAS)*

The Presidents of the member states of the OAS agree:

a. To mobilize financial and technical resources within and without the hemisphere to contribute to the solution of problems in connection with the balance of payments, industrial readjustments, and retraining of the labor force that may arise from a rapid reduction of trade barriers during the period of transition toward the common market, as well as to increase the sums available for export credits in intra-Latin American trade. The Inter-American Development Bank and the organs of both existing integration systems should participate in the mobilization of such resources.

b. To mobilize public and private resources within and without the hemisphere to encourage industrial development as part of the integration process and of national development plans.

c. To mobilize financial and technical resources to undertake specific feasibility studies on multinational projects for Latin American industrial firms, as well as to aid in carrying out these projects.

d. To accelerate the studies being conducted by various inter-American agencies to promote strengthening of capital markets and the possible establishment of a Latin American stock market.

e. To make available to Central America, within the Alliance for Progress, adequate technical and financial resources, including those required for strengthening and expanding the existing Central American Economic Integration Fund, for the purpose of accelerating the Central American economic integration program.

f. To make available, within the Alliance for Progress and pursuant to the provisions of the Charter of Punta del Este, the technical and financial resources needed to accelerate the preparatory studies and work involved in converting LAFTA into a common market.

CHAPTER II

MULTINATIONAL ACTION FOR INFRASTRUCTURE PROJECTS

The economic integration of Latin America demands a vigorous and sustained effort to complete and modernize the physical infrastructure of the region. It is necessary to build a land transport network and improve all types of transport systems to facilitate the movement of persons and goods throughout the hemisphere; to establish an adequate and efficient telecommunications system and interconnected power systems; and jointly to develop international watersheds, frontier regions and economic areas that include the territory of two or more countries. In Latin America there are in existence projects in all these fields, at different stages of preparation or implementation, but in many cases the completion of prior studies, financial resources, or merely the coordination of efforts and the decision to bring them to fruition are lacking.

The Presidents of the member states of the OAS agree to engage in determined action to undertake or accelerate the construction of the infrastructure required for the development and integration of Latin America and to make better use thereof. In so doing, it is essential that the groups of interested countries or multinational institutions determine criteria for assigning priorities, in view of the amount of human and material resources needed for the task.

As one basis for the criteria, which will be determined with precision upon consideration of the specific cases submitted for study, they stress the fundamental need to give preferential attention to those projects that benefit the countries of the region that are at a relatively lower level of economic development.

Priority should also be given to the mobilization of financial and technical resources for the preparation and implementation of infrastructure projects that will facilitate the participation of landlocked countries in regional and international trade.

In consequence, they adopt the following decisions for immediate implementation:

1. To complete the studies and conclude the agreements necessary to accelerate the construction of an inter-American telecommunications network.

2. To expedite the agreements necessary to complete the Pan American Highway, to accelerate the construction of the Bolivarian Highway (Carretera Marginal de la Selva) and its junction with the Trans-Chaco Highway and to support the studies and agreements designed to bring into being the new highway systems that will join groups of countries of continental and insular Latin America, as well as the basic works required to develop water and airborne transport of a multinational nature and the corresponding systems of operation. As a complement to these agreements, negotiations should be undertaken for the purpose of eliminating or reducing to a minimum the restrictions on international traffic and of promoting technical and administrative cooperation among land, water, and air transport enterprises and the establishment of multinational transport services.

3. To sponsor studies for preparing joint projects in connection with watersheds, such as the studies commenced on the development of the River Plate basin and that relating to the Gulf of Fonseca.

4. To allocate sufficient resources to the Preinvestment Fund for Latin American Integration of the IDB for conducting studies that will make it possible to identify and prepare multinational projects in all fields that may be of importance in promoting regional integration. In order that the aforesaid Fund may carry out an effective promotion effort, it is necessary that an adequate part of the resources allocated may be used without reimbursement, or with reimbursement conditioned on the execution of the corresponding projects.

5. To mobilize, within and outside the hemisphere, resources in addition to those that will continue to be placed at the disposal of the countries to support national economic development programs, such resources to be devoted especially to the implementation of multinational infrastructure projects that can represent important advances in the Latin American economic integration process. In this regard, the IDB should have additional resources in order to participate actively in the attainment of this objective.

CHAPTER III

MEASURES TO IMPROVE INTERNATIONAL TRADE
CONDITIONS IN LATIN AMERICA

The economic development of Latin America is seriously affected by the adverse conditions in which its international trade is carried out. Market structures, financial conditions, and actions that prejudice exports and other income from outside Latin America are impeding its growth and retarding the integration process. All this causes particular concern in view of the serious and growing imbalance between the standard of living in Latin American countries and that of the industrialized nations and, at the same time, calls for definite decisions and adequate instruments to implement the decisions.

Individual and joint efforts of the member states of the OAS are essential to increase the incomes of Latin American countries derived from, and to avoid frequent fluctuations in, traditional exports, as well as to promote new exports. Such efforts are also essential to reduce any adverse effects on the external earnings of Latin American countries that may be caused by measures which may be taken by industrialized countries for balance of payments reasons.

The Charter of Punta del Este, the Economic and Social Act of Rio de Janeiro and the new provisions of the Charter of the OAS reflect a hemispheric agreement with regard to these problems, which needs to be effectively implemented; therefore, the Presidents of the member states of the OAS agree:

1. To act in coordination in multilateral negotiations to achieve, without the more highly developed countries' expecting reciprocity, the greatest possible reduction or the elimination of tariffs and other restrictions that impede the access of Latin American products to world markets. The Government of the United States intends to make efforts for the purpose of liberalizing the conditions affecting exports of basic products of special interest to Latin American countries, in accordance with the provisions of Article 37. a) of the Protocol of Buenos Aires.

2. To consider together possible systems of general nonreciprocal preferential treatment for exports of manufactures and semimanufactures of the developing countries, with a view to improving the condition of the Latin American export trade.

3. To undertake a joint effort in all international institutions and organizations to eliminate discriminatory preferences against Latin American exports.

4. To strengthen the system of intergovernmental consultations and carry them out sufficiently in advance, so as to render them effective and ensure that programs for placing and selling surpluses and reserves that affect the exports of the developing countries take into account the interests of the Latin American countries.

5. To ensure compliance with international commitments to refrain from introducing or increasing tariff and nontariff barriers that affect exports of the developing countries, taking into account the interests of Latin America.

6. To combine efforts to strengthen and perfect existing international agreements, particularly the International Coffee Agreement, to obtain favorable conditions for trade in basic products of interest to Latin America and to explore all possibilities for the development of new agreements.

7. To support the financing and prompt initiation of the activities of the Coffee Diversification Fund, and consider in due course the creation of other funds to make it possible to control the production of basic products of interest to Latin America in which there is a chronic imbalance between supply and demand.

8. To adopt measures to make Latin American export products more competitive in world markets.

9. To put in operation as soon as possible an inter-American agency for export promotion that will help to identify and develop new export lines and to strengthen the placing of Latin American products in international markets, and to improve national and regional agencies designed for the same purpose.

10. To initiate such individual or joint action on the part of the member states of the OAS as may be required to ensure effective and timely execution of the foregoing agreements, as well as those that may be required to continue the execution of the agreements contained in the Charter of Punta del Este, in particular those relating to foreign trade.

With regard to joint action, the Inter-American Committee on the Alliance for Progress (CIAP) and other agencies in the region shall submit to the Inter-American Economic and Social Council (IA-ECOSOC), for consideration at its next meeting, the means, instruments, and action program for initiating execution thereof.

At its annual meetings, IA-ECOSOC shall examine the progress of the programs under way with the object of considering such action as may ensure compliance with the agreements concluded, inasmuch as a substantial improvement in the international conditions in which Latin American foreign trade is carried on is a basic prerequisite to the acceleration of economic development.

Latin American Consensus of Viña del Mar[1]

THE MEMBER COUNTRIES of the Special Committee for Latin American Coordination (CECLA), Meeting at the Ministerial Level at Viña del Mar, Chile, to examine the conditions surrounding international cooperation and the way in which this influences our external situation, and to propose new approaches that will take due account of current conditions in the Hemisphere, have agreed on the following common position for establishing jointly with the United States of America new bases for inter-American economic and social cooperation.

In the Declaration to the Peoples of America, the Charter of Punta del Este, the Economic and Social Act of Rio de Janeiro, and the Declaration of the Presidents of America, the Governments of Latin America and the Government of the United States spelled out obligations and programs of common action that incorporate the aspirations of the Latin American countries to promote the development and progress of the region. Up to the present time those obligations and programs have not enjoyed adequate implementation and attention.

The governments of the member states of the Special Committee for Latin American Coordination (CECLA) reaffirm the validity of the principles and purposes contained in the aforementioned instruments and the necessity of full compliance with the commitments and action specified therein.

Furthermore, they reiterate the principles contained in the Charter of Alta Gracia and the Charter of Tequendama, of which acceptance by the United States and support by that country vis-à-vis other industrialized nations will represent a positive contribution to the efforts of the Latin American countries to arrive at more equitable standards in the international community.

1. Reprinted from Organization of American States, Inter-American Economic and Social Council, "Special Meeting of CECLA at the Ministerial Level," Viña del Mar, Chile, May 15 to 17, 1969, OEA/Ser.H/X.14, CIES/1403 (English), June 16, 1969; processed. Bracketed phrases in the text are from the OAS document.

192

Notwithstanding the fact that the solution of the problems of development has been a matter of predominant concern in the international community, the decisions, recommendations, principles, and action programs thus far adopted, although valuable in themselves, have not been sufficient. Therefore, the member countries of CECLA believe it to be imperative to agree on more effective forms of inter-American and international cooperation.

The concepts stated in the following paragraphs, which have no antagonistic or negative import, are the logical consequence of the long process of reaffirmation of the characteristic values of Latin America and take stock of its common interests.

I

Nature and Substance of Inter-American and International Cooperation

1. The member countries of CECLA affirm the individual personality of Latin America. The process of development of the region and the changes that are at work in each of its countries, joined with the changes occurring in the world at large, demand far-reaching changes in the terms and conditions of relations between Latin America and the other members of the international community.

Inescapably, therefore, the Latin American countries must try to reach solutions fashioned according to their own criteria, reflecting their national identity.

2. Determined to overcome underdevelopment, they reiterate their conviction that economic growth and social progress are the responsibility of their peoples and that attainment of national and regional objectives depends fundamentally on the effort of each country, supported also by closer cooperation, coordination, and harmonization of policies and attitudes among the Latin American nations, which factors find relevant expression in the decision of the Presidents of the countries of Latin America to move to a common market.

3. The achievement of these objectives depends in great measure on the recognition and assumption of their responsibilities by the international community and, in particular, the countries that today carry greater weight in world decisions.

Acceptance of these responsibilities and fulfillment of the duties deriving from them are indispensable for the most rapid and fullest use and mobilization of internal resources and, consequently, for wider and more complete inter-American and international cooperation to supplement the individual effort of each country. These factors will likewise contribute significantly toward the process of Latin American economic integration.

4. During the last decade inter-American and international cooperation for the development of Latin America has fallen far short of satisfying the aspirations of the countries of the region as those have been defined in important forums and in inter-American and world documents. The resolutions, decisions, and

declarations of the Bogotá Conference of 1948; the Act of Bogotá of 1960; the Declaration of the Peoples of America and the Charter of Punta del Este of 1961; the Charter of Alta Gracia of 1964; the Economic and Social Act of Rio de Janeiro of 1965; the Protocol of Buenos Aires and the Declaration of the Presidents of America of 1967; the Action Plan of Viña del Mar and the Charter of Tequendama, both of the same year, and the Declaration of Santo Domingo of 1968, all inspired by the ideal of Latin American unity, have sought to actuate in a coherent and progressive manner far-reaching reforms in the economic and commercial relations between Latin America and the United States, as well as between the developing countries in general and the highly industrialized nations, based on principles of cooperation, solidarity, respect for national sovereignty and the self-determination of peoples, and the need for a just international division of work that will favor, and not obstruct, as it has done in the past, the rapid social and economic progress of the developing countries.

5. As the present decade nears its end, the economic and scientific-technological gap between the developing world and the developed nations has widened and is continuing to widen, and the external obstacles that act as a brake on the rapid economic growth of the Latin American countries not only have not been removed; they are on the increase. The persistence of these obstacles manifests itself with particular intensity, for example, in the tariff and nontariff restrictions that impede access to the great world markets under equitable or favorable conditions for the raw, semi-processed, and manufactured products of the aforesaid countries; in the progressive deterioration of the volume, terms, and conditions of international financing assistance, which is practically offset by the burden of service on existing debts, with the resultant serious impairment of the Latin American countries' capacity to import; in the disturbances stemming from the functioning of the international monetary system; in the conditions of ocean transport, that shackle and raise the cost of Latin America's foreign trade; and in the difficulties of transferring modern technology to the countries of the region, difficulties which slow down its use and adaptation to their particular requirements and the modernization of their structures of production.

6. The situation described demands, on the one hand, fulfillment of the general commitments contained in the Charter of the Organization of American States and the Economic Agreement of Bogotá; in the Act of Bogotá, the Charter of Punta del Este, and the Economic and Social Act of Rio de Janeiro; in the Protocol of Buenos Aires and the Declaration of the Presidents of America; and on the other hand it requires a new plan of inter-American and international cooperation for the realization of the aspirations of the Latin American countries. The majority of those aspirations have been identified and defined precisely and presented clearly to the rest of the world. Their attainment might have made it possible to solve or prevent many of the problems that those countries have faced, and to lay sound foundations for effective international cooperation.

7. Specific operative measures, which will be set forth in detail below, must be adopted; they must be designed to remove the external obstacles that hold back the rapid development of the Latin American countries.

Those measures must be based on the principles already accepted by the inter-American and international communities, that guarantee the political and economic independence of the countries concerned. Care must be taken to keep particularly in mind the principles of the juridical equality of states; nonintervention in the internal or external affairs of other states, that is, no kind of action that interferes with the personality of the state and the political, economic, and cultural elements that constitute it; respect for the validity of treaties; the sovereign right of every country to dispose freely of its natural resources; and the fact that economic cooperation cannot be made subject to political or military conditions; and furthermore, the concept that no state may apply or encourage coercive measures of an economic or political nature to force the sovereign will of another state in order to obtain advantages of any kind from it, but on the contrary should make every effort to avoid the adoption of policies, actions, and measures that may jeopardize the economic and social development of another state.

8. The principles of solidarity underlying inter-American cooperation in the political field and in matters of security should necessarily be applied also in the economic and social field. Their nonobservance in this regard can disrupt relations among the countries and imperil their peace and security.

9. The effectiveness of the measures that have been and may in the future be taken depends to a considerable extent on the adaptation of the machinery of inter-American cooperation to the political and economic requirements described above and on their being made genuinely operative.

It will be necessary for the organizations and agencies of cooperation within the hemisphere and world systems to vitalize their action and redirect it toward the central development goals. This action must likewise be based on a full knowledge of the economic and social situation as it prevails in each country, and on respect for the decisions and national programs adopted by each government. A continuing evaluation of programs and their results is also a necessary requirement for greater efficacy in cooperation.

10. These common goals should be complemented by coordinated and effective action on the part of the Latin American countries in the various international forums, institutions, and agencies of cooperation of which they form part. In this way the solidary action of Latin America will have greater weight on a world-wide scale and will lead to attainment of the ends pursued.

II

Proposals on Operative Measures

11. On the basis of these statements, principles, and affirmations, the Latin American countries, on jointly proposing a dialogue with the United States, have decided to convey to it their principal aspirations with respect to inter-

national trade, transportation, financing, investments and invisible items of trade, scientific and technological development, technical cooperation, and social development, with a view to achieving, through appropriate action and negotiation, solid advancement in inter-American cooperation. In these areas they believe it necessary:

A. TRADE

12. To insist on effective compliance with status quo commitments with respect to basic products and to manufactures and semimanufactures. To reiterate the necessity for the functioning of the machinery of consultation contemplated in UNCTAD and GATT prior to the adoption of measures that may mean retrogression in the treatment of imports of Latin American products. To perfect such machinery at the inter-American level, in accordance with the Declaration of the Presidents of America.

13. To continue action in favor of the elimination of customs duties and other nontariff barriers (such as quantitative, security, health, and other such rules and restrictions) which affect the access and marketing of basic commodities. To negotiate with the United States schedules for the elimination of such restrictions in that country's market for Latin American products of special interest, jointly identifying the existence of such obstacles. To promote the holding of a round of special negotiations in GATT for basic commodities that were not properly considered in the last round of negotiations.

14. To emphasize the vital importance of complying with the calendar set by UNCTAD II for agreements on basic commodities which will incorporate provisions guaranteeing equitable and remunerative prices for Latin American exports; respect for commitments established in existing agreements; the conclusion of new agreements, and, insofar as necessary, the broadening of their spheres of action.

15. To review and require the modification or the nonimplementation of policies of encouragement for the uneconomic production of basic products that may prejudice the sale of Latin American commodities on the world markets, and a periodic review of such policies.

16. To carry on joint efforts for the elimination within a fixed period of time of the discriminatory preferences that prejudice the selling of Latin American basic commodities in the markets of certain developed countries, suggesting the adoption of measures or action that will facilitate or induce the renunciation of such preferences by the developing countries receiving them.

17. To demand the effective functioning of consultation machinery in regard to the marketing of surpluses and the disposal of reserves, and that it operate with respect for the general principles already accepted in this field, likewise preventing the disruptions in Latin America's flow of trade caused by the AID tied loans and the dumping of surpluses.

18. To review the existing bilateral and multilateral systems of food aid, for the purpose of substantially expanding the multilateral programs on the basis of the principles approved in CECLA Resolution 9/68M.

19. To reiterate the urgency of putting into force the system of general, non-reciprocal, and nondiscriminatory preferences in favor of the exports of manufactures and semimanufactures of developing countries within the time limits provided and with due observance of the calendar of programmed meetings. In this regard action should be considered that will enable the countries of relatively less economic development to make full use of the advantages that may result.

20. To eliminate, according to a jointly agreed schedule, restrictions on imports of manufactured and semimanufactured products of importance to Latin America, tying this in closely with the system of general preferences. In this connection, to give special attention to the problem of the application of escape clauses, which requires the adoption of adequate criteria and machinery for consultation. To avoid in this context the application of discriminatory practices of any kind.

21. To identify jointly industrial sectors or branches in which the adoption by the United States of measures for the modification, within adequate time limits, of certain productive structures might help to improve and expand trade in the United States market for manufactures and semimanufactures of special interest to Latin America. The effect of such measures would be reviewed periodically.

22. By means of greater technical and financial cooperation, to strengthen, expand, and make more flexible the national and regional mechanisms for the promotion of exports, systematizing Latin American trade information and seeking the cooperation of official and private organizations in the United States in order to intensify and diversify Latin American exports; and also facilitating the supplying of zones or areas with products originating in the same area.

23. To emphasize the importance of active United States support of the proposals of Latin America with respect to other areas, as agreed in the Declaration of the Presidents of America. Compliance by the United States with its own commitments will considerably strengthen the value of such support.

B. TRANSPORTATION

24. To prevent, as far as possible, increased operating costs that occur outside the Latin American area from being reflected in increases in ocean freight rates that may affect exports of particular interest to the countries of Latin America.

25. To advocate reductions in ocean freight rates in inter-American trade when a reduction in the operating costs occurs for the vessels in the ports, on the basis of the effective improvement of each port, instead of the average productivity of an aggregate number of ports.

26. To recognize the right of the Latin American countries to adopt measures for the development of their national and regional merchant marines. Provided that such measures of support are based on equitable sharing of the cargoes generated by the various currents of trade, national or regional, as the case may

be, they will not be considered discriminatory and shall not be cause for decisions that would annul them.

27. To increase inter-American bilateral and multilateral, financial and technical cooperation for the expansion and modernization of the merchant marines of the countries of Latin America and, in accordance with their own programs, the development of their maritime industry and the improvement of port facilities and other elements of the infrastructure of transportation in general.

C. FINANCING, INVESTMENTS, AND INVISIBLE ITEMS OF TRADE

28. Inter-American financial cooperation, which characteristically supplements domestic efforts, should be governed by the following basic premises:

a. It should be a real transfer and be granted in accord with national development policies and plans, since it will guarantee an adequate and sustained volume of financial resources and the right of the receiving country to determine its priorities, thereby improving the efficacy of the external financing in the face of situations that require an overall approach;

b. Lending countries and international financing agencies should base their cooperation on economic and social criteria that respect the receiving country's concept of development;

c. It is indispensable that external financial cooperation not be made subject to conditions that limit the national capacity to adopt decisions in the field of the receiving country's basic economic policies;

d. Preferential attention should be given to the countries of relatively less economic development in the area;

e. Provisions or criteria that tie the use of loans to the purchase of goods and services in specific countries or of specific origin should be eliminated;

f. It is imperative to strengthen a genuine multilateralization of external financial cooperation. By reason of their multilateral nature the international financing agencies should avoid allowing possible bilateral programs between countries to influence their decisions;

g. It is necessary to create effective machinery that will make it possible to liberalize external credit, reduce interest rates, and broaden the volume and terms of loans, taking into account circumstances such as the pluriennial nature of certain projects or programs, and to propose the creation of an Interest Equalization Fund, whose resources, as well as those required by other possible mechanisms, should be provided by contributions of international financing agencies and of developed countries;

h. Greater participation by public agencies in the channeling or use of external financing is desirable, and

i. Measures are required to ensure that the terms of external financing are no less favorable for Latin America than they are for other developing areas of the world.

29. It is considered indispensable that external financing be completely freed of elements that impose special conditions, because of their multiple effects

on the economy of Latin America, such as: the artificial creation of trade currents, including those resulting from application of the additionality concept; the requirements for an excessive component of local expenditures and investments; the creation of superfluous agencies; possible undue influence on internal decision; the compulsory use of specified ocean shipping lines, and the making of purchases on the basis of inadequate lists which represent high costs and distort the trade of the region. As a possible temporary solution the use of AID loans or other similar funds for purchases in Latin America is envisaged.

30. To emphasize the need for resuming U.S. financial support to the International Development Association, and support to Latin America in facilitating the use of its credits by all the countries of the region, by changing for this purpose the standards of eligibility and by not tying such credits to specific conditions.

31. The access of the Latin American countries and their regional and subregional organizations to the capital markets of the United States should be facilitated, by decreasing costs and giving greater flexibility to the administrative and other requirements that now make such access difficult.

32. Available funds should be increased and improvements made in the utilization of the mechanisms for financing Latin American exports, taking into account the need for such credits to be granted under terms and conditions that will make it possible to maintain and improve the competitive position of Latin American products and their trade on international markets, including the use of soft loans when the matter depends basically on the financing terms. In this sense it is considered important to revise the conditions for the use of Inter-American Development Bank funds, in order to expand preshipment credits, provide for the availability of financing for exports of manufactures and semimanufactures and not limit them to trade among Latin American countries.

33. It should be agreed that private foreign investment should not be considered as assistance, nor should it be computed as part of financial cooperation for development. Private foreign investment, subject to national decisions and priorities, should operate in favor of the mobilization of domestic resources, generate income or prevent expenditures of foreign exchange, promote savings and national technological research, represent a real technological contribution, and participate as an element supplementing national investment, preferably associated with it—these being factors that have not always prevailed. Concern is expressed at the global magnitude of the flow of external financing that it [private foreign investment] has originated, and at the excessive use of local financing resources, the effect of certain marketing agreements that disrupt competition in the internal or external markets, and the possible resultant effects on the economic development of the region.

34. Interest is expressed in increased international cooperation in the financing of multinational projects and the extension of such cooperation to projects for the promotion of economic integration, this being a reflection of decisions of the integration agencies in their specific field. This cooperation should be provided in conformity with the Declaration of the Presidents of America.

35. Insistence is placed on the necessity of greater participation by Latin America in the discussions on the reform of the international monetary system, including those that may take place outside the sphere of the International Monetary Fund and, particularly, within the so-called Group of Ten. The prompt ratification and activation of the provisions on Special Drawing Rights and the search for mechanisms that will make it possible to obtain additional financing for development at the opportune time are considered matters of importance.

36. The importance of expanding tourist travel to the Latin American countries is pointed out, by avoiding the adoption of measures that would obstruct it and supporting by means of technical and financial assistance the improvement of services in this field and improvement of the tourism infrastructure.

37. All countries making up the inter-American system should be included in the annual country reviews made by CIAP, in order to study the execution of commitments undertaken, including those national policies that may impinge on the economic development of the Latin American countries.

D. SOCIAL DEVELOPMENT

38. It is reiterated that:

a. Their [the Latin American countries] economic development should be conducive to effective social transformation, whose basic goals should be to attain substantial improvements in the standards of living of the population, particularly in rural areas, and to bring less privileged or marginal groups into active participation in the process of economic and social progress and full enjoyment of its benefits.

b. Investments for social development are one way of raising standards of living of the people, a factor of great importance for the increase of productivity and a better distribution of income; therefore, they deserve preferential attention, taking into account the particular situation of each country.

c. The goals set forth in the Declaration of the Presidents of America on the social development of Latin America can reach full and prompt fruition only if there is a considerable increase in international technical and financial cooperation for social development, which cooperation should be provided on the basis of the programs and policies of each country, with due consideration for national characteristics.

To that end, the financial cooperation should be granted without discrimination and on especially flexible terms; therefore, mechanisms such as the Fund for Special Operations of the Inter-American Development Bank (whose resources should be increased in due course) should be used more widely.

E. TECHNICAL COOPERATION

39. It is affirmed that the following principles should be observed in the field of technical cooperation:

a. Technical cooperation should be a joint undertaking of the parties concerned. Its volume, processes, and form of coordination should be fitted to the national objectives of each country, according to its economic and social development plans.

b. Technical cooperation should be channeled through the national coordinating agencies of each country or, as the case may be, of regional or subregional agencies.

c. Technical cooperation should be directed toward supporting and supplementing the national programs of each country and the agencies in charge of the execution of those programs, but not toward replacing such programs or agencies.

d. Multilateral technical cooperation should be strengthened and substantially increased.

e. Latin American experts should be used in so far as possible in programs of technical cooperation.

f. Technical cooperation should not be cut down as the countries of Latin America achieve more advanced and complex stages in their growth; rather it should be adapted to the new conditions in the development process.

g. In attention to the needs and responsibilities involved in the process of national and regional development, technical cooperation should be made available basically on nonreimbursable terms.

F. SCIENTIFIC AND TECHNOLOGICAL DEVELOPMENT

40. For the fulfillment of their economic and social development programs, the countries of Latin America recognize that it is necessary vigorously to promote a process of scientific and technological development, based on maximum domestic effort and supplemented by international cooperation. In this sense the countries of Latin America will adopt a concerted action plan, through a broad program of scientific and technological cooperation that requires the help of international cooperation, especially of the United States.

41. It is imperative to carry out fully the Action Program agreed upon by the Presidents of America with respect to science and technology. To that end, and in view of the fact that scientific and technological development requires resources of an order of magnitude much in excess of the amount currently being invested at the national and regional levels, it becomes necessary to have available special funds for such development, which should be granted without repayment commitments.

On the basis of the complementarity of efforts mentioned, the United States of America should:

42. Support the Latin American countries in respect to science and technology, channeling its cooperation in consideration of the goals and priorities set by those countries and through the pertinent national and regional organizations.

43. Adopt suitable methods to improve the transfer of technology to the region. In this respect it should:

a. Contribute to the improvement of scientific and technological information through the training of experts and assistance in setting up national information centers, which would make it possible to create regional scientific and technical information machinery, including information on patents, trade-marks, licenses, etc.

b. Intensify assistance for improving the region's scientific and technological infrastructure, by means of the following measures, among others: increased exchange of scientists; promotion of cooperative programs of research on problems of importance to Latin America; strengthening and supplementing the necessary physical facilities for scientific and technological research.

44. Improve the transfer of science and technology among the countries of Latin America, for which purpose it should:

a. Substantially increase its financial support of the multinational projects contained in the Regional Program of Scientific and Technological Development; and

b. Support the efforts for cooperation among Latin American countries in relation to teaching and research, among both state and private organizations or universities.

45. Assist in the efforts of the Latin American countries to speed up the establishment of their own science and technology, for which effect it should:

a. Encourage research work in the Latin American countries by United States concerns that have branches or affiliates there, using national or regional scientific and technological ability;

b. Study, within the framework of Latin American national or regional programs, the execution in Latin America of certain specific scientific and technological research programs of interest to the region that are presently being carried out in the United States by government or paragovernment bodies;

c. Support the national development programs prepared by the countries of Latin America to encourage scientific and technological development; and

d. Support national efforts toward integration of the action of the entrepreneurial, governmental, university, and technological research sectors in order to increase the capacity for original research.

46. It is also necessary to agree between the countries of Latin America and the United States on joint international action to promote the region's scientific and technological development. In that regard the United States should:

a. Collaborate in the review of existing international conventions on patents, for the purpose of improving for developing countries the terms of access to industrial knowledge and processes and of eliminating restrictive practices, thereby making possible the more effective use of the benefits of science and technology covered by the said instruments, as well as the rapid and effective utilization of such benefits in industry in the aforesaid countries.

The cooperation of the United States in this field should include facilities for wider access, with assurances of equitable, nondiscriminatory treatment, to industrial processes that are subject to licenses, and to contracts for technica services. To that effect it is necessary to promote on an urgent basis a join study of the problems involved in the transfer and absorption of technology where patents are concerned.

b. Act jointly with the countries of Latin America in advocating that the international financing institutions and credit organizations in the developed countries grant them loans on advantageous terms for scientific and technological research, within the framework of national priorities.

c. Similarly, advocate that in the financing of development projects funds always be included for the research that such proiects may require, using the scientific and technological capacity of the countries of the region.

d. Give its support to the holding (on an urgent basis) of a conference on the application of science and technology to Latin American development.

Selected Bibliography

Economic Policies toward Developing Countries

Asher, Robert E. *Development Assistance in the Seventies: Alternatives for the United States.* Washington: Brookings Institution, 1970.

Bernstein, Marvin D. (ed.). *Foreign Investment in Latin America: Cases and Attitudes.* New York: Knopf, 1966.

Commission on International Development, Lester B. Pearson, Chairman. *Partners in Development.* New York: Praeger, 1969.

Gallagher, John, and Ronald Robinson. "The Imperialism of Free Trade," *Economic History Review,* 2d Ser., Vol. 6 (August 1943).

Geiger, Theodore. *The Conflicted Relationship: The West and The Transformation of Asia, Africa and Latin America.* New York: McGraw-Hill, 1967.

Hirschman, Albert O. *How to Divest in Latin America, and Why.* Essays in International Finance No. 76. Princeton: Princeton University, International Finance Section, 1969.

————, and Richard M. Bird. *Foreign Aid—A Critique and a Proposal.* Essays in International Finance No. 69. Princeton: Princeton University, International Finance Section, 1968.

Inter-American Development Bank. *Multinational Investment, Public and Private, in the Economic Development and Integration of Latin America.* Round Table, Bogotá, April 1968. Washington: Inter-American Development Bank, n.d.

Johnson, Harry G. *Economic Policies Toward Less Developed Countries.* Washington: Brookings Institution, 1967.

Johnson, Leland L. *U.S. Private Investment in Latin America: Some Questions of National Policy.* Santa Monica, California: Rand Corp., July 1964.

Kindleberger, Charles (ed.). *The International Corporation.* Cambridge, Mass.: M.I.T. Press, 1970.

Mikesell, Raymond F. *The Economics of Foreign Aid.* Chicago: Aldine, 1968.

———, and Associates. *Foreign Investment in the Petroleum and Mineral Industries: Case Studies of Investor-Host Country Relations.* Baltimore: Johns Hopkins Press for Resources for the Future, 1971.

Nelson, Joan M. *Aid, Influence, and Foreign Policy.* New York: Macmillan, 1968.

Pincus, John. *Trade, Aid and Development: The Rich and Poor Nations.* New York: McGraw-Hill, 1967.

Task Force on International Development. *U.S. Foreign Assistance in the 1970s: A New Approach.* Report to the President. Washington: Government Printing Office, 1970.

United Nations. *A Study of the Capacity of the United Nations Development System.* 2 Vols. Geneva: United Nations, 1969.

U.S. Congress. House. Subcommittee on Foreign Economic Policy of the House Committee on Foreign Affairs. *The Involvement of U.S. Private Enterprise in Developing Countries.* House Report 1271. 91 Cong. 1 sess. Washington: Government Printing Office, 1968.

Vernon, Raymond (ed.). *How Latin America Views the U.S. Investor.* New York: Praeger, 1966.

Inter-American Relations

Burr, Robert N. *Our Troubled Hemisphere: Perspectives on United States-Latin American Relations.* Washington: Brookings Institution, 1967.

Connell-Smith, Gordon. *The Inter-American System.* London: Oxford University Press, 1966.

Dávila, Carlos. *We of the Americas.* Chicago: Ziff-Davis Publishing Co., 1949.

Dozer, Donald Marquand. *Are We Good Neighbors? Three Decades of Inter-American Relations, 1930–1960.* Gainesville: University of Florida Press, 1959.

Dreier, John C. "New Wine and Old Bottles: The Changing Inter-American System," *International Organization,* Vol. 22 (Spring 1968).

———. *The Organization of American States and the Hemisphere Crisis.* New York: Harper & Row for the Council on Foreign Relations, 1962.

García Calderon, Francisco. *Latin America: Its Rise and Progress.* New York: Charles Scribner's Sons, 1913.

Gregg, Robert W. (ed.). *International Organization in the Western Hemisphere.* Syracuse: Syracuse University Press, 1968.

Hanson, Simon G. *Five Years of the Alliance for Progress: An Appraisal.* Washington: Inter-American Affairs Press, 1967.

Levinson, Jerome, and Juan de Onís. *The Alliance That Lost Its Way.* Chicago: Quadrangle Books, 1970.

Lowenthal, Abraham F. "Alliance Rhetoric Versus Latin American Reality," *Foreign Affairs,* Vol. 48 (April 1970).

May, Herbert K. *Problems and Prospects of the Alliance for Progress: A Critical Examination.* New York: Praeger, 1968.

Organization of American States. *The Alliance for Progress and Latin-American Development Prospects: A Five-Year Review, 1961–1965.* Baltimore and London: Johns Hopkins Press, 1967.

Perloff, Harvey S. *Alliance for Progress: A Social Invention in the Making.* Baltimore: Johns Hopkins Press for Resources for the Future, 1969.

Rogers, William D. *The Twilight Struggle: The Alliance for Progress and the Politics of Development in Latin America.* New York: Random House, 1967.

U.S. Congress. Senate. Committee on Foreign Relations. *Latin American Summit Conference.* Hearings. 90 Cong. 1 sess. Washington: Government Printing Office, 1967.

U.S. Presidential Mission for the Western Hemisphere, Nelson A. Rockefeller, Chairman. "Quality of Life in the Americas." New York: The Mission, 1969; processed. Reprinted in *Rockefeller Report on Latin America,* Hearing before the Subcommittee on Western Hemisphere Affairs of the Senate Committee on Foreign Relations. 91 Cong. 1 sess. Washington: Government Printing Office, 1970.

Wood, Bryce. *The Making of the Good Neighbor Policy.* New York: Columbia University Press, 1961.

Economic Integration and Development

Baerresen, Donald W. "A Method for Planning Economic Integration for Specific Industries," *Journal of Common Market Studies,* Vol. 6 (September 1967).

Balassa, Bela. *Economic Development and Integration.* Mexico City: Centro de Estudios Monetarios Latinoamericanos, 1965.

———. *The Theory of Economic Integration.* Homewood, Illinois: Irwin, 1961.

Cooper, C. A., and B. F. Massell. "Toward a General Theory of Customs Unions for Developing Countries," *Journal of Political Economy,* Vol. 73 (October 1965).

Denison, Edward F., assisted by Jean-Pierre Poullier. *Why Growth Rates Differ: Postwar Experience in Nine Western Countries.* Washington: Brookings Institution, 1967.

Gehrels, Franz. "Customs Union from a Single-Country Viewpoint," *Review of Economic Studies,* Vol. 24 (1956–57).

Johnson, Harry G. *Money, Trade and Economic Growth.* London: Allen & Unwin, 1962.

Krause, Lawrence B. *European Economic Integration and the United States.* Washington: Brookings Institution, 1968.

Lipsey, R. G. "The Theory of Customs Unions: A General Survey," *Economic Journal,* Vol. 70 (September 1960).

Maizels, Alfred, assisted by L. F. Campbell-Boross and P. B. W. Rayment. *Exports and Economic Growth of Developing Countries.* London: Cambridge University Press, 1968.

Martirena-Mantel, Ana María. "Integración y desarrollo económico," *El Trimestre Económico*, Vol. 36 (April–June 1969).

Meade, James E. *The Theory of Customs Unions*. Amsterdam: North-Holland Publishing Co., 1966.

Mikesell, Raymond F. *Liberalization of Inter-Latin American Trade*. Washington: Pan American Union, 1957.

Nguyen Tien Hung, G. "Economies of Scale and Economic Integration," *Finance and Development*, Vol. 5 (June 1968).

Sakamoto, Jorge. "Industrial Development and Integration of Underdeveloped Countries," *Journal of Common Market Studies*, Vol. 7 (June 1969).

Scitovsky, Tibor. *Economic Theory and Western European Integration*. London: Allen & Unwin, 1958.

United Nations Conference on Trade and Development. *Trade Expansion and Economic Integration among Developing Countries*. Sales No. 67.II.D.20. New York: United Nations, 1967.

Viner, Jacob. *The Customs Union Issue*. New York: Carnegie Endowment for International Peace, 1950.

Wionczek, Miguel S. "Requisites for Viable Economic Integration," in Joseph S. Nye, Jr. (ed.), *International Regionalism: Readings*. Boston: Little Brown, 1968.

Economic Integration and Development in Latin America

Baerresen, Donald W., Martin Carnoy, and Joseph Grunwald. *Latin American Trade Patterns*. Washington: Brookings Institution, 1965.

Brown, Robert T. *Transport and the Economic Integration of South America*. Washington: Brookings Institution, 1966.

Carnoy, Martin (ed.). *Industrialization in a Latin American Common Market*. An ECIEL study. Washington: Brookings Institution, 1971.

Castillo, Carlos. *Growth and Integration in Central America*. New York: Praeger, 1967.

Centro de Estudios Monetarios Latinoamericanos. *Cooperación financiera en América Latina*. Mexico City: CEMLA, 1963.

Cochrane, James D. "Central American Economic Integration: The Integrated Industries Scheme," *Inter-American Economic Affairs*, Vol. 19 (Autumn 1965).

———. "U.S. Attitudes Toward Central American Economic Integration," *Inter-American Economic Affairs*, Vol. 18 (Autumn 1964).

Dell, Sidney. *A Latin American Common Market?* London: Oxford University Press, 1966.

González del Valle, Jorge. "Monetary Integration in Central America: Achievements and Expectations," *Journal of Common Market Studies*, Vol. 5 (September 1966).

Griffin, Keith B. "Potential Benefits of Latin American Integration," *Inter-American Economic Affairs*, Vol. 17 (Spring 1964).

———, and Ricardo Ffrench-Davis. "Customs Unions and Latin American Integration," *Journal of Common Market Studies*, Vol. 4 (October 1965).

Grunwald, Joseph, and Philip Musgrove. *Natural Resources in Latin American Development*. Baltimore: Johns Hopkins Press for Resources for the Future, 1970.

Haas, Ernst B., and Philippe C. Schmitter. "Economics and Differential Patterns of Political Integration: Projections about Unity in Latin America," *International Organization*, Vol. 18 (Autumn 1964).

————. *The Politics of Economics in Latin American Regionalism: The Latin American Free Trade Association after Four Years of Operation*. Denver: University of Denver, 1965.

Hansen, Roger D. *Central America: Regional Integration and Economic Development*. Washington: National Planning Association, 1967.

Harberger, Arnold C. (ed.). "Key Problems of Economic Policy in Latin America," *Journal of Political Economy*, Vol. 78, Supplement (July–August 1970).

Herrera, Felipe. "The Inter-American Development Bank and the Latin American Integration Movement," *Journal of Common Market Studies*, Vol. 5 (December 1966).

————, José Antonio Mayobre, Carlos Sanz de Santamaría, and Raúl Prebisch. "Proposals for the Creation of the Latin American Common Market submitted to the Governments of Latin America in 1965," *Journal of Common Market Studies*, Vol. 5 (September 1966).

Karnes, Thomas L. *The Failure of Union: Central America, 1824–1960*. Chapel Hill: University of North Carolina Press, 1961.

McClelland, Donald H. "The Common Market's Contribution to Central American Economic Growth: A First Approximation," in Ronald Hilton (ed.), *The Movement Toward Latin American Unity*. New York: Praeger, 1969.

Navarrete, Jorge E. "Latin American Economic Integration—A Survey of Recent Literature," *Journal of Common Market Studies*, Vol. 4 (December 1965).

Nye, Joseph S., Jr. *Central American Regional Integration*. International Conciliation No. 562. New York: Carnegie Endowment for International Peace, March 1967.

Organization of American States. *External Financing for Latin American Development*. Baltimore and London: Johns Hopkins Press, 1971.

Perloff, Harvey S., and Rómulo Almeida. "Regional Economic Integration in the Development of Latin America," *Economía Latinoamericana*, Vol. 1 (November 1963).

Prebisch, Raúl. *Change and Development—Latin America's Great Task*. Report submitted to the Inter-American Development Bank. New York: Praeger, 1971.

————. "The Economic Development of Latin America and Its Principal Problems," *Economic Bulletin for Latin America*, Vol. 7 (February 1962).

————. *Towards a Dynamic Development Policy for Latin America*. New York: United Nations, 1963.

Triffin, Robert. "International Monetary Arrangements, Capital Markets and Economic Integration in Latin America," *Journal of Common Market Studies*, Vol. 4 (October 1965).

United Nations. Conference on Trade and Development. *Payment Arrangements among the Developing Countries for Trade Expansion: Report of the Committee of Experts.* Sales No. 67.II.D.8. Geneva: United Nations, 1966.

————. Economic Commission for Latin America. *The Latin American Common Market.* New York: United Nations, 1959.

————. *Possibilities for Integrated Industrial Development in Central America.* New York: United Nations, 1964.

U.S. Congress. Joint Economic Committee. Subcommittee on Inter-American Economic Relationships. *Latin American Development and Western Hemisphere Trade.* Hearings. 89 Cong. 1 sess. Washington: Government Printing Office, 1965.

Urquidi, Víctor L. *Free Trade and Economic Integration in Latin America.* Berkeley: University of California Press, 1962.

Vanek, Jaroslav. "Payments Unions among the Less Developed Countries and their Economic Integration," *Journal of Common Market Studies,* Vol. 5 (December 1966).

Wionczek, Miguel S. (ed.). *Economic Cooperation in Latin America, Africa, and Asia: A Handbook of Documents.* Cambridge, Mass.: M.I.T. Press, 1969.

————. *Latin American Economic Integration: Experiences and Prospects.* New York: Praeger, 1966.

————. *Latin American Free Trade Association.* International Conciliation No. 551. New York: Carnegie Endowment for International Peace, January 1965.

Index

Act of Bogotá, 4, 71–72
Agency for International Development (AID), 84–89, 93, 96
Agriculture, 21, 23–24, 109, 143–44, 157
AID, *see* Agency for International Development
Aid-tying, 86–90
Alliance for Progress: and CACM, 66; formation, 5, 75; and regional integration, 75–76, 99; and U.S. policy, 4, 17, 77
Almeida, Romulo, 79n
Andean group: Andean Development Corporation, 56–58, 160; Andean Subregional Integration Agreement, 57, 150; Bogotá Declaration, 56; complementarity agreements, 57; equitable benefits policy, 37; foreign investment, 58–59, 116–17; formation, 55; future of, 61; industrial program, 57–58; investment code, 116–17, 132; membership, 56–57; tariffs, 58. *See also* Latin American Free Trade Association
Andean Subregional Integration Agreement, 57, 150
Argentina: development level, 20, 97; foreign aid, 86; foreign investment, 110; and LAFTA, 52; Montevideo conference, 40; and regional integration, 13, 67, 160; trade, 138, 141, 147

Baerresen, Donald W., 33n
Balassa, Bela, 21n, 32n, 145n

Bemis, Samuel F., 67n
Bhagwati, Jagdish, 88n
Bird, Richard M., 93n
Blaine, James G., 67–68, 73
Bogotá Declaration, 56
Bolívar, Simon, 39
Bolivarian Highway, 126
Bolivia: and Andean group, 58–59; development level, 97; investment code, 116; and LAFTA, 50, 52; Montevideo conference, 40; trade, 148
Brazil: development level, 20; foreign aid, 86; foreign investment, 110; GNP level, 13; and LAFTA, 52; Montevideo conference, 40; population, 13; and regional integration, 13, 160; trade, 138, 141, 147
Brown, Robert T., 125n–128n
Burr, Robert N., 9n

CABEI, *see* Central American Bank for Economic Integration
CACM, *see* Central American Common Market
Campbell-Boross, L. F., 146n
Cárdenas, Jose C., 119n
Caribbean Free Trade Area (CARIFTA), 59–61
Caribbean Development Bank, 61
Carnoy, Martin, 33n, 34n, 37n, 91n, 99n, 120n, 125n
Carretera Marginal de la Selva, 126
Castañeda, Jorge, 67n

211